The Right to Development in the African Human Rights System

The right to development (RTD) seeks to address global inequities hidden in world politics and global institutions through the game of influences played by powerful actors. The negative impacts of the Atlantic slave trade, colonialism and the subjugation of Africa through globalisation and its institutions are key factors that have caused Africa and African people claiming their RTD.

This book examines how the African continent protects the right to development, examining the nature of the RTD and controversies surrounding it and how it is implemented. The book then goes on to explore the RTD at the regional level including through the jurisprudence of the African Commission and the African Court on Human Rights, at the sub-regional level including in sub-regional courts and tribunals, at the national levels through case studies and through the African Union governance institutions. Through this examination, the author unveils what the prospects and challenges are to the realisation of the RTD in Africa.

Serges Djoyou Kamga is Associate Professor at the Thabo Mbeki African Leadership Institute, University of South Africa.

Global Africa
Series Editors: Toyin Falola and Roy Doron

1 **Dissent, Protest and Dispute in Africa**
Edited by Emmanuel M. Mbah and Toyin Falola

2 **Environment and Identity Politics in Colonial Africa**
Emmanuel M. Mbah

3 **Poverty Reduction Strategies in Africa**
Edited by Toyin Falola and Mike Odugbo Odey

4 **Literature and Culture in Global Africa**
Tanure Ojaide

5 **Gendering Knowledge in Africa and the African Diaspora**
Contesting History and Power
Edited by Toyin Falola and Olajumoke Yacob-Haliso

6 **The African Metropolis**
Struggles over Urban Space, Citizenship, and Rights to the City
Edited by Toyin Falola and Bisola Falola

7 **Africa's Big Men**
Predatory State – Society Relations in Africa
Edited by Kenneth Kalu, Olajumoke Yacob-Haliso and Toyin Falola

8 **The Right to Development in the African Human Rights System**
Serges Djoyou Kamga

The Right to Development in the African Human Rights System

Serges Djoyou Kamga

Routledge
Taylor & Francis Group
LONDON AND NEW YORK

First published 2018 by Routledge

2 Park Square, Milton Park, Abingdon, Oxfordshire OX14 4RN
52 Vanderbilt Avenue, New York, NY 10017

Routledge is an imprint of the Taylor & Francis Group, an informa business

First issued in paperback 2020

British Library Cataloguing-in-Publication Data
A catalogue record for this book is available from the British Library

Library of Congress Cataloging-in-Publication Data
Names: Kamga, Serges Djoyou (Serges Alain Djoyou Kamga), author.
Title: The right to development in the African human rights system/Serges Djoyou Kamga.
Description: New York, NY : Routledge, 2018. | Series: Global Africa ; 8 | Includes bibliographical references and index.
Identifiers: LCCN 2017048347 | ISBN 9780815350408 (hbk) | ISBN 9781351142489 (e-book)
Subjects: LCSH: Human rights—Africa. | Right to development—Africa.
Classification: LCC KQC572. K36 2018 | DDC 342.9608/5—dc23
LC record available at https://lccn.loc.gov/2017048347

ISBN: 978-0-8153-5040-8 (hbk)
ISBN: 978-0-367-59319-3 (pbk)

Typeset in Times New Roman
by Apex CoVantage, LLC

Contents

1 Introduction

1.1. Introduction and overview

There is a plethora of scholarly works and especially books on the right to development (RTD). Nevertheless, these books focus mostly on the RTD at the global level. Although there are some chapters in books[1] and articles[2] on the RTD in Africa, the only book on the RTD on the continent is a 34-page book written back in 1989[3] when the contents and the justiciability of the RTD were yet to be tested. Therefore, there is absolutely no doubt that there is a gap on the literature on RTD in the African human rights system. This book seeks to close this gap by providing the first volume that explores the RTD in its entirety in Africa. This introductory chapter is divided into five parts including this introduction. The second part examines the historical development of the RTD; the third subsection focuses on its theoretical foundation; the fourth part presents the scope of the book and the fifth part provides concluding remarks.

1 E. Bello. 'Article 22 of the African Charter on Human and Peoples' Rights' In Bello, E. and Adjibola, B. (eds.) *Essay in Honour of Judge Taslim Olawale Elias* (Martinus Nijhoff 1992); O. C. Okafor. '"Righting" The Right to Development: A Socio-Legal Analysis of Article 22 of the African Charter of Human and Peoples' Rights' In Marks, S. (ed.) *Implementing the Right to Development: The Role of International Law* (Friedricht Ebert Stiftung 2008); O. C. Okafor. 'A Regional Perspective: Article 22 of the African Charter on Human and Peoples' Rights' in UN Human Rights Office of the High Commissioner (ed.) *Realizing the Right to Development – Essays in Commemoration of 25 Years of the United Nations Declaration on the Right to Development* (UN 2013), 373–383; R. Rich. 'The Right to Development: A Right of Peoples?' In Crawford, J. (ed.) *The Rights of Peoples* (Clarendon Press 1988).

2 N. J. Udombana. 'The Third Word and the Right to Development: Agenda for the Next Millennium' (2000) 22 *Human Rights Quarterly* 759; S. D. Kamga and C. M. Fombad. 'A Critical Review of the Jurisprudence of the African Commission on the Right to Development' (2013) 57(2) *Journal of African Law* 196; S. D. Kamga. 'The Right to Development in the African Human Rights System: The *Endorois* Case' (2011) *De Jure* 381; C. R. Mahalu. 'Human Rights and Development: An African Perspective' (2009) 1(1) *Leiden Journal of International Law* 15; O. Oduwole. 'International Law and the Right to Development: A Pragmatic Approach for Africa' (2014) *International Institute of Social Studies* 1; G. W. Shepherd. 'The African Right to Development: World Policy and the Debt Crisis' (1990) 37(4) *Africa Today* 5.

3 T. A. Aguda. *Human Rights and the Right to Development in Africa* (Nigerian Institute of International Affairs 1989).

1.2. The right to development: historical background

To trace the historical background of the RTD, it is important to understand the subjugation of Africa through the slave trade, colonialism and the economic alienation of Africa in post-colonial time.

1.2.1. The slave trade

Through slave trade that could be qualified as the most shameful trade of all times, or rather 'the moral decay of the modern world'[4] African people were exploited, abused and dehumanised. They were brutalised and sold like cattle; their families which are 'the epicenter of African social existence'[5] and the glue that hold communities together, were broken. Cultures and traditions were destroyed or to use Ama's words, Africans were victims of a 'cultural genocide'[6] as they were loaded into ships to be taken across the Atlantic as slaves. In this process of 'destruction of black civilisation',[7] the continent lost its men and women power, its human resources that could have been used for its development.[8] The shipping of Africans (mostly men) from the continent reduced the population of Africa. In this respect, although Africa is huge in terms of land, its population is less than 800 million and the slave trade played a major role in depopulating the continent, even though some human lives were lost to wars and diseases.[9]

Moreover, as result of slave trade, African people lost their dignity. In his analysis of the South African example, Terreblanche shows how the Dutch, Portuguese, English and the French stole the dignity or self-worth of the South African people by trading them like mere animals while stealing their resources to build the global North.[10]

Similarly, West African communities were devastated. Out of about 12 million Africans shipped across the Atlantic, almost 6.3 million were from West Africa.[11] Like in Southern Africa, the West of the continent was torn apart and looted by

4 K. Beckman. 'Imperialism' In M. K. Asante and M. Ama (eds.) *Encyclopedia of Black Studies* (Sage 2005), 269.

5 M. K. Asante. 'Afrocentric Criticism' In M. K. Asante and M. Ama (eds.) *Encyclopedia of Black Studies* (Sage 2005), 64.

6 M. Ama. 'Cultural Genocide' In M. K. Asante and M. Ama (eds.) *Encyclopedia of Black Studies* (Sage 2005), 209.

7 C. Williams. *The Destruction of Black Civilization: Great Issues of a Race From 4500 B.C. to 2000 A.D* (Third World Press 1974).

8 W. Rodney. *How Europe Underdeveloped Africa* (London: Tanzanian Publishing House 1973). www.blackherbals.com/walter_rodney.pdf (Accessed 20 May/August 2017).

9 T. Falola. 'Africa and Slavery in a Global Context' The UNESCO Slavery Route Project (ed.). www.unesco.org/fileadmin/MULTIMEDIA/HQ/CLT/images/Falola_Eng.pdf, p 3 (Accessed 12 April 2017).

10 S. Terreblanche. *History of Inequality in South Africa 1652–2002* (University of Natal Press 2002), 8–14 & 153.

11 M. Bump. 'Ghana: Searching for Opportunities at Home and Abroad' (2006). www.migrationpolicy.org/article/ghana-searching-opportunities-home-and-abroad (Accessed 21 April 2017); also

the architects of the slave trade who captured the populations and their freedoms through 'wars and raiding expeditions' to use Falola's words.[12] The impact of the slave trade on Africa in general cannot be overemphasised. Taking Africans from their communities was disruptive 'to traditional patterns of trade and seasonal movements'.[13] Nunn demonstrates the direct correlation between present-day Africa's development challenges and the slave trade.[14] He provides empirical evidence to the fact that the poorest African countries are those that produced the highest number of slaves.[15]

Even though a narrow African political elite was involved in and sustained the slave trade for their self-interest, the entire trade was informed by a Western-sponsored global economy in which Africans were to provide the labour force, Europe the capital and the Americas the land to produce sugar cane, cotton and tobacco.[16] Consequently, as correctly observed by Falola, '[t]he African chiefs, no matter how much blame is apportioned to them, neither created this global economy nor served as its main financial managers'[17] or its main architects. Some of these local agents who participated in the transatlantic slave trade were either forced to be involved, or threatened or corrupt, but they were never the primary designers of the capitalist system which needed the shipping of Africans across the Atlantic to survive.

In the final analysis, not only the Atlantic slave trade has frustrated Africa's development throughout the four centuries of its operations, it has equally prepared the ground for further underdevelopment by Europeans through colonialism.

1.2.2. Colonialism

Subsequent to the slave trade, in 1884 in Berlin, the African continent was shared like a piece of cake by Western powers. Qualified as savage in need of 'civilisation', the peoples of Africa witnessed the entry of colonial masters in their territories. Building on the legacy of the slave trade, these invaders orchestrated the destruction of local communities and cultural identity as well as intensive looting of lands and other resources.[18] The nature of forced labour used by colonialists to build infrastructure to export African goods and resources was similar to the

see P. D. Curtin who argues that 11.5 million slave were taken from Africa. P. D. Curtin. *The Atlantic Slave Trade* (UW 1969).

12 T. Falola. *The African Diaspora: Slavery, Modernity, and Globalization* (University Rochester Press, 2013), 35.

13 Ibid.

14 N. Nunn. 'The Long-Term Effects of Africa's Slave Trades' (2008) *Quarterly Journal of Economics* 139; Also C. Ngang. 'Towards a Right-to-Development Governance in Africa' (2017) *Journal on Human Rights* 3.

15 Nunn (n 14) 2.

16 Falola (n 9).

17 Ibid.

18 V. Y. Mudimbe. *The Invention of Africa: Gnosis, Philosophy and the Order of Knowledge* (Indiana University Press 1988), 4.

one used by slave masters on farms and other enterprises. Echoing Lovejoy and Hogendorn,[19] Falola points out that during the colonial area, the global quest for African goods and resources informed the continued reliance on 'slave labor to produce and carry raw materials to the coastal cities', and consequently 'slavery had a slow death, surviving in some places till the 1930s'.[20] This is to say, the replacement of slavery by colonialism did not see the end of enslavement of Africans as numerous colonial administrations replicated slavery labour practices crafted in blatant inequity.[21]

The other highlight of colonialism was the implementation of Western-style administration and education. Although not always responsive to local realities, the Western-style administration was imposed on people who adapted or sank. The entire initiative was characterised by extreme violence and death. This is evidenced by the letters from Jarvis, a volunteer in Rhodes's settler-army, during the establishment of the colony Rhodesia (current Zimbabwe).[22] Explaining the situation to his family, Jarvis wrote:

> I hope the natives will be pretty well exterminated. There are 5500 niggers in this district and . . . our plan of campaign will probably be to proceed against this lot and wipe them out, then move towards Bulawayo wiping out every nigger and every kraal we can find . . . you can be sure that there will be no quarter and everything black will have to die, for our men's blood is fairly up.[23]

Similarly in West Africa and specifically in Nigeria, brutality and extreme aggressiveness were the methods which led to the death of numerous kings who dared to resist the penetration of colonial masters.[24] Any resistance to such penetration was described as 'barbaric' acts of violence by 'primitive' people and needed to be addressed with more ferocity.[25] This clearly demonstrates the cruelty of the process which was simply inacceptable.

Even though the colonial masters invested in infrastructure and education, the former was generally made of roads needed to take the looted resources from the farm or mines to the habour and the so called-education aimed to teach Western

19 P. E. Lovejoy and Jan S. Hogendorn. *Slow Death for Slavery: The Course of Abolition in Northern Nigeria* (Cambridge University Press 1993).

20 Falola (n 9) 11.

21 For more, see S. Miers and R. Roberts (eds.). *The End of Slavery in Africa* (Madison: University of Wisconsin Press 1988); F. Cooper. *Decolonization and African Society: The Labor Question in French and British Africa* (Cambridge University Press 1996).

22 C. Ngwena. *What Is Africanness to Me? Contesting Nativism in Sexualities, Race and Culture* (PULP 2017).

23 Quoted in: B. Kiernan. 'From Irish Famine to Congo Reform: Nineteenth-Century Roots of International Human Rights Law' In R. Provost and P. Akhavan (eds.) *Confronting Genocide* (Springer 2011), 13–43 42. P. Brendon. *Decline and Fall of the British Empire 1781–1997* (Vintage books 2010), 571. Also Ngwena (n 22).

24 T. Falola. *Colonialism and Violence in Nigeria* (Indiana University Press 2009).

25 Ibid.

languages to local people in order to communicate with them, brain-wash them and colonise 'every aspect of [their] lives including their consciousness, mind, memory and intellect'.[26] In other words, infrastructure building in Africa was informed by Western interests and not the need to empower the native populations who after all did not really matter.[27] In reality, the underdevelopment of Africa was engineered by the colonial masters who disguised their evil deeds by building so-called infrastructure which ultimately aimed to ensure their supremacy.[28] In the process, they physically removed people from their land and natural resources. Daes writes:

> The legacy of colonialism is probably most acute in the area of expropriation of indigenous lands, territories and resources for national economic and development interests. In every part of the globe, indigenous peoples are being impeded from proceeding with their own forms of development consistent with their own values, perspectives and interests.[29]

Moreover, they developed a negative narrative on Africa to convince Africans and the world that people are of less value. Mbembe explains the narrative in these words:

> the African human experience constantly appears in the discourse of our times as an experience that can only be understood through a negative interpretation. Africa is never seen as possessing things and attributes properly part of 'human nature'. Or, when it is, its things and attributes are generally of lesser value, little importance, and poor quality. It is this elementariness and primitiveness that makes Africa the world par excellence of all that is incomplete, mutilated, and unfinished, its history reduced to a series of setbacks of nature in its quest for humankind.[30]

These words echo the view of Hegel, who to justify colonialism described Africa as 'Unhistorical, Undeveloped Spirit, [and] still involved in the conditions of mere nature.'[31] Given the intensity of the painful subjugation suffered by African

26 Falola (n 12) 35; also Ngũgĩ wa Thiong'o. 'Decolonise the Mind, Secure the Base', Public Lecture at Wits University 2 March 2017; also Ngũgĩ wa Thiong'o. *Something Torn and New: An African Renaissance* (Basic Civitas Books 2009).

27 A. Hrituleac. 'The Effects of Colonialism on African Economic Development: A Comparative Analysis Between Ethiopia, Senegal and Uganda'. Masters Dissertation Aarhus University 2011), 14–15.

28 W. Whatley and R. Gillezeau. 'The Impact of the Slave Trade on African Economies' (2009) *Department of Economics University of Michigan* 6.

29 *Indigenous peoples and Their Relationship to Land*, Final Working Paper Prepared by the Special Rapporteur, E-I Daes, un Doc E/CN.4/Sub.2/2001/21, at 21; J. Gilbert. *Indigenous Peoples' Land Rights Under International Law- From Victims to Actors* (Brill 2016), 250.

30 A. Mbembe. *On the Postcolony* (Wits University Press 2001), 1.

31 G. W. F. Hegel. *The Philosophy of History*. Translated by J. Sibree (1956) 91–98, cited in L. R. Gordon. 'African Philosophy's Search for Identity: Existential Considerations of a Recent Effort' (1997) 98 *CLR James Journal*, 101–102.

countries, the latter could only aspire to self-determination, to their development, to reclaim the human dignity of their peoples. This state of affairs led to development of pan-African ideology which called for the right to self-determination and independence of Africa[32] which became an essential element on which the RTD was developed and advanced.[33] In fact, the ideology of pan-Africanism indicated that it was time to move away from colonialism and its narrative which

> impose[d] its rule upon the present and the future of a dominated country. [to move from a doctrine which] is not satisfied merely with holding a people in its grip and emptying the native's brain of all form and content. [from a doctrine based on] a kind of perverted logic, [which] turns to the past of the oppressed people, and distorts, disfigures and destroys it.[34]

Sharing this view, Asante defines the scope of research in this century as anchored on the need to free Africa from the burdens of colonialism. He writes:

> The real work of this century is not going to be about race, colour, or Black Studies but rather about the deep quest for African identity, liberated from mental enslavement on the continent and in the Diaspora, and gaining United Africa based on democratic power and founded on the realization of the dreams of Marcus Garvey, DuBois, Kwame Nkrumah, Muammar Gaddafi, and Cheikh Anta Diop.[35]

The idea of pan-Africanism signalled that it was time to claim the RTD in Africa. This was formulated by Nkrumah in these terms:

> If the outside world refuses us its sympathy and understanding, we have at least *the right* to ask *it to leave us alone to work out our destiny in ways that seem most apposite to our circumstances and means, human as well as material.* In any event, we are determined to overcome the disruptive forces set against us and to forge in Africa . . . the African's ability to manage his own affairs.[36]

1.2.3. Subjugation of Africa in post-colonial time

After their independence and their integration into the community of nations, developing countries observed that the world order was far from being conducive

32 K. Nkrumah. *Africa Must Unite* (Fredericka Praeger Publisher1963), 10. For more on Pan Africanism see chapter 6 of this book.

33 A. Anghie. 'Whose Utopia? Human Rights, Development and the Third World' (2013) 22(1) *Qui Parle: Critical Humanities and Social Sciences* 66.

34 F. Fanon. *The Wretched of the Earth* (Présence Africaine 1967), 169.

35 M. K. Asante. *As I Run Toward Africa* (Boulder, CO: Paradigm 2011), 269.

36 Nkrumah (n 32) xv. My emphasis.

to their development. Global financial and trade arrangements through the international financial institutions (IFIs), namely the World Bank and the International Monetary Fund (IMF) and the General Agreement on Tariffs and Trade (GATT) and later the World Trade Agreement, simply failed developing countries. Consequently, they gathered through the Group of 77 (G77), the largest intergovernmental organisation of developing countries in the United Nations[37] to claim the establishment of a New International Economic Order (NIEO) that could allow them to realise their development.

The need to ensure the development of Third World countries was not negotiable and the G77 urged the global community to adopt 'a new international division of labour oriented towards the accelerated industrialisation of developing countries', and establish a conducive international environment for the development of all.[38] These ideas were reiterated in 1967, at the first Ministerial Conference of the G77 in Algiers, Algeria where the Charter of Algiers was adopted. In the first sentence of this Charter, the G77 emphasised that their members were unified by the need to attain their 'economic and social development',[39] and this was going to be achieved solely through the setting up of a new world order. More importantly, at the same conference, the expression 'right to development' was verbalised for the first time when Dodou Thiam, the then foreign Minister of Senegal, unambiguously declared:

> Our task is to denounce the old colonial compact and to replace it with a new right. In the same way that developed countries proclaimed individual rights to education, health and work, we must claim here, loud and clear, that the nations of the Third World have *the right to development.*[40]

This view was echoed two years later in the same city of Algiers by the anti-imperialist Catholic Archbishop Emeritus, Cardinal Léon-Étienne Duval, when after a critique of the development injustices inflicted on the global South by the global North, he explicitly reminded the international community that '*the right to development* should be proclaimed for the Third World'.[41]

This call for the RTD was then carried forward in academia by Keba M'baye who was Chief Justice of Senegal at the time. In his address in 1972 at the International Institute of Human Rights in Strasbourg, France, M'baye presented development as a human right,[42] and the idea filtered down in various political

37 www.g77.org.

38 The G77 Declaration 1964 adopted in Algiers, Algeria: para 1.

39 The Charter of Algiers, 1967, part 1.

40 L. Meillan. 'Le Droit au Dévelopment et les Nations Unies: Quelques Réflexions' (2003) *Droit en Quart Monde* 14; F. Ouguergouz. *The African Charter on Human and Peoples' Rights: A Comprehensive Agenda for Human Dignity and Sustainable Democracy in Africa* (Kluwer Law International 2003); Okafor (n 1) 374.

41 Ouguergouz (n 40) 298. My emphasis.

42 K. M'baye. 'Le droit au développement comme un droit de l'homme' (1972) 5 *Revue des droits l'homme* 505–534.

fora and became part and parcel of discussions at the UN which adopted its first resolution on the right in 1977.[43] In essence, at the onset, the RTD that originated from Africa[44] was considered as the channel to diagnose and remedy the 'structural and systemic root causes of inequality and underdevelopment' in developing countries.[45]

The demand for the establishment of a NIEO was attended to by the international community in 1974 through the adoption of the Declarations on the Establishment of the International Economic Order[46] as well as through the adoption of the Charter on the Economic Rights and Duties of States[47] which reiterate the need for a world order in which the asymmetrical relationship between the global South and the global North will become history.

In short, the NIEO Declaration underscores the importance to respect the equal sovereignty of States, their sovereignty over their resources, self-determination and the requirement to ensure international cooperation, equal participation of States in global affairs, which are all fundamentals of the RTD. Tadeg writes: the RTD 'provides a unique opportunity to promote an international economic order that is based on equity social justice, and one that integrates human rights in different dimensions'.[48]

In sum, the negative impacts of the Atlantic slave trade, colonialism and the subjugation of Africa through the so-called 'globalisation'[49] and its institutions are 'the most critical historical developments'[50] which resulted in Africa and African people claiming their RTD. After this overview of the historical background of the RTD, the following section focuses on its theoretical context.

1.3. The right to development: theoretical foundations

The RTD is based on the cosmopolitanism philosophy which stands for global justice without consideration of state borders as all human beings have the same moral standards.[51] Originally, the term 'Cosmopolitanism' came from the Greek words 'cosmos' which means world and 'polis' which designates city, together forming 'cosmopolis' or world city.[52] The 'world city' derives from the Stoic idea

43 Resolution 4 (XXXIII) on 1977 adopted without vote by the Committee on Human Rights.

44 Ngang (n 14) 3.

45 'The Politics of the Possible – The Way Ahead for the Right to Development' (2011) *International Policy Analysis* 2. http://library.fes.de/pdf-files/iez/08156.pdf (Accessed 9 August 2016).

46 UN Resolution 3201 (S-VI).

47 UN Resolution 3281 (XXIX).

48 M. A. Tadeg. 'Reflections on the Right to Development: Challenges and Prospects' (2010) 10 *African Human Rights Law Journal* 325–344.

49 Beckman (n 4) 70.

50 Falola (n 9 above) 1.

51 P. Kleingeld and E. Brown. 'Cosmopolitanism'. http://plato.stanford.edu/entries/cosmopolitanism/ (Accessed 9 August 2016).

52 M. Jones. 'Cosmopolitanism: How to Be a Citizen of the World'. www.motherjones.com/politics/2006/02/cosmopolitanism-how-be-citizen-world (Accessed 10 August 2016); also C. Jones. *Global Justice: Defending Cosmopolitanism* (Oxford University Press 1999).

advocating that all human beings possess a natural faculty of reason and are therefore citizens of the same community notwithstanding their various dissimilarities.[53] Hence, cosmopolitanism is world citizenship without consideration of race, gender and other status. Diogenes declared himself as 'a citizen of the world'[54] and not of Sinope, his country of birth.

In essence the cosmopolitanism theory simply requests the establishment of a world without discrimination based on race, sex, religions, disability or any other grounds including nationality. It urges the establishment of world characterised by global justice, equity and fairness where human dignity is a reality for all. In this context, everyone's rights or needs should be realised without considering his/her citizenship because humanity is similar all over the world. To use the words of Hayden and Tan, respectively, 'human status has a global scope'[55] and 'cosmopolitan justice' ignores borders,[56] or cultures.

Given that the achievement of the RTD entails harmonious international relations, the latter should be informed by cosmopolitanism or characterised by an anti-hegemonic agenda. Such relations are not guided by imperial inclinations, but by fairness, respect and equity at the centre of states' transactions. Accordingly, at the global level, international cooperation shall be designed to foster global ethics and moral responsibility concerning the well-being of human kind in general.

Crafted in the cosmopolitanism philosophy, the RTD reposes on equity and fairness and practically seeks to address global inequities hidden in world politics and global institutions through the game of influences played by powerful actors. The cosmopolitanism theory is the platform through which the human race in general can develop equally and be freed from poverty, hence its significant place at the centre of the RTD discourse.[57]

1.4. Scope of the book

As indicated at the onset, notwithstanding the abundance of literature on the RTD, there is undeniably no book on the RTD in the African human rights system where the right is binding. Even though the discussion on the nature of the RTD contains debates at the global level which are necessary to explain and provide a broad understanding of the RTD, this book will focus mainly on the RTD in the African human rights system. The latter is made of laws and initiatives at the regional, sub-regional and even national levels with special attention to how they advance

53 Ibid.; also Kamga and Fombad (n 2) 198.

54 Jones (n 52). Ibid.

55 P. Hayden. *Cosmopolitan Global Politics* (Ashgate 2005), 11.

56 K-C. Tan. *Justice Without Borders: Cosmopolitanism, Nationalism and Patriotism* (Cambridge University Press 2004), 1.

57 See generally, M. E. Salomon. 'Legal Cosmopolitanism and the Normative Contribution of the Right to Development' In S. Marks (ed.) *Implementing the Right to Development – The Role of International Law* (Friedricht Ebert Stiftung 2008), 19.

the right under investigation. To this end the book will be divided into seven chapters including this introduction.

The second chapter explores the nature of the RTD. It examines the substance of the right, the controversy on the right within academic circles and at the UN. The third chapter focuses on the implementation of the right in identifying the duty bearers as well as the right holders. While the former comprises the state, the international community, transnational companies, multilateral organisations, international financial institutions as well non-governmental organisations (NGOs) as duty bearers of the RTD, the latter is made of individuals, peoples and the state when it claims the right on behalf of its people. The fourth chapter looks at the place of the RTD in the African regional system. It investigates how the RTD is received in Africa and especially how it cascades from the regional level, the sub-regional level and to national levels in selected jurisdictions, where it is explicitly provided for in the constitution, and where constitutionalism is conducive for its attainment. Namely, these jurisdictions are Cameroon, Uganda, Malawi and Ethiopia, which have provided for the RTD in their constitutions, and South Africa which is said to have one of the best constitutions in the world in terms of human rights guarantee.[58] Subsequently, Chapter 5 explores the jurisprudence of the African Commission on the RTD with special attention to the *Bakweri Land Claims Committee v Cameroon*[59] (*Bakweri* case), the first ever inter-state complaint brought before the African Commission, *Democratic Republic of the Congo v Burundi, Rwanda, and Uganda.*[60] *Centre for Minority Rights Development (CEMIRIDE) (on behalf of the Endorois) v Kenya*[61] (*Endorois* case) and *SERAC v Nigeria*[62] (*SERAC* case). In addition, it unpacks the Ogiek case through which the African Court rendered its first judgement on the RTD. Chapter 6 focuses on the reception of the RTD by the African Union governance institutions, namely the African Union Assembly (AU Assembly), the Executive Council, the Permanent Representatives' Committee (PRC), the Peace and Security Council (PSC), the Pan-African Parliament, the New Partnership for Africa's Development (NEPAD) and the African Peer Review Mechanism (APRM). Finally, Chapter 7 provides concluding remarks and looks at what should be done prospectively to secure the realisation of the RTD in Africa.

1.5. Concluding remarks

This chapter introduced the book by showing that so far there is no book focusing on the RTD in Africa, hence the necessity of this volume. Subsequently, it

58 J. C. Mubangizi. *The Protection of Human Rights in South Africa: A Legal and Practical Guide* (Juta 2004), 71.

59 *Bakweri Land Claims Committee v Cameroon*, Communication No 260/2002, AHRLR (2004) 43.

60 Communication 227/99. *Democratic Republic of the Congo v Burundi, Rwanda, and Uganda* Annex IV, 20th Annual Activity Report of the African Commission, 111.

61 Communication 276/2003.

62 *SERAC & Another v Nigeria*, ACHPR, 2001, Banjul, the Gambia, and www.achpr.org.

presented the historical and theoretical underpinnings of the RTD. It found that historically, the RTD can be located in the slavery trade, colonialism and the economic domination of Africa in post-colonial time, which led to the claim for the NIEO. Theoretically, the RTD is crafted in the cosmopolitanism philosophy which calls for a better world where boundaries and inequalities as well as exclusion are non-existent. It then proceeded to present the structure of the book to be divided into seven chapters with a special focus on the RTD in the African human rights architecture where it is obligatory.

2 Unpacking the right to development

2.1. Introduction

At the centre of this chapter is the following question: What is the nature or constitutive elements of the RTD?[1] The RTD is one of the most controversial issues in the human rights discourse. Grounded in the third generation human rights or solidarity rights, the RTD was first brought to academia in 1972 by Keba M'baye, in his Inaugural Lecture at the International Institute of Human Rights in Strasbourg, France.[2] Subsequently, several international undertakings aiming to incorporate the right in global standards were adopted.[3] Nevertheless, the right remains contentious. While developing countries base their claim for resources transfer on the RTD perceived as a fundamental right, developed countries believe the right is a fallacy.[4]

The aim of this chapter is to explore the nature of the RTD. With a special attention to the right at a global level, this chapter is a background to the next one that focuses on the implementation of the right. The chapter is divided into four parts including this introduction. The second part examines the content of the RTD, the third part focuses on the controversy on the right in academic arenas and at the UN level and the fourth and final part provides concluding remarks.

2.2. The content of the right to development

This subsection examines the substance of the RTD. It provides a brief overview of the right as described by the United Nations Declaration on the Right to Development (UNDRTD). However, a thorough analysis of the right will be the feature

1 This chapter builds on 'the nature of the right to development' discussed in S. D. Kamga. 'Human Rights in Africa: Prospects for the Realisation of the Right to Development under the New Partnership for Africa's Development'. LLD Thesis (University of Pretoria 2011), Chapter 3.

2 K. M'baye. 'Le Droit au Développement Comme un Droit de l'Homme' (1972) 5 *Revue des Droits L'Homme* 505.

3 Examples: Human Right Commissions Resolutions 4 (XXXIII) of 21 February 1977, 4 (XXXV) of 2 March 1979, 36 (XXXVII) of 11 March 1981, and 1985/44 of 14 March 1985.

4 E. S. Nwauche and J. C. Nwobike. 'Implementing the Right to Development' (2005) 2(2) *Sur International Journal of Human Rights* 93.

of the subsections addressing the controversy on the right.[5] According to article 1 of UNDRTD, the RTD is:

1 [A]n inalienable human right by virtue of which every human person and all peoples are entitled to participate in, contribute to, and enjoy economic, social, cultural and political development, in which all human rights and fundamental freedoms can be fully realized.
2 The human right to development also implies the full realization of the right of peoples to self-determination which includes, subject to the relevant provisions of both International Covenants on Human Rights, the exercise of their inalienable right to full sovereignty over all their natural wealth and resources.

This suggests that the RTD has five main features:[6]

1 The RTD is absolute or cannot be bargained away.
2 It is a process securing the right to partaking or participation.
3 It is a process in which all human rights and essential or fundamental freedoms should be achieved.
4 It is an individual and collective right.[7]
5 The RTD echoes the right of people to self-determination.

2.2.1. *The right to development as a non-negotiable right*

The RTD is not negotiable, or is inalienable. The term 'inalienable' of the first paragraph of the 1986 UNDRTD highlights the importance of the RTD that cannot be encroached upon, that cannot be negotiated. It originates from the natural law theory which posits that all human beings are entitled to human rights by virtue of their humanity.[8] Besides the 1986 UNDRTD, the inalienable character of the RTD is also emphasized by the 1994 International Conference on Population and Development (ICPD).[9] Accordingly, the RTD cannot be set aside for any reason including the lack of development. The right is inherent to the nature of mankind and should be fulfilled in a sustainable manner. In this regard, human beings are the subject of development and as such should be the centre of all development initiatives.

5 See section 2.3 of this chapter.
6 For more on these features, see S. D. Kamga. 'The Right to Development and the Post-2015 Agenda' In S. Zondi and P. Mthembu (eds.) *From MDGs to Sustainable Development Goals* (IGD 2017).
7 This will be discussed in the next chapter under the section allocated to the right holders of the RTD (Chapter 3 section 3.3).
8 On natural law theory, see generally C. F. Alford. *Narrative, Nature, and the Natural Law: From Aquinas to International Human Rights* (Palgrave Macmillan 2010); P. Zagorin. *Hobbes and the Law of Nature* (Princeton University Press 2009); R. P. George (ed.) *Natural Law Theory: Contemporary Essays* (Clarendon Press 1992).
9 ICPD, principle 3.

However, the RTD loses its inalienable character when the state is at the same time duty bearer and beneficiary of the right. In this context as will be seen while analysing the concept of people in the African human rights system, people's rights are easily distorted by the state.[10]

2.2.2. The right to partaking is central to the right to development

Although the RTD incorporates all human rights and freedoms, the prescription on the right to participation[11] or partaking is plainly indicated through the expression 'every human person and people are entitled to participate'.[12] Participation is the basis of development. The entitlement to participate ensures that no one is left out on any ground, whatsoever. The right to participation underscores the prohibition of discrimination and highlights the need for transparency and accountability in the development process. Women,[13] youth,[14] indigenous groups,[15] persons with disability[16] and other vulnerable groups should be part of designing the process and be involved in the distribution of the benefit of development. The right to participation builds on article 21 of Universal Declaration which provides as follows:

1 Everyone has the right to take part in the government of his country, directly or through freely chosen representatives.
2 Everyone has the right of equal access to public service in his country.
3 The will of the people shall be the basis of the authority of government; this shall be expressed in periodic and genuine elections which shall be by universal and equal suffrage and shall be held by secret vote or by equivalent free voting procedures.

This provision highlights the importance of participation to any society. In a similar vein, building from article 25 of the International Covenant on Civil and Political Rights (ICCPR)[17] and the common article 1 of the two 1966 Covenants, the importance of the right to participation was underscored by the 1990

10 See Chapter 5, section 5.2.1.6 of this book.
11 This right will be further discussed in Chapter 5 of this book.
12 The 1986 UNDRTD, art 1.
13 ICPD, principle 4; Beijing Declaration, art 13.
14 ICPD, principle 6.13.
15 ICPD principle 14; Declaration on indigenous people, art 41.
16 2006 Convention on the Rights of Persons with Disabilities (CRPD).
17 Art 25 of ICCPR reads: 'Every citizen shall have the right and the opportunity without any of the distinctions mentioned in articles 2 and without unreasonable restrictions:

(a) To take part in the conduct of public affairs, directly or through freely chosen representatives;
(b) To vote and to be elected at genuine periodic elections which shall be by universal and equal suffrage and shall be held by secret ballot, guaranteeing the free expression of the will of the lectors;
(c) To have access, on general terms of equality, to public service in his country'.

African Charter for Popular Participation in Development and Transformation[18] which aimed to ensure a meaningful participation of African peoples in Africa's development.[19]

Drawing from the natural law theory according to which all human beings are created with natural rights, it could be argued that the right to participation is an inalienable human right and is in line with the RTD, even though it is necessary to note that participation without sufficient resources will not lead to the achievement of the RTD.

2.2.3. The right to development as a combined human right

Article 1 of UNDRTD underscores the combined or composite character of the RTD by underlining that not only does development have to deal with economic, social, cultural and political well-being, but it is also a process in which no human right or freedom should be forgotten. It includes 'all human rights and fundamental freedoms'. Put differently, economic, social and cultural rights as well as civil and political rights are the substance of the RTD. Prior to the 1986 UNDRTD, the African Charter on Human and Peoples' Rights (ACHPR or the African Charter) which is the only instrument in which the RTD is binding, noticeably underlined the composite character of the RTD which includes economic, social and cultural rights with a strong stance for respect of freedoms. Its article 22 reads:

1 All people shall have the right to their economic, social and cultural development with due regard to their freedom and identity and in the equal enjoyment of the common heritage of mankind.
2 States shall have the duty, individually or collectively, to ensure the exercise of the right to development.

For that reason, the RTD far from being based on favour or charity, is an entitlement. However, as will be demonstrated later, this seems to be a case for

18 The African Charter for Popular Participation in Development and Transformation; UN doc. A/45/427 of 22 August 1990.

19 Art 3 reads: 'The Conference was organized out of concern for the serious deterioration of the human and economic conditions in Africa in the decade of the 1980s, the recognition of the lack of progress in achieving popular participation and the full appreciation of the role popular participation plays in the process of recovery and development'. According to article 4, the objectives of the African Charter for Popular Participation for Development and Transformation were to:

(a) Recognise the role of people's participation in Africa's recovery and development efforts
(b) Sensitise national governments and the international community to the dimensions, dynamics, processes and potential of a development approach rooted popular initiatives and self – reliant efforts
(c) Recommend actions to be taken by governments, the United Nations system as well as the public and private donors agencies in building environments for authentic popular participation in the development process and encourage people and their organizations to undertake self-reliant development initiatives.'

disagreement on the right in question because some members of the international community like the United States of America (USA) for example want to associate the RTD with charity, humanism and matters of foreign policy.

Similar to the 1986 UNDRTD and the ACHPR, the Vienna Declaration recognises and explains the composite aspect of the RTD in these words:

> The World Conference on Human Rights reaffirms the right to development, as established in the Declaration on the right to development, as a universal and inalienable human right and an integral part of fundamental human rights.[20]

Put differently, the Vienna Declaration which was universally approved, recognises that the RTD implies a process ensuring the realisation of 'all human rights and fundamental freedoms'. Notably paragraph 5 of the Vienna Declaration reads:

> All human rights are universal, indivisible and interdependent and interrelated. The international community must treat human rights globally in a fair and equal manner, on the same footing, and with the same emphasis. While the significance of national and regional particularities and various historical, cultural and religious backgrounds must be borne in mind, it is the duty of States, regardless of their political, economic and cultural systems, to promote and protect all human rights and fundamental freedoms.

Explaining the composite character of the RTD, Baxi writes that the vital factor is the 'organic linkage between human rights' and not the individual recognition of each human right.[21] Furthermore, he claims that the liberal concept of 'rights' is somewhat confusing in the context of the RTD where the 'emphasis is placed on a large number of 'neighbouring rights' considered indispensably interlinked to the task of the realisation of the right to development'.[22] The composite feature of the RTD could also be understood within the context of Sen's capability theory. In this view, realising the RTD necessitates empowering people through various freedoms including from fear and from want. Unlike other human rights that are straightforward, the RTD is not, hence the polemic on the nature of the RTD which is multifaceted or multidimensional.[23]

In shedding more light on the nature and content of the RTD, Baxi shows while the human rights discourse debates on the place of civil and political rights (freedom) versus socio-economic rights (bread) 'the issues is not really "bread" and or "freedom" but rather who has how much of each, for how long, at what cost to

20 Vienna Declaration and Programme of Action adopted by the World Conference on Human Rights in Vienna on 25 June 1993, part I, para 10.

21 U. Baxi. 'The New International Economic Order, Basic Needs and Rights: Note Towards Development of the Right to Development' (1983) 23 *India Law Journal* 235.

22 Ibid.

23 The composite feature of the RTD underscores the indivisibility and interdependency of human rights elements of the RTD.

others and why [?]'.[24] According to Baxi, the RTD should be informed by equity and fairness in the sharing of world resources; the main question should be centred on 'redistribution, access and needs'.[25]

For Sengupta the RTD is a vector of rights. He contends that the RTD will be on the right track if at least one element of the vector is realised while none of other elements are tempered with or violated.[26] Whyte disagrees and claims that Sengupta's view would imply that 'Chinese', whose civil rights are systematically violated, have experienced no development in the last ten years, or perhaps they have developed, but without their right to development improving'.[27]

In response to what Whyte sees as incoherence, it could be argued that, to be a constitutive element of the RTD, 'economic growth must satisfy the basic conditions of facilitating the realisation of all other human rights.'[28] Hence the need to ensure consistency between policies implemented to enhance economic growth with human rights standards.

This opinion is echoed by Sen's capability theory which also highlights the composite character of the RTD. In this regard, the RTD is an empowering right through which other human rights are realised. It calls for the removal of 'unfreedoms'. Accordingly, the realisation of the RTD goes through the realisation of the right to education, health, food and association which empower the poor to reach their potential, and such freedoms multiply people's choice in their realisation. According to human capability theory, the RTD is consistent with article 28 of the Universal Declaration of Human Rights (UDHR) and can be defined as 'a people's claims to social and economic arrangements that protect them from the worst abuses and deprivations, and that enable them to enjoy their security and dignity as human beings'.[29] It is the right to 'functionings' or the right to the things that a person can do or be.[30] Therefore, assessing the RTD implies a critical examination of the overall

24 U. Baxi. 'Human Rights, Accountability and Development (1978) 18 *Indian Journal of International Law* 279.

25 Ibid.

26 A. Sengupta. 'The Human Right to Development' In B. Andreassen and S. Marks (eds.) *Development as a Human Right: Legal, Political and Economic Dimensions* (Harvard School of Public Health, Francois Xavier Bagnoud Center For Health and Human Rights 2006), 17.

27 J. Whyte. 'Book Review: Development as a Human Right edited by Bard A. Andreassen and Stephen P. Marks, Harvard University Press, London England, 2006' (2007) 1(1) *The Electronic Journal of Sustainable Development* 2.

28 A. Sengupta. 'Development Cooperation and the Right to Development' http://tanzaniagateway.org/docs/Development_cooperation_and_the_Right_to_Development.pdf (Accessed 27 December 2016), 4.

29 P. Vizard. 'The Human Development Capability Approach and Human Rights' (2006) 4 *Human Development and Capability Association* briefing note (on file with author); also P. Vizard, S. Fukuda-Parr and D. Elson. 'Introduction: The Capability Approach and Human Rights' (2011) 12(1) *Journal of Human Development and Capabilities 1–22*. http://sakikofukudaparr.net/wp-content/uploads/2016/06/The-Capability-Approach-and-Human-Rights.pdf (Accessed 8 August 2017).

30 M. Nussbaum. 'Capabilities and Human Rights' (1997) 66 *Fordham Law Review* 285; also D. Bilchitz. *Poverty and Fundamental Rights: The Justification and Enforcement of Socio-Economic Rights* (Oxford University Press 2007), 10–17.

development process. Such an examination should take into account the allocated financial resources, the planning and should give equal attention to development objectives and their strategies of implementation, without neglecting the causes of underdevelopment. In fact, the capability theory shifts poverty from non-rights (liberal theory) to rights and compels everyone, state or institution in a position to help to do so, as will be shown in the next chapter. This is in line with the United Nations Development Programme (UNDP's) perspective claiming that eradicating poverty is more than a major development challenge, but a human right one.[31]

From a different perspective, the multidimensional character of the RTD does not serve the purpose of the RTD in question which is to eradicate poverty. This association of human rights renders the RTD vague, complicates its implementation and keeps it in a stage of mere rhetoric.[32] Allan Rosas calls for a comprehensive clarification of the right.[33] This means the significance of the RTD is unclear. The more the RTD is expanded to include all possible aspects of development, the more difficult it becomes to specify what would count as a violation or infringement of the right, since almost anything may count as such, and the responsibility of not fulfilling it becomes correspondingly diffused and unidentifiable. In other words, it does not help to have a basket filled with human rights if none of them can be fulfilled. Donnelly argues that 'the paradox of rights is that the fewer you possess, the more important they become',[34] hence the argument that the content of the RTD should be narrowed down and not include all aspects of development, but rather focus on the context of 'economic development' which was at the origin of the right in question.[35]

The criticism of the composite aspect of the RTD and even its existence raises the questions of its justiciability and feasibility. In other words, the RTD is not justiciable and feasible. This is the liberal concept of 'right' secured in Dworkin's philosophy which argues that rights are exclusively individual,[36] or 'individualistic, adversarial, and negative and therefore must be susceptible to a private judicial remedy'.[37] It is however submitted that the political agitation/naming and shaming as well as public interest litigation (PIL) can assist in ensuring respect for collective rights.

31 UNDP Report 2005, 73.

32 E. Bello. 'Article 22 of the African Charter on Human and Peoples' Rights' In E. Bello and B. Adjibola (eds.) *Essay in Honour of Judge Taslim Olawale Elias* (Martinus Nijhoff 1992), 462.

33 A. Rosas. 'The Right to Development' In A. Eide, C. Krausus and A. Rosas (eds.) *Economic Social and Cultural Rights* (Martinus Nijhoff 2001), 251.

34 J. Donnelly, quoted from J. K. Hansen and H-O. Sano. 'The Implications and Value Added of a Right Based Approach' In B. Andreassen and S. Marks (eds.) *Development as a Human Right: Legal, Political and Economic Dimensions* (Harvard School of Public Health, Francois Xavier Bagnoud Center For Health and Human Rights 2006), 41.

35 D. Bentham. 'The Right to Development and Its Corresponding Obligations' In A. Andreassen and S. P. Marks (eds.) (Harvard School of Public Health, Francois Xavier Bagnoud Center For Health and Human Rights 2006), 83.

36 R. Dworkin. *Taking Rights Seriously* (Duckworth 1977), xi.

37 J. M. Woods. 'Justiciable Social Rights as a Critique of the Liberal Paradigm' (2003) 38 *Texas International Law Journal* 766.

On the first point, although the rule of law is necessary to enforce human rights, it is not the only road. In fact, social and political agitations can give birth to appropriate legislations and raise awareness on the issues in order to change the conditions. Supposing that there is no law or legislation involved, this book posits that social and political pressure, naming, awareness raising and disgracing are other ways to compel violators of human rights to stop their evil deeds and protect human dignity. The power of popular insurrection was seen in Ukraine during what was called the 'Orange Revolution' in 2006, when citizens, in winter, went to the street and forced the President of the Republic out of office without using a legal process. A similar situation happened in November 2008 in Thailand where the population peacefully forced the Prime Minister out of office without any legal process. Furthermore, in North Africa, popular insurrection described as the Arab Spring ousted Presidents Ben Ali and Osni Mubarack in Tunisia and Egypt respectively. According to the Nobel Prize winner Amartya Sen, the value of a human right is not linked to its feasibility.[38] In other words, the aptitude to make something a legal entitlement is not necessary to make that thing a human right.[39] Therefore, if the state lacks the capacity to establish a legal system to protect the RTD, this shortcoming does not affect the nature of the right which is inherent to all human beings.

On the opposite side of the debate, Whyte argues that 'Sen rejects the idea that the standard of human rights implies corresponding obligation, that if you have a proper claim to something, then some individual or institution is obliged to provide you with that something'.[40] He further argues that Sen confounds the RTD with belief in this right.[41] Prior to Whyte, this reasoning led Donnelly to reject the RTD because of its non-justiciability. Accordingly, individuals cannot hold it against their states, or individual *qua* individual.[42]

It is contended that human rights should not be confused with legal rights because human rights precede law and derive from the concept of human dignity.[43] Human rights are first and foremost 'commitments to social ethics'.[44] To use Sen's words,

> [t]he validity of these rights can be questioned only by showing that they will not survive public scrutiny, but not – contrary to a common temptation – by pointing to the fact that in many repressive regimes that prevent open public discussions in one way or another, these rights are not taken seriously.[45]

38 A. Sen. 'Human Rights and Development' In B. Andreassen and S. Marks (eds.) *Development as a Human Right: Legal, Political and Economic Dimensions* (Harvard School of Public Health, Francois Xavier Bagnoud Center For Health and Human Rights 2006), 3.

39 Ibid., 3.

40 Whyte (n 27).

41 Ibid.

42 J. Donnelly. 'In Search of the Unicorn: The Jurisprudence and Politics of the Right to Development' (1985) 15 *California Western International Law Journal* 485.

43 U. Baxi. 'From Human Rights to the Right to be Human: Some Heresies' In S. Kothari and H. Sethi (eds.) *Rethinking Human Rights* (Tripathy 1989), 187.

44 Sen (n 37) 3.

45 Ibid.

The question becomes, why hide behind the justiciability of the RTD to claim that it is not a right? Is there any international court to sue states that do not comply with the provision of the International Covenant on Economic, Social and Cultural Rights (ICESCR) or the ICCPR? For instance, according to the ICESCR, education should be free, but various African countries are still charging school fees. At the national level, the provisions pertaining to socio-economic rights are very often located in general principles of states' policy and are therefore not justiciable. This does not make socio-economic rights less of a human right. Consequently, the non-justiciability of the RTD (at the global level) should not destroy its qualification as a human right. Nonetheless, it is worth noting that if someone is deprived of his or her socio-economic rights or civil and political ones, he or she can petition the relevant body and not so for the RTD, though the natural character of the latter gives it a significant value.

On the second point of PIL, it could be argued that the RTD, though very often located in general Directives Principles of State Policy[46] may just be as justiciable as any right contained in a national bill of rights. This can be done through the PIL mechanism which is an interpretation of the law through which judges protect public interest by infusing principles of States policies into the binding constitutional provisions to foster the spirit of social justice.[47] This approach is well demonstrated by Indian jurisprudence.[48]

2.2.4. *The right to self-determination: an essential element of the right to development*

The right to self-determination which 'contains all the aspiration of freedom'[49] is another basis of the RTD as it embodies 'the ideal of a people to pursue its own destiny'.[50] It is underlined by article 1(2) of the UNDRTD. According to this provision, the RTD will never be a reality if there is no right to self-determination. In this regard, the second purpose in article 1 of the UN Charter is to 'develop friendly relations among nations based on respect for the principle of equal rights and self-determination of peoples and to take other appropriate measures to strengthen universal peace.' Accordingly, relations amongst states should be based on the principle of equality between them. This equality implies their right to freedom to

46 Principles of state policy are generally not justiciable.

47 For more on PIL, see Circle of Rights – Economic, Social & Cultural Rights Activism: A Training Resource 'Justiciability of ESC [Economic Social and Cultural] Rights-the Indian experience' at www1.umn.edu/humanrts/edumat/IHRIP/circle/justiciability.htm (Accessed 27 December 2016).

48 See for example *Francis Coralie Mullin v The Administrator, Union Territory of Delhi* (1981) 2 SCR 516; *Keshavananda Bharati v State of Kerala* (1973) 4 SCC 225, para 1707; *Bandhua Mukti v Union of India* (1984) 3 SCC 161; *Shanti Star Builders v Narayan K. Totame* (1990) 1 SCC 520; *Olga Tellis v Bombay Municipal Corporation* (1985) 3 SCC 545.

49 J. Gilbert. *Indigenous Peoples' Land Rights Under International Law: From Victims to Actors* (1st ed.) (Transnational Publishers 2006), 200.

50 Ibid.

choose their political system, to administer their wealth and resources which can be understood as their right to self-determination. This is fundamental in realising universal peace as well as fighting poverty or providing an 'adequate standard of living'.

According to this provision, there is no doubt that the beneficiary of the right to self-determination is a sovereign state on the international plane. This interpretation of self-determination is substantiated by the provision of the ICESCR and the ICCPR in their common article 1(1) which reads as follows: 'all peoples have the right of self-determination. By virtue of that right, they freely determine their political status and freely pursue their economic, social and cultural development'. This provision is confirmed by the Vienna Declaration,[51] the Charter of Economic Rights and Duties of the States (CERDS),[52] the United Nations Educational, Scientific and Cultural Organisation (UNESCO) Convention on the Protection and Promotion of the Diversity of Cultural Expressions[53] as well as the UN Declaration on the Rights of Indigenous Peoples.[54] For most of these instruments, self-determination is a group right or 'people's right'. But it seems that in the international arena, self-determination refers to sovereign entities like states.[55]

In sum, the RTD is inalienable, connected or 'interlinked' with the right to self-determination and is a multifaceted human right which comprises civil and political rights as well as socio-economic and cultural rights. It emphasises the right to participation, the right to self-determination and the principle of universality, interdependency and indivisibility of human rights. As will be shown later, it is an individual as well as a collective right. However, this description of the RTD, though based on the first article of the UNDRTD, is controversial.

2.3. The right to development: a contentious human right

This section shows that the RTD is a subject of disagreement in academic arenas as well as at the UN level.

51 Vienna Declaration, part 1, para 2; also art 4 of the NIEO Declaration, 26(k) and 14(e) of Copenhagen Declaration.

52 Art 2 'Every State has and shall freely exercise full permanent sovereignty, including possession, use and disposal, over all its wealth, natural resources and economic activities'.

53 Art 2(2).

54 Art 3.

55 For more on the nature of the RTD, see Concluding Observation on Canada, UN Doc. CCPR/C/79/Add.105 (1999), para 8; Concluding Observations on Mexico, UN Doc. CCPR/C/79/Add.109 (1999); Concluding Observations on Norway, UN Doc. CCPR/C/79/Add.112 (1999); Concluding Observations on Australia, UN Doc. CCPR/CO/69/AUS (2000); M. Scheinin. 'Advocating the Right to Development Through Complaint Procedures Under Human Right Treaties' In A. Andreassen & S. Marks (eds.) *Development as a Human Right: Legal, Political and Economic Dimensions* (Harvard School of Public Health, Francois Xavier Bagnoud Center For Health and Human Rights 2006), 276; Communication No 547/1993 *Makuika et al v New Zealand* (27 October 2000) where the it is argued that the right to self-determination is an individual human right; See 2000 Report of the Human Rights Committee, Vol. II, UN Doc. A/56/40 (Vol. II), 11–29.

2.3.1. The controversy in academic arenas

In academic circles, the debate on the nature of the right under study goes from the concept of development law to the RTD *per se.*

2.3.1.1. The disagreements on development law

This subsection unveils the link between the law of development[56] and the RTD. The theory advanced here is the positivist one claiming that law is the source of rights and that a right emanates from the law. From this standpoint, it could be said that the law of development sets out the legal or normative framework for pursuing development by the addressees in that law, i.e. states both as individual or collectives. The law of development which may be in the form of customary international law, treaties, statutes, case law and charity law, amongst others, consists of principles, objectives and even steps to be taken towards attaining development or particular levels of development. The RTD is therefore secured in the law of development. The latter, also called international development law or international economic development law was fashioned by a group of academic lawyers around *l'Annuaire Francais de Droit International* with prominent names such as Michel Virally and Maurice Flory in the driving seat.[57]

The discussion about international law and development may be seen as a feature of the broader controversy about the nature and the identity of international law between those who view international law as a normative system and those who discard the notion of rules in favour of a process and a policy, goal-orientated approach.[58] It is a question opposing supporters of the Fitzmaurice School of thought, who believe in the classic sources of international law made of a set of neutral value-free rules, to be impartially and universally applied to the supporters of French School of the *Droit international du development* (DID) who are of the view that international legal norms are shaped by social, economic and ideological factors.[59]

According to the Fitzmaurice School of thought, the only sources of international law are the traditional ones listed in article 38 of the ICJ Statute established in 1922. The wording of article 38 of ICJ is as follows:

1 The Court, whose function is to decide in accordance with international law such disputes as are submitted to it, shall apply:

   (a) International conventions, whether general or particular, establishing rules expressly recognised by the contesting states

56 For more on this concept, see G. Schwarzenberger. 'Meanings and Functions of International Development Law' In F. G. Snyder and P. Slinn (eds.) *International Law of Development: Com paratives Perspectives* (Professional Books 1987), 49.

57 Ibid.

58 P. Slinn. 'Differing Approaches to the Relationship Between International Law and Development' In F. G. Snyder and P. Slinn (eds.) *International Law of Development: Comparatives Perspectives* (Professional Books 1987), 28.

59 Ibid.

(b) International custom, as evidence of a general practice accepted as law
(c) The general principle of law recognised by civilized nations
(d) Subject to the provision of article 59,[60] judicial decisions and the teachings of the most highly qualified publicists of the various nations, as subsidiary means for the determination of rules of law.

2 This provision shall not prejudice the power of the court to decide a case *ex aequo et bono*[61] if the parties agree thereto.

The ICJ Statute clearly identifies the sources of international law. According to the Fitzmaurice School, to be included in international law, development should find its sources in article 38 of the ICJ Statutes. From this standpoint, there is no such thing as the RTD.

However, since 1922 when the ICJ was established, international law has evolved and unilateral acts, equity, resolutions of the UN General Assembly or Declarations and *Jus Cogens* were added to the traditional sources of international law.[62] This view is sustained by the French school of thought which believes that international law is not static, but develops in response to societal needs. In responding to societal needs, law can be used to eradicate poverty, address social inequities and encourage interdependence between nations. Opponents of this theory warn about confusion of law as it is (*lex lata*) with law as it should be (*lex feranda*). For instance, they argue that it is an illusion to believe that there is a system of international law underpinned by the principle of social interdependency of states and functioning in the interest of all.[63] In this respect, Slinn argues that confusing *lex lata* and *lex feranda* will lead to a vagueness which will affect the reliability of the international legal system and create confusion between law, morality and ideology.[64] In the same vein, Sir Robert Jennings offered a caution related to the concept of the NIEO in these terms:[65]

> Unless the formal test of what it is international law and what it is not can be tightened, clarified and disciplined, we shall find international law becoming

60 Art 59 of the ICJ Statute reads: 'The decision of the Court has no binding force except between the parties and in respect of that particular case'.

61 To decide a case *ex aequo et bono* means to decide otherwise than in accordance with the applicable law.

62 H. Thirlway. 'The Sources of International Law' In D. Evans (ed.) *International law* (Oxford University Press 2006), 135; for more on the *jus cogens* nature of the RTD, see F. Murray-Bruce 'Should Anybody be Poor – An Analysis of the Duties and Obligations of the International Community to the Eradication of Poverty and Growth of Sustainable Development in Light of the *jus cogens* Nature of the Declaration of the Right to Development' (2005) bpress legal series' Working paper No 725.

63 B. Cheng. *International Law, Teaching and Practice* (Stevens and Sons 1982), 514; also Slinn (n 58) 30.

64 Slinn (n 58) 31.

65 Ibid.

more and more a series of expressions in juridical guise of the ambitions of different political and economic pressure groupings.

This view is shared by Alfredsson who believes that claiming the RTD on the ground of the NIEO and other resolutions is a 'risky form of legal gymnastics' and cautions about using political preferences as law.[66] From this standpoint, it is important to abandon the concept of development law because it is legally incompatible with other basic concepts of international law, it is not binding and it is therefore not part of classical international law. Consequently, it can be argued that the form of an instrument is the only criteria to evaluate the intent to be bound. If parties want to be bound by an agreement, the best way to show that they are serious about the agreement and accept its binding character is to put it in a treaty form and not wait for their intention to be guessed or subjected to speculation. Following this logic, Kratochwil argues that a non-binding instrument or soft law is nothing, but 'a weak institutionalization of the norm-creation process by prodding the parties to seek more specific law-solutions within the space laid out in the declaration of intent.'[67] In other words, an international agreement not concluded as a treaty (sources of classical international law) is everything, but not law. The logical conclusion would be that outside Africa, the law of development is not binding since it is grounded on declarations at a global level.

Nevertheless, general principles of law as recognised by civilised nations constitute international law. Therefore, aspects of the development law, though grounded in general principles, are a source of the RTD. However, this view remains the subject of controversy. In this regard, Alfredsson – founding his argument on the hierarchy of sources of international law – aptly argues that a general principle of law cannot overcome a vigorous states' opposition to the development of the same principle to treaty and customary rank.[68] According to him, it would not happen because a general principle 'fills gaps in existing laws and does not override the other two primary sources [International convention and international custom] or to pre-empt on ongoing legislative debate which is loaded with disagreement and opposition or significant reservations by major participants'.[69]

Though this view makes sense, it can be put aside on the ground that, based on the sovereign equality of all states, international rules are equivalent, sources are equivalent, and procedures are equivalent[70] since all of them express the

66 G. Alfredsson. 'The Right to Development: Perspective From Human Rights Law' In L. A. Rehof and C. Gulmann (eds.) *Human Rights in Domestic Law and Development Assistance Policies of the Nordic Countries* (M. Nijhoff 1989), 84.

67 Kratochwil quoted G. Maggio and O. J. Lynch. 'Human Rights, Environment, and Economic Development: Emerging Standards in International Law and Global Society' Revised Draft, November 15, 1997 (on file with author).

68 Alfredsson (n 66) 84.

69 Ibid.

70 P-M. Dupuy. *Droit International Public* (Dalloz 1995), 14; for more on the debate on the normative force of the sources of international law, see C. M. Chinkin. 'The Challenge of Soft Law:

will of states.[71] More importantly, international law is evolving and addresses problems of the international society as they arise. It should be responsive of society problems. Are poverty and underdevelopment international problems? If the answer is yes, then the international community shall take action through international law to address such issues. Stressing the importance of non-binding instruments, Brownlie claims that when a resolution of the UN General Assembly (non-binding) touches on subjects that deal with the UN Charter, it may be regarded as an 'authoritative interpretation of the Charter'.[72] It could therefore be argued that the RTD, though secured in a UN General Assembly Resolution, but dealing with 'the better standard of living' incorporated in the UN Charter, has a normative force.

Furthermore, international law is dynamic and is frequently adjusted to respond to international crises whether they are linked to genocide, terrorism or abject poverty. In this perspective, the binding force of an instrument is not always in its form or label. The core question lies in the substance of the text and the intent to be bound. In other words, what is the true intention of the parties while signing the agreement? What is the content of the agreement?

The *Qatar-Bahrain Maritime Delimitation* case[73] demonstrates that the binding character of an agreement does not lie in its form, but in its content and in the intent of the parties. In a matter of Maritime delimitation and territorial dispute between Qatar and Bahrain, under the mediation of Saudi Arabia, the two countries agreed to transmit the dispute to the ICJ in case they did not reach a compromise. The agreement was made through an exchange of letters and a document called 'Minute' and signed by the parties as well as Saudi Arabia. However, when Qatar took the matter to the ICJ, Bahrain in its counter argument claimed that both parties had agreed to submit the dispute to the ICJ jointly and argued that the letters and 'Minute' giving jurisdiction to the ICJ were not legally binding instruments and were not treaties. The ICJ found that these instruments were 'international agreements creating rights and obligations for the parties'. It cited the *Anglo-Iranian Oil Co case*[74] to highlight that an agreement between a state and another entity may be binding even if it is not a treaty. Viewed from this angle, it could be argued that the law of development is law with a binding force at a global level. For those who believe that the law of development is nothing but a 'nice aspiration', Pellet replies that

Development and Change in International Law' (1989) 38 *International and Comparative Law Quarterly* 549; P. M. Dupuy. 'Soft Law and the International Law of Environment' (1991) 12 *Michigan Journal of International Law* 420.

71 In this regard, see the *'Lotus judgment* (1927), PCIJ, Ser A, No10, 18.

72 I. Brownlie. *Principles of Public International Law* (Oxford University Press 2003), 715.

73 *Maritime Delimitations and territorial questions between Qatar and Bahrain, Jurisdiction and Admissibility*, Judgment, *Qatar v Bahrain* (1994) 1 July. www.icj-cij.org/docket/files/87/6995.pdf (Accessed 27 December 2016).

74 *Anglo-Iranian Oil Co. Preliminary Objections, United Kingdom v Iran*, Judgment (22 July1952) ICJ Reports 93.

> [t]he law is not an ideal philosophy or a kind of mental game, but rather a guide for concrete social behaviour. International law does not appear in an abstract way, but in a social environment, in a given society.[75]

In the same perspective, the ICJ stated:[76]

> A rule of international law, whether customary or conventional, does not operate in a vacuum; it operates in relation to facts and in the context of a wider framework of legal rules of which it forms only a part.

According to these two views, international law is more than just pure *lex lata*. It should respond to the needs of the international community at a given time. In fact, it could be argued that development law is a law which addresses development issues that were not on the table when the sources of international law as provided for by the ICJ Statutes were drafted. According to Flory, the DID is *'cette nouvelle réalité juridique qu'est l'inegalité économique des Etats'*,[77] in other words, the international development law is this new legal reality which addresses economic inequality between states. Again, the form of the instrument or its location in the traditional sources of international law is not the yardstick of its normative force. In fact, non-binding instruments have many valuable attributes and may well be a substitute to a law-making treaty. In law-making through non-binding instruments, states agree to more details because the consequences of non-compliance are limited, the mechanism avoids the slowness attached to treaty ratification and the resulting document is flexible and may be the evidence of international support and consensus on a given topic.

However, it is difficult to consider mere declarations, codes of conduct, guidelines and other promulgations from the UN as law. The same applies to operational directives of multilateral development institutions as well as resolutions and other statements by NGOs. All these instruments are mere objectives with no legal strength. By the same token, Dupuy refers to soft law as 'either not yet or not only law'.[78] Accordingly, soft law is different from law as it is non-binding and the use of treaties or conventions as law making process should be the rule. In this perspective, Alliot argues that, the law of development can develop successfully by 'the elaboration of individual initiatives between two or more states, rather than by attempting the creation and imposition of an elaborate structure from

75 A. Pellet. 'A New International Legal Order: What Legal Tools for What Changes?' In F. G. Snyder and P. Slinn (eds.) *International Law of Development: Comparatives Perspectives* (Professional Books 1987), 118.

76 I.C.J. Advisory Opinion of December 20, 1980, interpretation of the agreement of 25 March 1951 between the W.H.O and Egypt, No 10, Rep, 16.

77 Slinn (n 57).

78 Dupuy quoted G. Maggio and O. J. Lynch. 'Human Rights, Environment, and Economic Development: Emerging Standards in International Law and Global Society' Revised Draft, November 15, 1997 (on file with author).

above'.[79] In other words, Alliot is a proponent of treaty law for the development of development law. Nonetheless, he does not address how the shortcomings of treaty law such as slowness and wastage of time (for examples) attached to treaty ratification will be addressed in the process. Alliot condemns the use of legislation as tools of emphasising desirable future goals, without any real hope of their being implemented.[80] He further argues that this approach may weaken the authority of the law itself.[81] Sharing his view, Chamelier believes that development cannot be a legal objective and maintains that the international legal system is incapable of transformation towards the realisation of development goals.[82] This view was sustained by Dupuy in the *Texaco v Libya* case[83] when he said that article 2 of the 1974 CERDS[84] 'must be analysed as a political rather than as a legal declaration concerned with the ideal strategy of development and as such, supported only by non-industrialised states'.[85] In other words, article 2 of CERDS, was not law,

79 A. Alliot. 'The Law of Development and the Development of Law' In F. G. Snyder and P. Slinn (eds.) *International Law of Development: Comparatives Perspectives* (Professional Books 1987), 84.

80 A. Alliot. 'Towards the Unification of Laws in Africa' (1965) 14 *International Comparative Law Quarterly* 366.

81 Ibid.

82 M. Chemelier-Gendreau. 'Relationship Between the Ideology of Development and Development Law' In F. G. Snyder and P. Slinn (eds.) *International Law of Development: Comparatives Perspectives* (Professional Books 1987), 57; also M. Hansungule. 'The Right to Development' 18, paper presented at the International Human Rights Academy jointly organised by University of Western Cape, Utrecht University, Ghent University, American University; October 2005, Sea Point, Cape Town, South Africa.

83 *Texaco Overseas Petroleum Company and California Asiatic Oil Company v Libya* (1978) (1) *International Legal Material* 30.

84 A/RES/29/3281, CERDS, art 2 (1). Every State has and shall freely exercise full permanent sovereignty, including possession, use and disposal, over all its wealth, natural resources and economic activities.

(2). Each State has the right:

a. To regulate and exercise authority over foreign investment within its national jurisdiction in accordance with its laws and regulations and in conformity with its national objectives and priorities. No State shall be compelled to grant preferential treatment to foreign investment;
b. To regulate and supervise the activities of transnational corporations within its national jurisdiction and take measures to ensure that such activities comply with its laws, rules and regulations and conform with its economic and social policies. Transnational corporations shall not intervene in the internal affairs of a host State. Every State should, with full regard for its sovereign rights, cooperate with other States in the exercise of the right set forth in this subparagraph;
c. To nationalize, expropriate or transfer ownership of foreign property, in which case appropriate compensation should be paid by the State adopting such measures, taking into account its relevant laws and regulations and all circumstances that the State considers pertinent. In any case where the question of compensation gives rise to a controversy, it shall be settled under the domestic law of the nationalizing State and by its tribunals, unless it is freely and mutually agreed by all States concerned that other peaceful means be sought on the basis of the sovereign equality of States and in accordance with the principle of free choice of means.

85 *Texaco Overseas Petroleum Company and California Asiatic Oil Company v Libya* (n 83) 30.

but a political provision; it was not *lex lata*. This position clearly establishes that development law is an ideal morality lacking enforceable legal standards because of its location in non-binding or soft instruments.[86]

Closer to the French school of thought, this book contends that international law is dynamic and changes according to contemporary problems. For instance, in the past climate change was not an issue of international law, but these days, it is.[87] Similarly, today in the context of globalisation, international law should address poverty; in fact international law is so fluid that Virally concluded that 'today there is a lack of sources of international law'.[88] As correctly argued by Flory, though international law is still concerned with peace and a sound relationship between states in the international community, the demands of this community are now broader than before and include economic and social matters[89] in order to ensure human welfare.

2.3.1.2. The disagreements on the right to development

The scholarly disagreements on the law of development demonstrate that the RTD itself is not universally accepted. Commenting on the book *Development as A Human Right: Legal, Political and Economic Dimensions*,[90] Whyte claims that the book is an intellectual disaster,[91] whereas Louise Arbour, former UN High Commissioner for Human Rights believes that it is 'excellent scholarly writing'.[92] This testifies to the controversy on the right in question. In the same vein, while the Algerian Bedjaoui and others see the RTD as the most important human right or 'the necessary condition for the achievement of all other human rights',[93] or as a 'right to rights',[94] as a 'basic right', as Henry Shue[95] put it or 'enabling right'[96] to use Abi-Saab words, it is also claimed that

86 P. H. Brietzke. 'Development as a Human Rite' In *The International Third World Legal Studies Association* (International Center or Law and Development 1984), 25.

87 Climate change issues are addressed through the Kyoto Protocol which is an international agreement linked to the UN Framework Convention on Climate Change.

88 M. Flory. 'A North-South Legal Dialogue: The International Law of Development' In F. G. Snyder and P. Slinn (eds.) *International Law of Development: Comparatives Perspectives* (Professional Books 1987), 21.

89 Ibid.

90 B. Andreassen and S. P. Marks (eds.). *Development as a Human Right: Legal, Political and Economic Dimensions* (Harvard School of Public Health, Francois Xavier Bagnoud Center For Health and Human Rights 2006).

91 Whyte (n 27).

92 Andreassen and Marks (n 90) iii.

93 M. Bedjaoui. 'The Difficult Advance of Human Rights Towards Universality in a Pluralistic World' Proceedings at the colloquium organised by the Council of Europe in co-operation with the International Institute of Human Rights, Strasbourg 17–19 April 1989; 32–47.

94 V. Dimitrievic. 'Is There a Right to Development?' paper presented at the annual convention of the International Studies Association, Cincinnati, March 1982 (on file with author).

95 H. Shue. *Basic Rights* (Princeton University Press 1980), 19–20; also W. P. Nagan. 'The Right to Development: Importance of Human and Social Capital as Human Rights Issues' (2013) 1 *CADMUS* 24–48.

96 M. E. Salomon. 'Legal Cosmopolitanism and the Normative Contribution of the Right to Development' In S. Marks (eds.) *Implementing the Right to Development – The Role of International Law* (Friedricht Ebert Stiftung 2008), 17.

> [t]he right to development is little more than a rhetorical exercise designed to enable the Eastern European countries to score points on disarmament and collective rights [and that] it also permits the Third World to "distort" the issues of human rights by affirming the equal importance of economic, social and cultural rights and by linking human rights in general to its "utopian" aspiration for a new international economic order.[97]

This strong stand against the RTD is supported by Donnelly who sees no legal or even moral reason for a RTD.[98] Even though he believes that it is correct to link human rights and development,[99] he also believes that 'the right to development is neither philosophically [nor] legally justified nor a productive means to forge such a linkage',[100] and he proceeds to explain 'how not to link human rights and development'[101] because such a right is a hindrance in the search for how to link human rights and development.[102]

Not far from Donnelly, Shivji, distancing himself from the cosmopolitanism understanding of the world, claims that the RTD is grounded 'on an illusory model of co-operation and solidarity'.[103] To Donnelly's claim that the RTD has no philosophical foundation, M'baye responds that any development endeavour has a human dimension that can be 'moral, spiritual and [even] material',[104] and to Shivji, he speaks as a cosmopolitan and locates the RTD in the realm of international 'solidarity which must be at the centre of all conducts, of all human politics, [of] man himself.[105]

In total disagreement with M'baye's contention, Bello criticises the RTD on the ground that it is

> [t]oo woolly and does not easily invite the degree of commitment that one expects unequivocally in support of an inescapable conclusion; . . . The right to development appears to be more like an idea or ideal couched in a spirit of adventure, a political ideology conceived to be all things to all men in a developing world, especially Africa; it lacks purposeful specificity; it is latent with ambiguity and highly controversial and "directionless;" it strikes a cord of the advent of the good Samaritan.[106]

97 P. Alston. 'Making Space for New Human Rights: The Case of the Right to Development' 3(1) *Harvard Human Rights Journal* (1998) 20.

98 J. Donnelly. 'In Search of the Unicorn: The Jurisprudence and Politics of the Right to Development' (1985) 15 *California Western International Law Journal* 473; also A. Vandenbogaerde. 'The Right to Development in International Human Rights Law: A Call for its Dissolution' (2013) 31(1) *Netherlands Quarterly of Human Rights* 187–209.

99 Donnelly (n 98 above) 477.

100 Ibid., 478.

101 J. Donnelly. 'The Right to Development: How Not to Link Human Rights and Development' In C. Welch (ed.) *Human Rights and Development in Africa* (State University of New York Press 1984), 261.

102 Donnelly (n 98) 478; also Donnelly (n 101) 274.

103 I. Shivji. *The Concept of Human Rights in Africa* (CODESRIA 1989), 82.

104 M'baye (n 2) 513.

105 Ibid., 523.

106 Bello (n 31) 462.

Sharing this view, Rosas argues that 'the precise meaning and status of the right is still in flux'.[107] In other words, the significance of the RTD is unclear. In support of this opinion, Gudmundur observes that it may be just to sustain that the RTD at least as provided for by the UNDRTD is not yet binding on states.[108] In this register, one of the most radical rejections of the RTD is from Ghai who argues that the right is dangerous for the human rights discourse as it

> [w]ill divert attention from the pressing issues of human dignity and freedom, obfuscate the true nature of human rights and provide increasing resource and support for state manipulation (not to say repression) of civil society and social groups and [lead] the international community for many years in senseless and feigned combat on the urgency and parameters of the right.[109]

Ghai's position is too extreme and seems to be a threat to the concept of human dignity itself, hence the correctness of Baxi's view that qualifies Ghai's as a 'cynical perspective'.[110] In fact, the law of development is 'not only a new discipline but also . . . a juridical technique for carrying on the struggle against underdevelopment,'[111] and this is in line with Eleanor Roosevelt's view, which in the early days of the UDHR observed: 'We are writing a Bill of Rights for the world, and . . . one of the most important rights is the opportunity for development'.[112] In agreement with this view and basing their arguments on the UN Charter,[113] on the Universal Declaration,[114] and on the 1966 International Covenant on Economic, Social and Cultural Rights,[115] Chowdury and De Waart claim that the RTD is a human right in international law.[116] The controversy among scholars filters down to the UN system.

2.3.2. Controversy at the UN

At the UN level, the disagreement on the RTD is characterised by the politicisation of the debate, the reflection of such politicisation in voting resolutions on the right and different approaches *vis a vis* the right by international organisations.

107 Rosas (n 32) 251.

108 Alfredsson (n 66) 84.

109 Y. Ghai. 'Whose Human Rights to Development' Human Rights Unit Occasional Paper (1989) as quoted by U. Baxi. *Human Rights in Post Human World: Critical Essays* (Oxford University Press 2007), 124.

110 Baxi (n 109) 124.

111 G. Espiell. 'The Right to Development' (2009) 5 *Revue des doits de l'homme* 190.

112 M. Glen Johnson, 'The Contribution of Eleanor and Franklin Roosvelt to Development of International Protection for Human Rights' (1987) 9 *Human Rights Quarterly* 19–48.

113 Art 55 and 56.

114 Art 28.

115 Art 2.

116 S. R. Chowdhury, E. Denters and P. Waart (eds.). *The Right to Development in International Law* (Martinus Nijhoff 1992), 10.

2.3.2.1. The politicisation of the debate

As indicated earlier, the idea of the RTD originated from the developing countries in the 1970s in their claim for a NIEO[117] to eliminate world injustice and allow Third World countries to enjoy their development. Right from the start, there were two opposing camps: one developed and the other developing. The latter made up of countries in the Non-Aligned Movement (NAM) complained about their poverty and underdevelopment which could not be resolved through years of decolonisation process as well as years of development co-operation[118] in which 'developing countries continue to face difficulties in participating in the globalisation process, and that many risk being marginalised and effectively excluded from its benefits'.[119] This claim did not sit well with the developed countries with the USA in the driving seat. As a result, throughout the numerous Working Groups on the RTD and the Open Ended Working Group led by Sengupta the Independent Expert on the right,[120] the latter was the topic of ideological and political battles.

The fighters were divided in four camps: first, the most dynamic members of the NAM in the Working Group on the RTD, known as the 'Like-Minded Group' made of Algeria, Bangladesh, Bhutan, China, Cuba, Egypt, India, Indonesia, Iran, Malaysia, Myanmar, Nepal, Pakistan, the Philippines, Sri Lanka, Sudan and Vietnam.[121] This group views the RTD as the roadmap to reduce global inequities and stand for the institution of fair trade rules, technology transfer from the North to the South and the abolition of developing countries' debts, amongst others.

A second group is made of more cautious developing countries that want to use human rights based approach in their national development plans and intend to keep good relations with the donor community at large.[122]

A third group comprises countries in transition and some wealthy countries. This group views the RTD as a bridge to enhance the North-South dialogue and is inclined to support the implementation of the right. The position of this group, especially the European Union (EU), is not always predictable because as Marks correctly observes, 'they will go along with a resolution if nothing particularly objectionable is inserted or will abstain'.[123]

The fourth group or the 'outsiders' is the one in which the USA always leads the votes against resolutions on the RTD. Japan, Denmark, Israel and Australia are the other members of this group. It is worth to note that the US rejection of the RTD is linked to its hegemonic ideologies implemented through the globalisation of capitalism.[124]

117 NIEO, UN G.A Res 3201 (S-VI), 1 May 1974.
118 S. Marks. 'The Human Right to Development: Between Rhetoric and Reality' (2004) 17 *Harvard Human Rights Journal* 139.
119 G.A. Res. 56/150, UN GAOR, 56th Sess., Supp. No. 49, at 341, UN Doc. A/56/150 (2001).
120 G.A. Res. 1998/72.
121 G.A. Res. 150, UN GAOR, 56th Sess., Supp. No. 49, at 341, UN Doc. A/2890 (2001).
122 Marks (n 118) 141.
123 Ibid.
124 Baxi (n 109) 128.

2.3.2.2. *The reflection of the politicisation of the debate on the voting pattern of right to development resolutions*

This division on the RTD characterises the proceedings at the international level. The disagreement was manifest during the vote of the General Assembly Resolution 41/128 of 1986 proclaiming development as a human right, where the USA cast the only negative vote and eight other countries abstained.[125] Even after 1986, the debates remain polarised at the UN. From 1998 to 2008, several resolutions on the RTD were adopted (some without votes) at the Commission on Human Rights (CHR or the Commission), (from 2006 Human Rights Council) and at the General Assembly.

An examination of the voting pattern on the resolutions on the RTD at the UN level shows the following lack of unanimity: In 1998, the resolution E/CN.4/RES/1998/72 was adopted at the CHR without a vote whereas at the General Assembly, 125 votes in favour, 1 vote against and 42 abstentions were recorded for the resolution A/RES/53/155. In 1999, the resolution E/CN.4/RES/1999/79 was adopted at the CHR without a vote and at the General Assembly 119 votes for, 10 against and 38 abstentions were recorded for the resolution A/RES/54/175. In 2000, the resolution E/CN.4/RES/2000/5 was adopted without vote at the CHR and the resolution A/RES/55/108 was also adopted without a vote at General Assembly. At the CHR in 2001 the EU (except the UK) was for the RTD, 3 abstentions (UK, Canada and the Republic of Korea) were recorded and Japan and the USA voted against.[126] The same year (2001), at the 56th session of the General Assembly (September – December) 123 votes in favour and 4 against (Denmark, Israel, Japan and the USA), with 44 abstentions were recorded.[127] The abstaining countries included Australia, Austria, Belgium, France, Germany, Norway, Sweden and the UK, who had voted for the resolution in the previous year.[128]

At its 57th session in December 2002, where the General Assembly adopted the conclusions of the Open Ended Working Group on the RTD, it recorded 133 votes in favour, 4 votes against (USA, Australia, the Marshall Islands and Palau), and 47 abstentions.[129]

At the CHR in April 2002, when the Commission (in the absence of the USA) was preparing the endorsement of the conclusions adopted by consensus at the third session of the Open Ended Working Group, 38 countries voted for the RTD, 15 countries including the EU (incorporating the UK), Canada, Japan and South Korea abstained and there was zero vote against, perhaps because the USA was not a member of the CHR in 2002.[130]

125 Denmark, Finland, Federal Germany, Iceland, Israel, Japan, Sweden and Great Britain.

126 Commission on Human Rights Res. 9, UN ESCOR, 57th Sess., at 68, UN Doc. E/CN.4/2001/167 (2001) (adopted by a vote of 48 to 2, with 3 abstentions).

127 G.A. Res. 150, UN GAOR, 56th Sess., Supp. No. 49, at 341, UN Doc. A/2890 (2001) (adopted on December 19, 2001).

128 GA Res. 55, UN GAOR, 55th Sess., Supp. No. 49, at 405, UN Doc. A/55/49, vol.1 (2000).

129 G.A. Res. 556, UN GAOR, 57th Sess., Supp. No. 49, UN Doc. A/57/49 (2002) (adopted on December 18, 2002, by a vote of 133 to 4, with 47 abstentions).

130 Commission on Human Rights Res. 69, UN ESCOR, Supp. No. 3, at 292, UN doc. E/CN.4/2002/200, Part I (2002); also L-H. Piron. 'The Right to Development: A Review of

The disagreement between UN member states was also visible in 2003 when the Commission decided to call upon its Sub-Commission on the Promotion and Protection of Human Rights to prepare a concept document assessing the avenues for the implementation of the RTD, including the adoption of an international legally binding instrument on the right, amongst others.[131] A total of 47 countries voted for the resolution; the USA, Australia and Japan voted against and 3 abstentions were recorded. In this vote, the USA stood strongly against the paragraph of the resolution considering the option of an international legal standard of a binding nature and attracted the attention of the General Assembly on the recorded votes of Australia, Canada, Japan and Sweden on the paragraph which were identical to its own.[132] The USA stood against the paragraph because it was not discussed in the Working Group[133] and on the ground that it was going to lead to wastage of resources. Danies, the US Representative to the Commission stated that:

> [The USA's] delegation opposed the proposal that the Sub-Commission should prepare a concept document on a legally binding instrument on the right to development because it would devote scarce resources to a project that would be unlikely ever to garner significant support.[134]

A similar trend of divergence on the RTD was observed in the same year (2003) at the General Assembly when 173 votes in favour, 3 against and 5 abstentions were recorded for the resolution A/RES/58/172. In the subsequent years the voting pattern on the RTD at the UN did not change, hence the following statistics:

> In 2004 at the CHR, 49 votes in favour, 3 against and abstentions 0 vote were recorded for the resolution E/CN.4/RES/2004/7 whereas at the General Assembly 181 votes for, 2 against and 4 abstentions were recorded for the resolution A/RES/59/159. In 2005 at the CHR, 48 votes for, 2 against and 0 abstention were recorded for the resolution E/CN.4/RES/2005/4 and at the General Assembly 172 votes for, 2 against and 5 abstentions were recorded for the resolution A/RES/60/157. In 2006, the first resolution of the Human Rights Council on the RTD (resolution A/HRC/RES/1/4) was adopted without vote, whereas at the General Assembly, 134 votes in favour, 54 against and no abstention were recorded for the resolution A/RES/61/169. The 2007

the Current State of the Debate. Report for the Department for International Development, April 2002. www.odi.org/sites/odi.org.uk/files/odi-assets/publications-opinion-files/2317.pdf 18 (Accessed 27 December 2016).

131 UN Human Rights Commission, Summary Record of the 63rd Meeting, 59th Sess; UN Doc. E/CN.4/2003/SR.63 (2003).

132 *Economic and Social Council Official Records*, UN Commission on Human Rights, 59th Sess., Supp. No. 3, at UN Doc. E/2003/23/E/CN.4/2003/135 (2003).

133 UN Human Rights Commission, Summary Record of the 63d Meeting, 59th Sess., at 3, 5. UN Doc. E/CN.4/2003/SR.63 (2003).

134 Statement by Joel Danies, US Representative to the UN Human Rights Commission, Summary Record of the 63rd Meeting, 59th Sess., at 5, 15, UN Doc. E/CN.4/2003/SR.63 (2003).

> Human Rights Council Resolution (A/HRC/RES/4/4) including issues related to the adoption of a legally binding instrument on the RTD was adopted without vote and the same concerns yielded 136 votes in favour, 53 against and 0 abstention for the resolution A/RES/62/161 at the General Assembly.

Again, the same pattern was followed in 2008 at the Human Rights Council when the resolution, A/HRC/RES/9/3 was adopted without vote; but interestingly, the General Assembly (including developed countries) voted overwhelmingly for the resolution A/RES/63/178 that not only endorsed the Working Group conclusions and the work plan of the High Level Task Force, it encompassed the language related to the 'consideration of an international legal standard of a binding nature'[135] which almost created chaos at the same forum in the previous year.[136] The 2008 General Assembly resolution was adopted by 182 votes in favour, 4 against (Marshall Islands, Palau, Ukraine and the USA), and 2 abstentions (Israel and Canada).

The shift in position by developed countries on the need to have a binding instrument on the right seems to suggest that a consensus on the right may not be far away. Nevertheless, it also seems that the unwillingness to have such a convention remains strong. In fact, by the look of things, the debate on the RTD at a global level has nothing to do with the concept of a human right to development *per se*, but is rather a political debate. Marks correctly observes that

> [t]he political discourse of the various working groups on the RTD and the Commission on Human Rights is often characterised by predictable posturing of political positions rather than practical dialogue on the implementation of the right to development.[137]

After the examination of UN member states' attitudes *vis a vis* the RTD, the next subsection assesses the behaviour of international organisations in respect of the right at the UN level.

2.3.2.3. *Different international organisations and different approaches to the right to development*

The lack of agreement on the RTD reaches international organisations at the UN level. These organisations have different approaches in taking part in debates on the RTD at the CHR. For instance, the EU participates very often through EU member states and a common EU position.[138] The International Monetary Fund (IMF) does not participate actively, but presents its views and updates on its

135 Resolution on the right to development, adopted by the GA on its 63rd session on 18 December 2008, UN Doc A/RES/63/178.

136 See General Assembly resolution on the right to development, adopted on its 62nd session, 13 March 2008 UN Doc. A/RES/62/161, para 10(d).

137 Marks (n 118) 141.

138 Piron (n 130).

programmes, while the World Bank participates fully through its Geneva representative and tries to better the RTD.[139] Lastly, the UNDP contributes concrete ideas to the discussion.[140]

In spite of these divergences on the RTD, the latter is now universally recognised and confirmed as shown at the 1993 World Conference on Human Rights in Vienna Declaration[141] where the juridical character of the RTD was reiterated without a single abstention or negative vote. Notwithstanding the controversy on the right under study, this book shares Alston's view when he says:[142]

> In terms of international human rights law, the existence of the right to development is a *fait accompli*. Whatever reservations different groups may have as to its legitimacy, viability or usefulness, such doubts are now better left behind and replaced by efforts to ensure that the formal process of elaborating the content of the right is a productive and constructive exercise.

As correctly argued by Okon, the RTD is now acknowledged by all[143] and the main question should focus on its implementation.

2.4. The legal force of the right to development

The aim of this section is to underline that notwithstanding its soft character, the RTD has a normative force. Non-binding instruments (such as the UNDRTD) are fundamental in testifying to the state practice and proving the *opinio juris* or intention to be bound as a proof of customary law. Following this perspective, Kratochwil argues that 'by legitimizing conduct which might diverge from the existing practices, soft law provides an alternative which can become a legally relevant crystallization for newly emerging customs or more explicit norms.'[144] From this standpoint, it can be argued that the RTD's source is in customary law because 25 years have passed since the UN General Assembly officially recognised the right in a Declaration,[145] 18 years since a consensus involving all governments was reached on it,[146] and 13 years since the Open Ended Working Group was

139 For more on the role of these institutions in fostering the RTD, see Chapter 3 of this book.

140 Piron (n 130) 20.

141 Vienna Declaration and Programme of Action (Vienna Declaration) 14–25 June 1993, UN General Assembly A/Conf.157/23 12 July 1993.

142 P. Alston. 'Development and the Rule of Law: Prevention Versus Cure as a Human Rights Strategy' In International Commission of Jurists (ed.) *Development, Human Rights and the Rule of Law* (1981) 31.

143 E. Okon. 'Poverty Alleviation and the Control of Public Revenue in Nigeria: Legal and Equitable Issues' (2007) 1 *Pretoria Student Law Review* 7.

144 Kratochwil (n 67)

145 The UNDRTD was adopted by the UN General Assembly in its Resolution 41/128 of 4 December 1986.

146 Vienna Declaration and Programme of Action 14–25 June 1993, UN General Assembly A/Conf.157/23 12 July 1993.

established and an Independent Expert on the right[147] was appointed as mentioned earlier. In addition, the UN High Level Task Force on the Implementation of the RTD was established[148] and remains operational. This extended and intense activity on the RTD demonstrates that it enjoys international recognition.

To the argument that the RTD enjoys a general international recognition, but is still short of state practice to gain the status of customary law,[149] it can be argued that for a practice to become customary law, the duration does not matter. What is needed is the consistency and generality of the practice.[150] It is instructive to note that even one practice is enough to create international customary law.[151] In this perspective, Cheng sustained that a well-worded General Assembly Resolution can create 'instant' customary law.[152] In this regard, Salomon argues that a mandatory language indicates 'the intent of parties to provide certain legal assurances'.[153] The language used in the UNDRTD is a well-crafted and mandatory language. For instance, the first article reads 'the right to development is an inalienable human right' and clearly highlights the individual and popular character of the right when it underlines that 'every human and all people' are entitled to it. Salomon observes that the UNDRTD is 'direct, unambiguous and leaves little scope for debate as whether the intention of the General Assembly was to declare the existence of a legally guaranteed right to development'.[154]

Nevertheless, General Assembly resolutions need a strong consensus because non-binding undertakings may be entered into in order to demonstrate the will of the international community to solve an urgent global matter over the objections of few states. Agreeing with such a perspective, Shelton is of the view that a resolution can be a parade to gather a consensus on an international urgent matter.[155] In such a case, the obligatory character or efficiency of the law remains questionable.

Nonetheless, in the case of the RTD, it can be argued that assessing *opinio juris* and defining the binding character of the law is less complicated. The 1986 UNDRTD was adopted by a very large majority with the only dissenting opinion coming from the USA. The 1993 Vienna Declaration produced a unanimous consensus, including that of the USA, that the RTD was a human right, hence the contention of this book that the recognition of the RTD as a human right (through the 1986 UNDRTD and 1993 Vienna Declaration) was the acknowledgement of

147 Commission on Human Rights, Resolution 1998/72 adopted without a vote on 22 April 1998 appointed Arjun Sengupta as the UN Independent Expert of the RTD.

148 The fifth session of the Working on the right to development recommended among other things the constitution of a High Level Task Force for the Implementation of the RTD within the framework of the Working Group. This recommendation was adopted at the 60th session of the Commission for Human Rights in its Resolution CHR 2004/7.

149 Sengupta (n 26).

150 Brownlie (n 72) 7.

151 B. Cheng. 'United Nations Resolutions on Outer Space: 'Instant' Customary Law?' (1965) 5 *Indian Journal of International Law* 23–24.

152 Ibid.

153 M. E. Salomon. *Global Responsibility for Human Rights* (Oxford University Press 2007), 89.

154 Ibid.

155 D. Shelton. 'International Law and Relative Normativity' In M. D. Evans (ed.) *International Law* (Oxford University Press 2006), 163.

its contribution to the norm-creating process and should have been in that account recognised as a norm of customary law. The RTD should have been binding by now because in 1984, one of the main arguments against it was that though the Commission on Human Rights was working 'on a Declaration on the topic' there was no international instrument recognising it,[156] but now there have been various instruments. So far, there are important developments as testified by the 1986 UNDRTD, 1993 Vienna Declaration, the appointment of a UN Independent Expert on the RTD and a UN Task Force on it as already mentioned.

In the same vein, Hansungule argues that though the UNDRTD, a product of a resolution of the UN General Assembly, is not legally binding, it 'may nevertheless be construed to constitute law or at the very least would evolve into law all factors being equal'.[157] Similarly, Brownlie claims that when a resolution of the UN General Assembly touches on subjects that deal with the UN Charter, it may be regarded as an 'authoritative interpretation of the Charter'.[158] From this angle, it can be claimed that the UNDRTD is binding because it deals with human well-being which is fundamental in the UN Charter and the ICESCR.[159] To use Baxi's words, 'the jurispotency of the Declaration (UNDRTD) has survived, and will transcend the well–manicured scepticism'.[160]

In spite of these strong views on the normative force of the UNDRTD, it is important to note that the latter remains in principle non-binding in international law and as such, its lack of universal legal backing stands on its way of becoming a hard law instrument.[161] Nonetheless, the development of international law led the world to a point of recognising obligations that transcend states' concern; these obligations are *erga omnes*, engaging the legal interest of the world at large, and are known as *jus cogens*. To use Kamrul Hossain's words '*Jus cogens* is the technical term given to those norms of general international law, that are argued as hierarchically superior, the literal meaning of which is compelling'.[162] Article 53 of the 1969 Vienna Convention on the Law of Treaties,[163] repeated *verbatim* by article 53 of the 1986 Vienna Convention on the Law of Treaties[164] states:

> A treaty is void, if at the time of its conclusion, it conflicts with a peremptory norm of general international law. For the purpose of the present convention, a peremptory norm of general international law is a norm accepted and

156 Donnelly (n 101) 267.
157 Also M. Hansungule. 'The Right to Development' 14, paper presented at the International Human Rights Academy jointly organised by University of Western Cape, Utrecht University, Ghent University, American University etc, October 2005, Sea Point, Cape Town, South Africa (on file with author).
158 Brownlie (n 72) 15.
159 ICESCR, art 11.
160 Baxi (n 109) 126.
161 Alfredsson (n 66) 84.
162 K. Hossain. 'The Concept of *jus cogens* in International Law' *The Daily Star* No 74 (on file with author); also in general see K. Hossain. 'The Concept of Jus Cogens and the Obligation Under The U.N. Charter' (2005) 3(1) *Santa Clara Journal of International Law* 71–97.
163 The Vienna Convention on the Law of Treaties, 1969, 1155 UNTS 331.
164 The Vienna Convention on the Law of Treaties Between States and International Organisations or Between International Organisations, 1986, UN Doc. A/Conf.129/15 (1986).

> recognised by the international community of states as a whole, as a norm from which no derogation is permitted and which can be modified only by subsequent norm of general international law having the same character.

In other words, a norm of *jus cogens* should be recognised as a norm of general international law; it should be accepted by the international community of states as a whole, enjoy immunity from derogation and be amendable only by a norm of the same rank. In its judgement in the *Nicaragua* case,[165] the ICJ confirmed that the doctrine of *jus cogens* was part and parcel of international law. It used the prohibition of the use of force to demonstrate 'a conspicuous example of a rule of international law having the character of *jus cogens*.'[166]

The RTD meets the criteria of *jus cogens*. Anchored in the promotion and protection of 'higher standards of living' for all, the RTD is recognised as a norm of general international law; the 1986 UNDRTD was passed with the blessing of 146 states, 8 abstentions and only one vote against.[167] The 1993 Vienna Declaration confirming the human rights nature of the RTD was unanimously applauded and so far has not been amended. In fact, the binding character of a *jus cogens* norm happens prior to the codification of the norms. This is clearly explained by Hossain who argues that codified norms such as 'treaties can at best be contributing factor in the development of *jus cogens* rules'[168] because 'a treaty cannot bind its parties not to modify its terms, nor to relieve themselves of their obligation under it, through a subsequent treaty to which all the parties to the first treaty have consented'.[169] He further argues that 'all existing, generally accepted *jus cogens* rules apply universally and none of the treaties which have codified these rules, have been universally ratified'.[170] It can therefore be argued that the RTD, anchored in the natural law theory had been a norm of *jus cogens* before its codification by the ACHPR, the UNDRTD and the Vienna Declaration.

Proponents of positivism are of the view that 'there is no simple criterion by which to identify a general rule of international law as having the character of *jus cogens*'.[171] Starting the debate from the case between *France v Turkey*[172] or the *Lotus* case in which the Permanent Court of International justice has stated that

> [I]nternational law governs relations between independent states. The rule of law binding upon states therefore emanate from their own free will as

165 Military and paramilitary activity in and against Nicaragua (*Nicaragua v USA)* (27 June 1986) (1986) ICJ Reports (1986) 100.

166 *Nicaragua v USA)* (27 June 1986) (1986) ICJ Reports (1986) 100.

167 Only the USA voted against the 1986 UNDRTD.

168 Hossain (n 162).

169 Ibid.

170 Ibid.

171 G. M. Danilenko. 'International Jus Cogens: Issues of Law-making' (1991) 2 *European Journal of International Law* 45.

172 *France v Turkey* PCIJ (7 September 1927), Series A, No. 10.

> expressed in conventions or by usages generally accepted as expressing principles of law.[173]

Consensualists can argue that though the *Nicaragua* case recognised *jus cogens*, the same case also acknowledged that 'in international law there are no rules, other than such rules as may be accepted by the state concerned'.[174] In other words, a rule of *jus cogens* is not binding on states which object to it or which are persistent objectors. Nevertheless, to use the words of the International Law Commission, 'it is not the form of a general rule of international law but the particular nature of the subject-matter with which it deals that may, in the opinion of the [International Law] Commission, give it the character of *jus cogens*'.[175] Therefore, echoing Rozakis, Danilenko is correct in arguing that

> [O]nce adopted, the peremptory norms bind the entire international community and in consequence a state can no longer be dissociated from the binding peremptory character of that rule even if it proves that no evidence exists of its acceptance and recognition of the specific function of that rule, or moreover, that it has expressly denied it.[176]

In the same line of thoughts, the chairman of the Drafting Committee during the Vienna Convention on the Law of Treaties, Yasseen explains that the sentence of article 53 of the Vienna Convention on the Law of Treaties 'accepted and recognised by the international community of states as a whole' did not mean that the universal acceptance and recognition of a rule of *jus cogens* was necessary.[177] He said:

> There was no question of requiring a rule to be accepted and recognised as peremptory by all states. It would be enough if a very large majority did so; that would mean that, if one state in isolation refused to accept the peremptory character of a rule, or if that state was supported by a very small number of states, the acceptance and recognition of the peremptory character of the rule by the international community as a whole would not be affected.[178]

In any case, the RTD passes the test; not only is it anchored in the natural law theory, but it also enjoys the support in modern legal theory. Apart from the adoption of the 1986 UNDRTD and Vienna Declaration, mentioned earlier, article 53 of the Vienna Convention on the Law of Treaties is declaratory of an already active international law with reference to *jus cogens*. As Murray-Bruce puts it

173 Ibid 19.
174 *Nicaraguay* case, ICJ Reports (1986) 135.
175 Danilenko (n 171) 45.
176 Ibid., 50.
177 Ibid., 54.
178 Ibid., 52.

> [W]ith the DRD's [Declaration on the right to development] purposes and objectives enshrined in the UN Charter – a peremptory norm of international law, a jus cogens from which there is no derogation – the Right to Development automatically espouses normative value and imposes legal and non derogable obligations on its duty holders.[179]

This view does not however, meet universal acceptance and is very much contested. Piron argues that there is no legally binding item on the RTD, though she acknowledges its 'moral or political force'.[180] Even though she has a good point, perhaps she should reconsider her view because there are instances where the binding character of an 'ambiguous obligation' is linked to the obligation deriving from its rights which are already part of a clear and precise obligation. In this regard, the RTD which might be viewed as an 'ambiguous obligation' made of socio, economic, civil and political rights, might be binding because its constituent rights are attached to the two International Covenants that are not ambiguous.[181] Furthermore, some obligations can be unclear or loose, but still be indispensable. Calling them 'imperfect obligations', Kant argues that they are important duties which can be attached to better formulated obligations called 'perfect obligations'.[182] For instance, the RTD can co-exist with the civil and political as well as socio-economic and cultural rights which are perfect obligations with a binding force. From this perspective, it will be correct to argue that the right in question is grounded in the ICESCR and the ICCPR.

It is contended that there is more than just moral force to the RTD because it can be argued that the binding force of the RTD derives from the principles of the UN Charter: sovereign equality of states, non-discrimination and the principles of inter-dependence and international co-operation.[183] Soft laws appear to be very instrumental to the creation of hard law. The path which led to the adoption of the two 1966 covenants seems to be followed by the RTD. This evolution clearly shows that a 'soft' instrument can produce hard ones and is therefore not a waste of time. A similar evolution seems to be happening on the RTD because 7 years after its declaration, a unanimous programme of action was undertaken by the international community. This evolution seems to indicate that a convention on the RTD is not far away. In fact, on behalf of the Non-Aligned Movement, Cuba recently called for the establishment of a convention on the RTD.[184]

179 Murray-Bruce (n 62) 16.

180 Piron (n 130) 14.

181 Sengupta (n 26) 10.

182 I. Kant. 'Critique of practical reason, quoted from A. Sen 'Human Rights and Development' In B. Andreassen and S. Marks (eds.) *Development as a Human Right: Legal, Political and Economic Dimensions* (Harvard School of Public Health, Francois Xavier Bagnoud Center For Health and Human Rights 2006), 7.

183 See UN Charter, Chapter 1 art 1 & 2 addressing the purpose and principles of the UN.

184 Twelfth session Working Group on the Right to Development, High-level task force on the implementation of the right to development, Fifth session (Geneva, 1–9 April 2009), A/HRC/12/WG.2/TF/2, para 11.

However, perhaps the strengthening of development law does not depend on the adoption of a binding instrument, but rather on 'interdependence–based reading and development informed reading of human right treaties [or instruments]'.[185] As De Feyter correctly observes, this will be in line with the Vienna Convention on the Law of Treaties,[186] according to which 'treaties [and other human rights instruments] are interpreted in the light of their context and their object and purpose'.[187]

In any event, the UNDRTD, though a soft instrument, has a normative value. In 1997 however, Nagendra Singh, President of the ICJ stated during a speech at the Vrige University (Free University, Amsterdam) affirmed that the RTD unquestionably exists, and that it is grounded on the essential principles of the UN Charter, especially those concerning the sovereign development of states, non-discrimination, interdependence and international cooperation.[188] In the same perspective, Professor Rais A Touzmohammadov argues that

> [T]he normative aspect of the content of the RTD is of course connected to those aspects that make it legally binding. It would be wrong to categorically reject the normative character of the right just because there is no appropriate multilateral treaty. In addition to the source of the right to development, there are now a number of aspects of the right to development that comes under the category of customary law.[189]

In other words, the mere fact that the expression 'right to development' is not explicitly mentioned in documents comprising the bill of rights does not destroy the validity of the right. Nevertheless, as correctly observed by Baxi, separating the UNDRTD from the initial texts on which it was based has weakened the document.[190] For instance, the UNDRD does not refer to the very empowering instruments such as the 1944 Declaration concerning the Aims and Purposes of International Labour Organisation (ILO) which amongst others condemn poverty, does not mention the Declaration on Social Progress and development,[191] the 1974 Declaration on the establishment of a NIEO and its Program of Action and the 1975 Charter on Economic Rights and Duties of the States (CERDS). Referring to these documents would have added more clarity to the UNDRTD which, though well recognised, is quite vague.

185 K. De Feyter. 'Towards a Multi-Stakeholder Agreement on the Right to Development' In S. Marks (ed.) *Implementing the Right to Development: The Role of International Law* (Friedricht Ebert Stiftung 2008), 98.
186 1969 Vienna Convention on the Law of Treaties, art 31, para 1.
187 De Feyter (n 185).
188 'What does "Defending the Right to Development" Mean Nowadays? Human Rights Commission 2002; Statement of the Working Group on the Right to Development. Joint written statement submitted by Centre Europe-Tiers Monde (CETIM) and AAJ. E/CN.4/2001/WG.18/CRP.15.
189 Ibid.
190 Baxi (n 109) 134.
191 G A Res 2542 (XXXI) 11 December 1969.

However, despite its broad recognition which gives it a normative force, at the national level, unlike in the African human rights system (to be discussed later in the book), the right remains non-binding as it is yet to be secured in a treaty or convention form.

2.5. Concluding remarks

The aim of this chapter was to examine the nature of the RTD. In so doing, it focused on the content of the right and studied the controversies on the right. It was found that the right is inalienable, is a multifaceted one made of civil and political rights, economic, social and cultural rights, right to participation and right to self-determination with a special emphasis on the interdependence, indivisibility and universality of all its elements. Apart from its composite feature, the right is also a claim for global justice, for fairness in sharing the world resources.

The right is very contentious in academic arenas where scholars battle on the concept of development law as well as the nature of the RTD *per se*. At the UN level, the debate has been turned into a political battlefield which is reflected in the voting patterns on UN resolutions on the RTD. The disagreement on the RTD is also illustrated through different attitudes adopted by international organisations in addressing the right. However, in spite of this disagreement, the right has been a subject of various undertakings at the national level and has a normative force, but remains non-binding at the international level where it is yet to be secured in a treaty or convention.

3 The implementation of the right to development

3.1. Introduction

Implementing a right entails giving effect to the right or turning it into reality. This suggests understanding what should be done by whom and to whom for the right to become reality. Put differently, who are the duty bearers and who are the right holders of the RTD? These questions are at the centre of this chapter.[1]

3.2. The duty bearers of the right to development

According the cosmopolitanism theory in which the RTD is crafted, the state, the international community, transnational companies, multilateral organisations, international financial institutions as well non-governmental organisations (NGOs) are duty bearers of the RTD. This suggests that states and non-state actors have the obligation to advance human dignity. Under the UNDRTD,[2] emphasis is put on the role of the state and the international community that shall rely on international cooperation to achieve the RTD. Accordingly, the state is the main or primary duty bearer and the secondary one is the international community. Therefore, while the state has the obligation to ensure the realisation of the RTD at the national level, the international community is also obliged at the international level.[3] The following section assesses the role of the state and the international community.

3.2.1. The state and the implementation of the right to development

Under the Maastricht Principles,[4] the state is presented as the primary duty bearer of human rights and this approach equally applies under the RTD discourse which

1 This chapter built on 'The nature of the right to development' discussed in S. D. Kamga. 'Human Rights in Africa: Prospects for the Realisation of the Right to Development Under the New Partnership for Africa's Development'. LLD Thesis (University of Pretoria 2011), Chapter 3.

2 Art 3.

3 The Vienna Declaration, part 1, para 10 (5); the ICCPR, art 2 and the UNDRTD, art 1(1) and (2).

4 The Maastricht Guidelines were adopted by a group of 30 experts in Maastricht from 22–26 January. 1997 (Maastricht Guidelines on Violations of the International Covenant on Economic, Social and Cultural Rights (1997)). The objective of the meeting was to 'elaborate on the Limburg Principles as regards the nature and scope of violations of economic, social and cultural rights and appropriate responses and remedies'.

compels the state to adopt policies that are 'favourable to the development of people and individuals'.[5] This obligation is clarified by the UNDRTD in these terms:[6]

1 States should undertake, at the national level, all necessary measures for the realisation of the right to development and shall ensure, inter alia, equality of opportunity for all in their access to basic resources, education, health services, food, housing, employment and the fair distribution of income. Effective measures should be undertaken to ensure that women have an active role in the development process. Appropriate economic and social reforms should be carried out with a view to eradicating all social injustices.
2 States should encourage popular participation in all spheres as an important factor in development and in the full realisation of all human rights.

This prescription is unequivocal in describing the actions to be taken by the state to fulfil the RTD which is well-presented in its composite nature to be respected by the duty bearer. It also expressly provides for the full inclusion of women in the development process. In other words, the state is obliged to design strategies and mechanisms to empower its citizens, to approach other states and various other stakeholders to play their role in ensuring that the RTD is achieved. This obligation is also captured by the 1993 Vienna Declaration as follows: 'Human rights and fundamental freedoms are the birth right of all human beings; their protection and promotion of human rights is the first responsibility of governments'.[7] This provision is not controversial and is well supported by the literature on human rights in general and the RTD in particular.[8] The 1995 World Summit for Social Development declared:

> [g]overnments should promote and protect all human rights and fundamental freedoms, including the right to development, bearing in mind the interdependency and mutually reinforcing relations between democracy, development and respect for human rights, and should make public institutions more responsive to people's needs.[9]

Accordingly, the duty bearer should not fail. Even the lack of resources excuse cannot be used as the state has the obligation to take steps including adopting a constitution characterised by the separation of powers, adopt legislative measures

5 The Preamble of the 1986 UNDRTD.
6 Article 8 of the UNDRTD.
7 Paragraph 1.
8 See in general A. Eide and A. Rosas. 'Economic, Social and Cultural Rights: A Universal Challenge' In A. Eide, C. Krause and A. Rosas (eds.) *Economic, Social and Cultural Rights* (Martinus Nijhoff 2001); also S. Marks. 'The Human Rights Approach to Development: Seven Approaches' In A. Sengupta, A. Negi and M. Basu (eds.) *Reflections on the Right to Development* (Sage 2005), 45–46. In the human rights discourse, state obligations are known as 'the Maastricht principles'.
9 Report of the World Summit for Social Development, Copenhagen, para 71, 6–12 March 1995. UN Doc. A/CON.166/9, 19 April 1995.

and other initiatives to foster the standard of living for all its citizens and establish necessary legal mechanisms to protect the enjoyment of these standards. In this respect, the state should be guided by the Vienna Declaration which calls on it to:

> Provide an effective framework of remedies to redress human rights grievances or violations. The administration of justice, including law enforcement and prosecutorial agencies and especially an independent judiciary and legal profession in full conformity with applicable standards contained in international human rights instruments are essential to the full and non-discriminatory realization of human rights and indispensable to the processes of democracy and sustainable development. In this context, institutions concerned with the administration of justice should be properly funded, an increased level of both technical and financial assistance should be provided by the international community.[10]

Put differently, the state should rely on regulations to ensure the enjoyment of the RTD. In this perspective, the level of freedom enacted should be conducive to development of a strong civil society which should be the necessary watchdogs for the RTD to become reality. In this respect, Sengupta argues that civil society organisations and NGOs in particular are key tools to secure participation, accountability and transparency in the implementation of the RTD.[11] This is to say, while taking action to secure the achievement of RTD, the government cannot omit to establish a conducive environment in which its activity should be scrutinised.

Whereas the state responsibility for achieving the RTD is agreed upon, the role of the international community is rather controversial in the right RTD discourse.

3.2.2. The international community and the realisation of the right to development

Even though the focus of this book is on the African human rights system, the international community has a role to play in making the RTD a reality in Africa. In other words, article 22(2) of the Banjul Charter should not limit international cooperation in realising the RTD to African states only because as Willy Brant rightfully observes, 'international cooperation is far too important to be left to [African] governments alone'.[12] In reality, a state's action to achieve the RTD is unlikely to be meaningful if is it not supported at the international level.[13] The

10 1993 Vienna Declaration, part 1, para 27.

11 A. Sengupta. 'Implementing the Right to Development' 17 (on file with author). The role of civil society in realising the RTD will be discussed extensively in section 3.2.2.4 of this chapter.

12 This Willy Brant Statement is the motto of The Friedrich Ebert Stiftung Foundation, available at www.feslb.org/(Accessed 24 September 2016).

13 B. Ramcharan. *The Right to Development in Comparative Law: The Pressing Need for National Implementation* (2010) 6.

international community comprises the UN member states, international non states actors, such as global institutions – namely the international financial institutions (IFIs) and the World Trade Organisation (WTO), and transnational companies (TNCs) and Non-Governmental Organisations (NGOs). This section will address the obligations of these duty bearers of the RTD respectively.

3.2.2.1. The UN member states' obligations for the realisation of the right to development

The notion of international responsibility for human rights was first advanced by the UN Charter, which does not only list conditions to secure development, but also calls on member states to act for the achievement of these purposes. In this vein, it compels UN member states to work together to improve the standard of living everywhere in the world.[14] In this context, humanity should precede national or individual interest. This means that through the UN Charter, the member states agree to give away aspects of their sovereignty for the sake of global happiness achievable through the realisation of the RTD.[15]

Besides the UN Charter, article 4 of the UNDRTD is unequivocal in urging UN member states to cooperate with each other in realising the RTD. Accordingly, they are obliged to work 'individually and collectively' in formulating international policies aiming to achieve the RTD. The international cooperation prescription is also at the centre of the Vienna Declaration which reads as follows:

> States should cooperate with each other in ensuring development and eliminating obstacles to development. The international community should promote an effective international co-operation for the realisation of the right to development and the elimination of obstacles to development.[16]

14 Art 55 of the UN Charter reads:

> With a view to the creation of conditions of stability and well-being which are necessary for peaceful and friendly relations among nations based on respect for the principle of equal rights and self-determination of peoples, the United Nations shall promote:

> a. higher standards of living, full employment, and condition of economic and social progress and development;
> b. solutions of international economic, social, health, and related problems; and international cultural and educational co-operation; and
> c. Universal respect for and observance of, human rights and fundamental freedoms for all without distinction as to race, sex, language, or religion.See also art 56 of the same instrument; art 1(3) of the UN Charter, art 22 UDHR, art 2(1) and 11 of the ICESCR, art 4, 23(4) and 24(4) of the CRC and art 32 of the Convention on Rights of People with Disabilities.

15 K. M'baye. 'Le Droit au Développement Comme un Droit de l'Homme' (1972) 5 *Revue des Droits L'Homme* 505–534. See also K. M'baye 'Emergency of the Right to Development as a Human Right in the Context of the New Economic Order'. paper presented to the UNESCO Meeting of Experts on Human Needs and the Establishment of a New International Economic Order, Paris 19–23 June 1978.

16 The Vienna Declaration, part 1, para 10.

This provision is echoed by Arts and Tamo who explicitly underline the sanctity of development cooperation as a vehicle without which the RTD may remain at the rhetorical level.[17]

Further, the international cooperation for the realisation of the RTD is also echoed through the notion of international solidarity[18] and moral universalism which suggest that 'individuals and political communities have a moral obligation to [their fellow citizens, and to] other societies in the form of both the wider society of states and the universal community of mankind'.[19] Put differently, those who have should not harm the have nots.[20] From an utilitarism viewpoint, the wealthy should be able to consider the common good before focusing on their personal interest, and for this to happen, it is essential to secure 'equal access to the means of personal and collective advancement and fulfillment in a climate of respect for the civilisations and cultures, both national and worldwide'.[21] This is in line with modern cosmopolitanism which epitomises the establishment of 'an emerging principle in international law "that holds" that there is a collective international responsibility for the human condition'.[22] This philosophy cascades down to the 2000 Millennium Declaration[23] which underlined the 'collective responsibility of states to uphold the principles of human dignity, equality and equity at the global levels'.[24] This was accentuated through the MDG number 8[25] which captured the need to rely on the international partnership to eradicate world poverty and to 'making the right to development a reality for everyone and to freeing the entire human race from want',[26] amongst others. Similarly, the 2015 Sustainable Development Goals (SDGs) underline the role of global partnership for the realisation of RTD in these terms: 'Strengthen the means of implementation and revitalise the global partnership for sustainable development'.[27]

However, the notion that international cooperation is central to the realisation of the RTD remains controversial. In this respect, Donnelly writes that 'States merely accept an obligation to take (unspecified) co-operative action to further (unspecified) human rights and they do not oblige themselves to undertake any particular course of action, let alone to protect or realise any particular human right'.[28] This dissenting view is reiterated by Rosa who does not see how the international

17 K. Arts and A. Tamo. 'The Right to Development in International Law: New Momentum Thirty Years Down the Line?' (2016) *Netherland International Law Review* 19–22.
18 R. Malhotra. 'Right to Development' Where Are We Today? In A. Sengupta, A. Negi, and M. Basu (eds.) *Reflections on the Right to Development* (Sage 2005), 130–131.
19 P. Hayden. *Cosmopolitan Global Politics* (Ashgate 2005), 34.
20 T. Pogge. 'World Poverty and Human Rights' (2005) 19 *Ethics and International Affairs* 74.
21 Malhotra (n 18) 131.
22 J. M. Woods. 'Justiciable Social Rights as a Critique of the Liberal Paradigm' (2003) 38 *Texas International Law Journal* Woods 793.
23 Millennium Declaration, GA res A/55/2, 8 September 2000.
24 Ibid., Sec I.2.
25 The targets for goal 8 are aid, trade and debt relief.
26 Millennium Declaration (n 23) sec III.12.
27 See the SDG no 17.
28 J. Donnelly. 'The Right to Development: How Not to Link Human Rights and Development' In Welch, C. (ed.) *Human Rights and Development in Africa* (State University of New York Press 1984), 262.

community can be held accountable for the realisation of the RTD.[29] In fact, current international order is not conducive to truly hold states accountable for failure to implement human rights and the RTD abroad. In this perspective, even though the SDGs[30] call upon the international community to ensure technology transfer, fair trade rules for all and equality between states, the international cooperation crafted under the SDG is not shaped around partnership based on shared responsibilities and informed by the need to achieve global justice. For this partnership to become reality, there is a need to establish viable mechanisms of accountability for all development actors.

Nevertheless, signing an international agreement to better people lives is not meaningless. Aaronson and Zimmerman correctly argue as follows:

> [t]he signing of the UN Declaration by the community of States was a commitment through multilateral mechanisms to further the enjoyment by all States . . . of access, on equal terms, to the trade and the raw materials of the world which are needed for their economic prosperity; to bring about the fullest collaboration between all nations in the economic field with the object of securing for all, improved labour standards, economic advancement and social security; . . . and they hope to see established a peace . . . which will afford assurance that all the men in all the lands may live out their lives in freedom from fear and want.[31]

This position is reinforced by Solomon who suggests that under the

> [UN] Charter, UN member states relinquish a degree of their sovereignty and instead accept international co-operation in the respect for, and observance of, human rights as a common purpose of their contemporary collective activities.[32]

In the same perspective, Baxi argues that the RTD will lose its significance

> [I]f it can be ethically said that the national of affluent societies owe no human rights obligations to non-nationals adversely and manifestly affected by economic and military polices of their governments.[33]

In sum, given that the RTD objective is to secure human dignity everywhere in the world, failure of UN member states to work towards achieving it may render the

29 A. Rosas. 'The Right to Development' In A. Eide, C. Krauses and A. Rosas (Martinus Nijhoff 2001), 251.

30 SDG 17 (n 26).

31 S. A. Aaronson and J. M. Zimmerman. *Trade Imbalance: The Struggle to Weigh Human Rights Concerns in Trade Policymaking* (Cambridge University Press 2008), 12.

32 M. E. Salomon. *Global Responsibility for Human Rights* (Oxford University Press 2007), 21.

33 U. Baxi. *Human Rights in Post Human World: Critical Essays* (Oxford University Press 2007), 149–150.

UN irrelevant. Therefore, the UN should take responsibility in securing mechanisms to hold its members responsible for global justice echoed through the RTD discourse.

3.2.2.2. *Global institutions' obligations for the realisation of the right to development*

The UDHR provides that everyone has the right to an 'adequate standard of living for himself and his family'[34] and to 'an international order in which [his] rights and freedom can be fully realized'.[35] This means that those who are behind global policies or those who craft the international order are bound to ensure that their actions do not hinder the realisation of human rights in general and the RTD in particular.[36] Therefore, global institutions such as the IFIs and the WTO that shape development agendas around the world have the responsibility to ensure that their activities do not hamper the realisation of the RTD.

3.2.2.2.1. THE IFIS' OBLIGATIONS FOR THE REALISATION OFTHE RIGHT TO DEVELOPMENT

The IFIs to be examined are the World Bank and the IMF. Both the International Bank of Reconstruction and Development Association and the International Development are known as the World Bank (the Bank). The Bank and the IMF were established in the aftermath of the 1944 Bretton Woods Conference.[37] The main objectives of the IFIs were to cater for economic growth; thus they play a fundamental role in the development arena, although they are not concerned with human rights or political issues. Article IV, section 10 of the Bank's Articles of Agreement is clear:

> *Political Activity Prohibited*
>
> The Bank and its officers shall not interfere in the political affairs of any members; nor shall they be influenced in their decisions by the political character of the member or members concerned. Only economic considerations shall be relevant to their decisions, and these considerations shall be weighed impartially in order to achieve the purposes stated in article I.

34 Art 25.

35 Art 28.

36 S. I. Skogly. 'The Role of the International Financial institutions in a Rights-Based Approach to the Process of Development' In A. Andreassen and S. P. Marks (eds.) *Development as a Human Right: Legal, Political and Economic Dimension* (Harvard School of Public Health, Francois Xavier Bagnoud Center For Health and Human Rights 2006), 288; also I. Skogly. *The Human Rights Obligations of the World Bank and the International Monetary Fund* (Cavendish 2001).

37 United Nations Monetary and Financial Conference, Bretton Woods, New Hampshire, USA, 1944. The World Bank Group is made of the International Bank for Reconstruction and Development (IBRD); the International Development Association (IDA), the International Finance Corporation (IFC); the Multilateral Investment Guarantee Agency (MIGA) and the International Centre for Settlement of Investment Disputes (ICSID).

Furthermore, article III, section 5 (b) imposes restrictions on political considerations in the Bank's financing activities:

> The Bank shall make arrangements to ensure that the proceeds of any loan are used only for the purposes for which the loan was granted, with due attention to consideration of economy and efficiency and without regard to political or other non-economic influences or considerations.

In the same vein, the IMF Articles of Agreement are similar *vis a vis* non-inclusion in politics. Article IV, section 3(b) on surveillance of exchange arrangement provides that '[t]hese principles shall respect the domestic, social and political policies of members, and in applying these principles the Fund shall pay due regard to the circumstances of members'. Similarly, schedule C 4 and 7 states that 'the Fund shall not object because of the domestic social or political policies of the member.'

According, to these provisions, the IFIs refuse to be part of internal affairs of their members. Human rights concerns were considered to be the 'affairs' of national governments. Following this logic, in 1960 the Bank refused to comply with the UN request not to give loans to South Africa and Portugal for reason of human rights violation. The Bank argued that the apartheid system of South Africa and the colonialism policies of Portugal were 'political affairs' of member states and had no economic impact on the loan criteria.[38] Therefore, these policies were not the Bank's business.

Over the years however, IFIs became important players in the field of development which had evolved to include human beings as its core element, hence the identification of development as:

> comprehensive economic, social, cultural and political process, which aims at the constant improvement of the well-being of the entire and of all individuals on the basis of active, free and meaningful participation in development and in the fair distribution of benefits resulting therefrom.[39]

Since development went beyond economic issues, IFIs could no longer stay away from human rights issues. Their argument classifying human rights as 'domestic concerns' could no longer hold because the human rights regime is international and extends beyond national jurisdictions. This is in line with Torsten's argument that 'the erstwhile Westphalian notion of State sovereignty has effectively been displaced by the emerging transboundary regimes'.[40]

38 M. Victoria. 'World Bank Power to Consider Human Rights Factors in Loans Decisions' (1979) 13 *Journal of International Law and Economics* 123.

39 Preamble of the 1986 UNDRTD, para 2.

40 A. Torsten. 'The Bretton Woods Institutions and Human Rights: Are the PRSPs Informed by Human Rights Consideration?' Chapter Contribution to an Anthology Entitled *Shared Responsibilities – Human Rights and Development in the 21st Century*, presented at the Annual Conference of the

The international Bill of Rights was also instrumental in getting the IFIs on board the human rights train. In its General Comment No 2 on article 22 of the CESCR,[41] the Committee on ESCR states:

> Recommendations in accordance with article 22 may be made to any 'organs of the United Nations, their subsidiary organs and specialized agencies concerned with furnishing technical assistance. The committee considers that this provision should be interpreted so as to include virtually all United Nations organs and agencies involved in any aspect of international development co-operation. It would therefore be appropriate for recommendations in accordance with article 22 to be addressed, *inter alia* to the Secretary General, subsidiary organs of the council such as the Commission on Human Rights, the Commission on social development and the Commission on the Statute of Women, other bodies such as the UNDP, UNICEF and CDP, agencies such as the World Bank and the IMF, and any other specialized agencies such as ILO, FAO, UNESCO and WHO.[42]

In the same light, the General Comment No 12 on the right to food states that:

> The international financial institutions, notably the international Monetary Fund (IMF) and the World Bank, should pay greater attention to the protection of the right to food in their lending policies and credit arrangement and in international measures to deal with the debt crisis. Care should be taken in line with the Committee's General Comment No 2, to ensure that the right to food is protected.[43]

In other words, IFIs are called upon to be attentive to human rights issues. This call was answered by the Bank in 1974 through the following policy Statement:

> The Bank and their affiliates are forbidden by their articles of Agreements to act from political motives; but the Bank Group cannot ignore conditions of obvious internal political instability or uncertainty which may directly or indirectly affect the economic prospects of a borrower. To this extent,

---

Association of Human Rights Institutes (AHRI), Vienna, 8–10 September 2006 (Working Group III) 4.

41 Art 22 of the CESCR reads: 'The Economic and Social Council bring to the attention of other organs of the United Nations, their subsidiary organs and specialised agencies concerned with furnishing technical assistance any matters arising out of the reports referred to in this part of the present Covenant which may assist such bodies in deciding, each within its field of competence, on the availability of international measures likely to contribute to the effective progressive implementation of the present Covenant'.

42 International technical assistance measures (Art 22): 02/02/90. Committee on ESCR, General Comment No 2.

43 Committee on ESCR, General Comment No 12 on the Right to Adequate Food, UN Doc E/C.12/1999/5, 12 May 1999.

> therefore, a country's political situation is taken into account in the investigation of proposals for financing.[44]

According to this statement, the bank acknowledges that it should consider more than just economic issues when issuing loans for development.

The IFI-sponsored 1980 Structural Adjustment Programmes (SAPs), however, did not take into consideration human rights. In fact these programmes had devastating effects in Africa.[45] Preaching free trade, market access and fiscal stability, the SAPs encouraged governments to introduce school fees, hospital fees and many other financial exigencies. This resulted in malnourishment, lack of education and health care as well as total poverty. The economic crisis and famine created by SAPs led an Intergovernmental Group of Experts to expressly urge the IFIs to respect the RTD in their operations in these terms:

> The Bretton Woods institutions (World Bank and IMF) should take account of *the right to development* in their guiding principles, decision-making criteria and programmes. The same is true of NGO's work at the international and national levels and whose activities relate to human rights, development and democracy. From this point of view, the ties between the World Bank and the IMF on the one hand, and the United Nations General Assembly and the Economic Social Council, on the other, should be strengthened. The IMF and the World Bank should be required to submit regular reports to the General Assembly and the Economic and Social Council to keep them informed of the extent to which these institutions are taking account of the right to development in their programmes and activities.[46]

Subsequently, the UN High Commissioner for Human Rights produced *Draft guidelines on a human rights approach to poverty reduction strategies* with a direct call on IFIs to be mindful of human rights in their activities. The *Draft guidelines* read as follows:

> global actors must be subject to accessible, transparent and effective monitoring and accountability procedures. If global actors fail to establish appropriate monitoring and accountability mechanisms in relation to their poverty reduction and human rights responsibilities, others should take steps do so.[47]

44 Torsten (n 40) 5.

45 B. Onimode, A. Adedeji and L. Agubuzu. *African Development and Governance Strategies in the 21st Century- Looking Back to Move Forward: Essay in Honour of Adebayo Adedeji at Seventy* (Zed Books in Association with the African Centre for Development & Strategy Studies 2004).

46 UN Doc, E/CN.4/1997/22, 21 January 1997, para 5. My emphasis.

47 The UN High Commissioner for Human Rights *Human Rights in Development: Draft Guidelines: A Human Rights Approach to Poverty Reduction Strategies* (2002) as quoted by Skogly (n 36) 296–297.

This is a clear injunction to IFIs to take responsibility in avoiding the violation of the RTD. According to Skogly, besides negative duties or obligation not to harm human rights, IFIs also have positive duties which compel them 'to take positive steps to achieve a certain result'.[48] This underlines the responsibility of the IFIs to take action to ensure that their sub-contractors respect human rights while implementing their projects.[49]

However, the real romance between human rights and the Bank started at the 50th anniversary of the Universal Declaration in 1998 when the Bank produced a booklet stating that 'the World Bank believes that creating the conditions for the attainment of human rights is central and irreducible goal of development'.[50] This shift of policy was also underlined by Joseph Stiglitz, then Senior Bank Vice President and Chief Economist who criticised the economic driven policies of the past. He stood for the ownership and participation of the beneficiaries for a successful development strategy in these words:

> We have seen again and again that ownership is essential for successful transformation: Policies that are imposed from outside may be grudgingly accepted on a superficial basis, but will rarely be implemented as intended. But to achieve the desired ownership and transformation, the process that leads to that strategy must be participatory. . . . It must involve and support groups in civil society.[51]

Stiglitz emphasises the right to participation and ownership which are fundamental elements of the RTD. Therefore, it can be argued that the adoption of these human rights principles was a shift towards catering for the RTD.

However, the recognition of the importance of the participation and ownership in the process of development did not amend the Bank's Articles of Agreement that keep the Bank away from 'political affairs' of its members, hence the view that ownership and participation can be easily interpreted as 'political affairs' with economic impact and thus remain in the confine of the Articles of Agreement.[52]

Nonetheless, the former Bank President, James D. Wolfensohn sees a nexus between development, human rights, poverty eradication and accountability. He clarifies the bank's position in these words:

> The Bank has long recognized that sustainable development requires both economic growth and social equity. There is, moreover, widespread recognition

48 Skogly (n 36) 289.

49 Ibid.

50 World Bank. 'Development and Human Rights: The Role of the World Bank' (1998) 2. http://siteresources.worldbank.org/BRAZILINPOREXTN/Resources/3817166-1185895645304/4044168-1186409169154/08DHR.pdf (Accessed 4 March 2017).

51 J. Stiglitz. 'Towards a New Paradigm For Development: Strategies, Policies, and Processes' Prebisch lecture, 19 October (1998) 21.

52 Torsten (n 40) 7–8.

> of the strong link between human rights and development. The connection between human rights and the attainment of the MDGs is also significant. The Bank's work substantially contributes to the realization of rights of people in a number of areas, such as health, education, gender, participation accountability, environmental, institutional reform activities and above all, the fight against poverty itself as a fundamental denial of human rights. Other Bank activities also contribute to the realization of human rights: these include fighting corruption, increasing transparency and accountability in governance. The Bank is currently reviewing its role with a view to making a more explicit link between human rights and our work, while at the same time remaining fully in compliance with our Articles of Agreement.[53]

It is important to note that dignitaries of the IMF were present at the forum where the 'RTD approach' to development was officially taken by Wolfensohn. It is contended that it was a 'RTD approach' because though the Bank did not amend its Articles of Agreements, it underlined human rights, participation and accountability which are the core elements of the 1986 UNDRTD. To be able to incorporate substantive aspects of the RTD in its policies, the Bank and the UN have established consultation on the RTD.[54] It could be argued that Wolfensohn's statement was a response to the Intergovernmental Group of Experts claiming that:

> The Bretton Woods institutions (World Bank and IMF) should take account of *the right to development* in their guiding principles, decision-making criteria and programmes. The same is true of NGO's work at the international and national levels and whose activities relate to human rights, development and democracy. From this point of view, the ties between the World Bank and the IMF on the one hand, and the United Nations General Assembly and the Economic Social Council, on the other, should be strengthened. The IMF and the World Bank should be required to submit regular reports to the General Assembly and the Economic and Social Council to keep them informed of the extent to which these institutions are taking account of the right to development in their programmes and activities.[55]

Most importantly the Committee on ESCR clarifies the IFIs human rights obligations in these terms:

> United Nations agencies involved in the promotion of economic, social and cultural rights should do their utmost to ensure that their activities are fully

53 J. Wolfensohn. 'Note of the President of the World Bank' In World Bank (ed.) *Statements Submitted to the Seventy-First Meeting of the Development Committee (Joint Ministerial Committee on the Boards of Governors of the Bank and the Fund on the Transfer of Real Resources to Developing Countries* (World Bank 2005).

54 UN Doc A/51/539, 23 October 1996 (Report of the Secretary General).

55 UN Doc, E/CN.4/1997/22,21 January 1997, para 5.

> consistent with the enjoyment of civil and political rights. In negative terms, this means that the international agencies should scrupulously avoid involvement in projects which, for example, involve the use of forced labour in contravention of international standards, or promote or reinforce discrimination against individuals or groups contrary to the provisions of all appropriate protection and compensation. In positive terms, it means that, wherever possible, the agencies should act as advocates of projects and approaches, which contribute not only to economic growth or to other broadly defined objectives, but also to enhanced enjoyment of the full range of human rights.[56]

As a result of their power, IFIs can remedy or prevent human rights violations. Taking the 1986 UNDRTD as a yardstick, IFIs can be involved only in development projects that meet the RTD criteria or projects informed by the right to participation, freedom of expression, non-discrimination, transparency and accountability. In this vein, Skogly adds that IFIs policies should enhance human rights such as the rights to education and food for example.[57]

In reality, the Bank remains attached to its Articles of Agreement which do not consider human rights. In June 2000, it approved the Chad-Cameroon oil pipeline project without looking at its impact on the *Bagyeli* people's rights.[58] The indigenous people known as *Bagyeli* were not informed on the possible consequences of the project in their community and did not receive any compensation for the effects of the pipelines crossing their lands. They were not consulted or involved in decision-making processes and an Indigenous Peoples Plan aiming to lessen the consequences of the pipeline on them failed to be in line with the World Bank's policy to protect individuals from harm caused by operations of the Bank.[59]

So far, the IMF has been inactive as far as incorporating human rights concerns in its policy. However, together with the Bank, the IFM initiated the Heavily Indebted Poor Country Initiative (HIPC) in 1996 before replacing it with Enhanced HIPC in 1999. The objective of these initiatives was to cancel debts owed by developing countries to the IFIs and regional development banks. To qualify for debt cancellation, applicants had to demonstrate the impact of the cancellation in reducing poverty, and this demonstration should be packaged in the form of a Poverty Reduction Strategy Paper (PRSP). To support countries in the preparation of their PRSP, the Bank published a *Sourcebook on Poverty Reduction Strategies* which was essentially a guideline on preparing a PRSP. Ultimately, the applicants had to demonstrate how the process of designing the PRSP was

56 Committee on ESCR, International technical assistance measure (Art 22), General Comments No 2, 1990, para 6.

57 S I Skogly *The Human Rights Obligations of the World Bank and the International Monetary Fund* (n 35)154–157.

58 See Forest Peoples Project: Annual Report 2001, 6–7. www.forestpeoples.org/documents/ann_rep/fpproj_ar_01.pdf (Accessed 4 March 2017).

59 Ibid.

participatory, transparent and the role of media in the process. Questions related to good governance, the rule of law, total accountability as well as a focus on health, education and nutrition were also part of the requirements.[60]

Although the PRSP Sourcebook did not allude to the Bill of Rights or any other human rights instruments, most of its requirements were human rights related. Food, health care, education and participation are all part of the Bill of Rights and essential for the realisation of the RTD.

A country such as Malawi that qualified for the initiative in 2002 had focused on improving its human rights record, among other things. The country referred to the ICCPR, the ICESCR, and section 12 and 13 of its Constitution protecting socio-economic rights.[61] To use Torsten's words, participation, good governance and human rights were 'all over the document.'[62] The fact that Malawi qualified for the Enhanced HIPC initiative evidenced the fact that in spite of IMF and the Bank's Articles of Agreements' failure to mention human rights as criteria for loans, these institutions understand that it is impossible to dissociate development and human rights. Nonetheless, how often does the Bank comply with its human rights' obligations?

Before the enactment of the HIPC, the Bank had established the Inspection Panel (the Panel) which is a three-member, non-judicial body created by Resolution 93–10 of the Bank's Executive Directors in 1993.[63] The Panel's duty is to protect individuals from harm caused by the operations of the Bank (with respect to its policies and procedures) as well as bank-funded projects. However, the panel appears to be a white elephant because it can only make recommendations to the Bank Executive Directors on the suitability of an investigation into the failure of the bank to meet its operational policies and procedure.[64] The weakness of the Panel was evidenced when during the China/Tibet Project,[65] the Panel was refused access to documents on the grounds that the Project was the property of the Chinese Government.[66] Amongst other constraints, the Panel is also limited in its protection of human rights because it does not receive individual complaints, but organisations' or associations' complaints only. It does not receive complaints related to human rights' violation by the Bank, but only complaints linked to operational procedures.

The responsibility of IFIs can also be located in their legal *personae*. This means they can be brought to court for not complying with human rights' obligation.[67]

60 Torsten (n 40) 12.

61 Ibid.; also Government of Malawi (2002) 85.

62 Torsten (n 40) 14.

63 C. Lumina. 'An Assessment of the Human Rights Obligations of the World Bank and the International Monetary Fund, With Particular Reference to the World Bank's Inspection Panel'. 14. Paper presented on the Development and Human Rights Course, Good Governance Programme at the Centre for Human Rights, University of Pretoria, on 12 April 2005 and 30 November 2005.

64 Ibid.

65 Ibid., 15; also China Western Poverty Reduction Project (Credit No. 3255-CHA and Loan No 4501-CHA).

66 Lumina (n 63).

67 For more on the IFIs legal personality, see Skogly (n 57) 64–70.

This is clarified by the ICJ that observes that international organisations are subjects of international law and as such they are bound by any obligations incumbent upon them under general rule of international law, under their constitutions or under international agreements to which they are parties.[68] In this perspective, the IFIs have been brought to court to comply with their human rights' obligations as shown in the *Chixoy Dam* case[69] discussed below.

The other human rights responsibility of IFIs also derives from the 2 Covenants: Article 16(2)(b) of the CESCR reads:

> The Secretary-General of the United Nations shall also transmit to the specialised agencies copies of the reports, or any relevant parts therefrom, from States Parties to the present Covenant which are also members of these specialized agencies in so far as these reports, or parts therefrom, relate to any matters which fall within the responsibilities of the said agencies in accordance with their constitutional instruments.

This provision allows the international community through the UN treaty bodies to monitor IFIs compliances with their human rights' obligations. In the same vein, article 18 of the same instrument provides:

> Pursuant to its responsibilities under the Charter of the United Nations in the field of human rights and fundamental freedoms, the Economic and Social Council may make arrangements with the specialized agencies in respect of their reporting to it on the progress made in achieving the observance of the Provisions of the present Covenant falling within the scope of their activities. These reports may include particulars of decisions and recommendations on such implementation adopted by their competent organs.

In the same perspective, article 40(3) of the ICCPR states that:

> The Secretary-General of the United Nations, may, after consultation with the Committee transmit to the specialised agencies concerned copies of such parts of the report as fall within their field of competence.

The reporting mechanism established by the UN treaty bodies aims to monitor how UN member states, UN agencies as well as IFIs comply with their human rights' obligations. This is evidenced by the three provisions referred to above. Earlier, it was argued that the RTD was made of socio-economic as well as civil and political rights. Therefore, the call to IFIs for compliance with these human rights is nothing but a call to comply with the RTD. This call to the IFIs has been reiterated

68 See *WHO v Egypt*, ICJ (25 March 1951) (1951) ICJ Reports 89–90.

69 For more on this case, see www.berkeleytravaux.com/reparations-maya-achi-guatemala-chixoy-dam-case/ (Accessed 4 March 2017).

by the court of law. In the *Chixoy Dam case*[70] submitted by the Centre for Housing Rights and Evictions to the Inter-American Court of Human Rights against the government of Guatemala, the World Bank and the Inter-American Development Bank (IBD) were taken to court to compensate for the violation of human rights of indigenous Rio Negro people in Guatemala. As a matter of fact, these indigenous people were violently displaced to make room for the construction of the Bank and IBD-sponsored Pueblo Viejo-Quixal Hydroelectric Project. After a protracted process, the parties agreed on the Reparation Plan of 2010[71] and in 2014 the US Congress called upon the Bank to implement the Chixoy Reparation Plan.[72] This development shows that the IFIs have human rights' responsibilities as seen through an analysis of the two 1966 Covenants. The validity of such responsibility is not conditioned by the justiciability of human rights, but by their simple existence in the international bill of rights and other instruments. This responsibility for the RTD derives from the obligation to do no harm in realising human rights which is a negative obligation under international human rights law.[73]

However, for some the IFIs cannot be responsible for poverty in the developing world. Proponents of this view, which include Cohen[74] and Rawls, argue that culture, religion and corruption are the causes of poverty and not global institutions. On the other side, Pogge rejects such a view and observes that corruption in the developing word is generally sponsored by Northern countries that benefit from it.[75]

In the final analysis, IFIs responsibility for human rights cannot be overemphasised for they play a prominent role in the world in shaping national development policies, hence they should be able to respond when these policies violate human rights. In fact, it is contended that economic growth in the midst of human rights violations is simply a fallacy, for the ultimate goal of growth should be to secure human dignity.

3.2.2.2.2. THE WTO'S OBLIGATIONS FOR THE REALISATION OF THE RIGHT TO DEVELOPMENT

Established during the Uruguay Round Agreements (URAs) of its predecessor, the General Agreement on Tariffs and Trade (GATT), the WTO aims to regulate global trade for the benefit of all nations.[76] It comprises 159 countries as of

70 Ibid.

71 See 'Plan de Reparacion de Daños y Perjuicios Sufridos por las Comunidades Afectadas por la Construcción de la Hidroeléctrica Chixoy'. www.internationalrivers.org/sites/default/files/attached-files/plan_de_reparacion1.final_.pdf (Accessed 4 March 2017).

72 See 'Reparations for the Maya Achi Chixoy Dam Affected'. www.internationalrivers.org/blogs/233/reparations-for-the-maya-achi-chixoy-dam-affected (Accessed 4 March 2017).

73 O. Oduwole. 'International Law and the Right to Development: A Pragmatic Approach for Africa' (2014) *International Institute of Social Studies* 3.

74 J. Cohen. 'Philosophy, Social Science, Global Poverty' In A. M. Jaggar (eds.) *Thomas Pogge and His Critics* (Polity Press 2010), 19.

75 T. Pogge (ed.). *Freedom From Poverty as a Human Right – Who Owes What to the Poor?* (Oxford University Press 2007).

76 'What is the WTO?'. www.wto.org/english/thewto_e/whatis_e/whatis_e.htm (Accessed 4 March 2017).

September 2016.[77] Apparently it is the adequate forum for the realisation of the RTD through trade, for it is the venue to ensure that international trade is fair and equitable; it is the venue where trade obstructions to Africa and other developing parts of the world can be addressed. In fact, its human rights/RTD responsibility can be retrieved from the preamble of the agreement establishing the WTO. Accordingly, the Member States of the WTO

> Recognizing that their relations in the field of trade and economic endeavour should be conducted with a view to *raising standards of living, ensuring full employment and a large and steadily growing volume of real income* and effective demand, and *expanding the production of and trade in goods and services*, while allowing for the optional use of the world's resources in accordance with the objective of sustainable development, seeking both to protect and preserve the environment and to enhance the means for doing so in a manner consistent with their respective needs and concerns at different levels of economic development.[78]

This provision underlines the need to secure and improve the standard of living, employment, secure income and expense of the production of goods and trade in a sustainable manner. These are all essential for the achievement of the RTD.

Even though for some the WTO does not have the legal personality to be held accountable for human rights violations, the *modus operandi* of the organisation has negative impacts on the realisation of human rights.[79] It is in this perspective that since the establishment of the WTO, developing countries have not benefited from its arrangements. On the contrary, severe poverty is created and sustained by these arrangements which benefit developed countries.[80] Developing countries' ability to realise their RTD is curtailed by protectionism, agriculture subsidies by rich countries to their farmers, and various other unfair trade rules and practices that push the developing world including Africa at the bottom of the trade pyramid. Foncesca writes:[81]

> The overall picture of international economy is one of imbalance: While the North preaches that governments in the developing world should not

77 Ibid.

78 Marrakesh Agreement establishing the World Trade Organization, United Nations Treaty Series, 33 International Legal Materials 1125 (1994), entered into force 1 January 1995. My emphasis.

79 J. Denkers and N. Jägers. 'The World Trade Organisation and Human Rights: The Role of Principles of Good Governance' (2008) 11(2) *Potchefstroom Electronic Law Journal* 101.

80 S. D. Kamga. 'The World Trade Orgnisation: For which world? Whose trade? And whose organisation?' In K. Kondlo (ed.) *Perspectives on Thought Leadership for Africa's Renewal* (Aisa 2014), 237–253

81 R. S. Foncesca. 'The World Trade Organisation: Africa's Dilemma' In H. Stephan and M. Power (eds.) *The Scramble for Africa in the 21st Century – From the Old World to the New* (Renaissance Press 2012), 241.

> subsidise their industries, the farmers of the developed world are subsidised to over produce. While the North preaches the need for the South to grant market access to industrial goods in the service sector, it denies market access to products from the South like agriculture. While the least developed countries lack the capacity to seriously influence the agenda of trade talks, multinational cooperation are powerful players often richer than governments and often to write their own rules.

In this perspective, the USA has a reputation of hampering the implementation of its URA commitments to eradicate its tariff and quota constraints on textile and clothing exports from developing countries. Even though the WTO provides a platform to discuss trade issues including their impact on African countries, it is yet to improve the conditions or human dignity in Africa. Nevertheless, it is important to recognise that the URA and even the WTO provide a framework where world poverty can be discussed. In August 2003, an agreement was reached on TRIPS and public health. This agreement aimed to empower poor countries to import medications for public health reasons under compulsory licences, but this did not yield a result; for by the end of the WTO Ministerial Conference organised in Hong Kong in 2005, several issues were still pending and are still affecting the enjoyment of the right to health in Africa and in the developing world in general.[82]

International trade so far is driven by self-interest and as such did not advance the realisation of human rights and the RTD especially in a very complex environment. Keet writes that WTO is a difficult platform where:

> Ruthless hard bargaining is driven by powerful corporate and national vested interests, not the polite diplomatic positioning or posturing of Heads of State. And, with the WTO Secretariat clearly biased towards the interests and demands of the most powerful member states, and the expansion of the liberalised global trade regime, the WTO is not a neutral open forum or assembly of nations where world leaders gather to debate and 'influence' each other's positions.[83]

Sharing this view, *The Economist* writes:

> Rich countries cut their tariffs by less in the Uruguay round than poor ones did. Since then, they have found new ways to close their markets, notably by imposing-antidumping duties on imports they deem 'unfairly cheap'. Rich countries are particularly protectionist in many of the sectors where

82 The effects of TRIPS on health care will be discussed in Chapter 5 of this thesis.

83 D. Keet. 'Proposals on the Role of Trade Within the New Partnership for Africa's Development (NEPAD) – Challenges and Questions' Presentation at workshop of African Trade unions organised by the National Labour and Economy Development Institute (NALEDI), 22–23 May 2003 (on file with author).

> developing countries are best able to compete, such as agriculture, textile and clothing. As a result, rich countries' average tariffs on manufacturing imports from poor countries are four times higher than those on imports from other rich countries. This imposes a big burden on poor countries . . . that could export $700 billion a year by 2005 if rich countries did more to open their markets.[84]

This shows how the WTO distances itself from the RTD discourse which ultimately seeks to improve the standards of living for all. Pogge argues that protectionism or policies echoed by the WTO are the causes of poverty in the developing world.[85] He goes on to argue that the WTO is tailored 'toward a better accommodation of the interests of the governments, corporations and citizens of the affluent countries'[86] to the detriment of the poor.

From a Pogges's perspective, it is submitted that all beneficiaries of this neoliberal approach to trade are harming the poor.[87] Although poor countries could be blamed for signing up to these unfair arrangements, it is important to note that these countries have no options for they find themselves in a difficult situation because as correctly observed by Pogge the 'one who failed to sign up [to the WTO regime] would find its trading opportunity even more severely curtailed'.[88]

The WTO should therefore take its responsibility in terms of fostering human rights and the RTD for all. As observed in the NEPAD framework, the WTO should move beyond protecting Western interest to 'negotiate more equitable terms of trade for African countries within the multilateral framework'.[89] In doing so it will be attending to the RTD concerns which is informed by three main issues in the trade arena, namely:

> 1 the impact on human rights derived of powerful actors *external* to the developing state advancing rules governing world markets that are widely criticised for being inequitable
> 2 the pervasive influence of international economic organizations that continue to espouse neoliberalism (or its more recent variant), and
> 3 the corresponding reduction in domestic autonomy that limits the ability of states – particularly poor and less influential states – to decide independently their own economic and social policies.[90]

84 *The Economist*, 25 September1989, 89 as quoted by Pogge (n 75) 34.

85 T. Pogge. 'Assisting the Global Poor' In K. D. Chatterje (ed.) *The Ethics of Assistance: Morality and the Distant Needy* (Cambridge University Press 2004), 278.

86 Pogge (n 75) 34.

87 Ibid., 34.

88 Ibid., 37.

89 NEPAD 2001, para 185.

90 M. E. Salomon. 'Legal Cosmopolitanism and the Normative Contribution of the Right to Development' In S. Marks (ed.) *Implementing the Right to Development – The Role of International Law* (Friedricht Ebert 2008), 19.

In the final analysis, given the pre-eminence of the WTO in shaping global trade policies, its responsibilities to ensure that its actions improve the quality of life everywhere cannot be discarded. In embracing its human rights responsibilities, the starting point could be to work towards 'the implementation of good governance principles, transparency and equal participation informed by the need to protect human rights'.[91]

In sum, the international institutions (IFIs and WTO) have human rights obligations and should comply with them. These obligations are negative, which entails 'obligation of conduct' and positive which entails 'obligation of results'.[92] Not only should international institutions' conduct not harm the poor, their actions should also enhance the realisation of human rights. Furthermore, beneficiaries of an unjust world order are all accomplices in harming the poor and should therefore be held responsible, hence the need to criminalise the RTD.[93]

3.2.2.3. Transnational companies' obligations for the realisation of the right to development

A transnational company (TNC) is a company operating beyond national boundaries or operating in different countries. Though such companies are not parties to human rights treaties, they should respect human rights based on the 1948 Universal Declaration, the 1986 UNDRT and the 1976 Organisation for Economic Co-operation and Development (OECD) Guidelines for multilateral enterprises. In addition, there are the 1977 ILO Tripartite Declaration of Principles concerning Multinational Enterprises and Social Policy Reform, the UN Global Compact launched in 2000 and the 2003 draft UN Norms on the Responsibilities of Transnational Corporations and Other Business Enterprises with Regard to Human Rights,[94] and the 2008 'Protect, Respect and Remedy Framework' produced by John Ruggie, the Secretary General Special Representative (SGSR), to investigate TNCs and human rights. These instruments call upon TNCs to comply with human rights standards as set out by the International Bill of Rights.

The Preamble of the 1948 Universal Declaration reads:

> Now, therefore, the General Assembly proclaims this Universal Declaration of Human Rights as a common standard of achievement for all peoples and all nations, to the end that every individual and *every organ of society*, keeping this Declaration constantly in mind, shall strive by teaching and education to promote respect for these rights and freedoms and by progressive measures, national and international, to secure their universal and effective

91 Denkers and Jägers (n 79) 88.

92 Skogly (n 35) 299.

93 Baxi (n 33) 153.

94 See UN doc. E/CN.4/Sub.2/2003/12/Rev.2, August 26, 2003.

> recognition and observance, both among peoples of Member States themselves and among the peoples of territories under their jurisdictions.[95]

This provision calls upon every entity in the society or 'organ of society' to ensure that human rights are observed. Such organs can be private, public or transnational companies which are important agents of development. This is a call on enterprises to achieve human rights and the RTD. This request is reinforced by article 3 of the UNDRTD which states that 'States have the primary responsibility for the creation of national and international conditions favorable to the realization of the right to development'. If states are the primary agents responsible for the realisation of the RTD (at national level), it can be argued that the secondary agents are TNCs who are often influential in setting policies at the domestic level.[96] Thus they should be a few steps behind the states in their task to promote, protect and fulfil human rights.

TNCs are however partisans of the 'stay away/trickle down' doctrine which is an economic doctrine according to which private enterprises should avoid being involved in political and human rights matters.[97] The rationale of such policies is that when businesses focus on commercial issues, their activities will trickle down and improve the well-being of the community. This logic ignores everything about human rights. Andreassen correctly observes that it 'avoids the question of responsibilities in cases where there is no trickle down and does not address the rule of conduct for production and corporate activities prior to the perceived trickle-down effects'.[98]

In addition, TNCs and other businesses refuse to take responsibility in human rights issues on the grounds that governments are the violators of human rights and not private companies. Following this perspective, the US envoy to Geneva, Switzerland, commented on the UN Norms on the Responsibilities of Transnational Corporations and Other Business Enterprises with Regard to Human Rights in these words:

> While it is true that private entities have been alleged to have been complicit in or even aided human rights abuses committed by governments, the fundamental cause of such abuses has been the action or inaction of the government, not the private entity.[99]

95 My emphasis.

96 S. D. Kamga and O. O. Ajoku PER. 'Reflections on How to Address the Violations of Human Rights by Extractive Industries in Africa: A Comparative Analysis of Nigeria and South Africa' 17(1) *Potchefstroom Electronic Law Journal* (2014) 455.

97 B. Andreassen. 'Development and the Human Rights Responsibility of Non – State Actors' In A. Andreassen and S. P. Marks (eds.) *Development as a Human Right: Legal, Political and Economic Dimensions* (Havard School of Public Health, Francois Xavier Bagnoud Center For Health and Human Rights), 122.

98 Ibid.

99 US Mission to International Organisations, Geneva, 'Re: Note verbal from the OHCHR of August 3, 2004' (GVA 2537), 30 September 2004.

This is a strange logic. How can human rights be protected if every time private companies are called to order, they point fingers at the government? TNCs and other development agents should respect the rule of law. This author agrees with Alston when he argues that all human rights regimes should stop violations of human rights by private entities or render themselves useless.[100] Fortunately, human beings and the poor in particular have another way out. TNCs and local businesses have a legal personality and can be taken to court directly. In addition, private entities have the 'indirect obligation' to respect the national law of their site of operation. In the same vein, Andreassen argues that if the government harbouring a TNC is unable or unwilling to uphold human rights, the home state of the company must act against the company. He calls such action 'legal extraterritoriality' which can be instrumental for keeping TNCs from abusing human rights in the course of their operations.[101]

The 1976 Organisation for Economic Co-operation and Development Guidelines (OECD Guidelines) for Multilateral Enterprises also reach out to TNC's to comply with human rights. After their adoption in 1976, the OECD Guidelines were revised four years later to emphasise the consideration of issues such as bribes, consumer interest and ethical standards of employment in the countries where TNCs operate. Most importantly, in the section allocated to 'general policy', companies are required to 'respect the human rights of those affected by their activities consistent with the host government's international obligations and commitments.' In addition, under the section allocated to Implementation Procedure, the OECD Guidelines establish a monitoring mechanism through a National Contact Point in each member state where complaints can be addressed and reports discussed. In general, the OECD Guidelines aim to build confidence and predictability in business in host governments, trade unions and other stakeholders.

Now, what is the impact of such a measure on the realisation of the RTD? Observance of the OECD Guidelines by companies is voluntary and not binding. In fact, it is almost like a 'gentlemen's agreement' with no pressure on enterprises to respect it. In this regard, Marinus Sekkel, Chairman of the OECD Committee on Investment and Multinational Enterprises states that 'the point of the exercise is not to name and shame companies, but to encourage them to do the right thing'.[102] However, it can be argued that this view holds within companies' policies. For the states subscribing to the OECD Guidelines, it can be the expression of their commitment to implement the guidelines in question,[103] thus protecting human rights and the RTD while businesses are making money.

100 P. Alston. 'The Not-a-Cat Syndrome: Can the International Human Rights Regime Accommodate Non-State Actors' In P. Alston (eds.) *Non State Actors and Human Rights* (Oxford University Press 2005), 19.

101 Andreassen (n 97) 127.

102 M. Sekkel. 'The OECD MNE Guidelines – An Overview'. *Business Brief* 1, No. 1 July 2003 (on file with author).

103 Report of the Sub-Commission on the Promotion and Protection of Human Rights, UN Doc. E/CN.4/2005/91, 7.

The 1977 ILO Tripartite Declaration of Principles concerning Multinational Enterprises and Social Policy Reform (the ILO Tripartite Declaration) in its Preamble paragraph 2 states its objectives which are to

> encourage the positive contribution which multinational enterprises can make to economic and social progress and to minimize and resolve the difficulties to which their various operations may give rise to concern either in the home or in the host countries or in both.

Furthermore, the tripartite Declaration through its paragraph 5 intends to

> guide the governments, the employers' and workers' organizations and the multinational enterprises in taking such measures and actions and adopting such social policies including, those based on the principles laid down in the constitution and the relevant Conventions and Recommendations of the ILO, as would further social progress.

The ILO Tripartite Declaration basically calls upon businesses to respect the rule of law and good governance principle while conducting business in the host country. The main criticism of this instrument is its 'soft' or non-binding character. However, it raises awareness on the issues at stake which are the promotion and protection of human rights. Thus it can be argued that subscribing to the ILO's standard is a good step towards the realisation of the RTD. In the same light, Andreassen correctly observes that disregarding ILO's standards will threaten 'sustainable and social development.[104]

The UN Global Compact launched in 2000 is another initiative aiming to protect human rights from companies. It can be defined as a UN initiative aiming to instigate businesses to comply voluntarily with human rights, labour and environment standards, as well as anti-corruption principles. Being part of the global process gives an opportunity to companies to expand their web of networks as well as exchange experiences and good practices. It also enhances access to various UN development strategies, convenes power with governments, businesses, civil society and other stakeholders. In addition, it increases legitimacy, reputation, as well as the brand value.

In spite of these motivations to join the Compact, human rights and the RTD still run the risk of being neglected for two reasons. First, the mechanism is voluntary and businesses might choose to ignore the compact and still make money like some Chinese companies do.[105] In fact, companies investing in Africa are not likely to join the Compact because there is poverty and people do not have a

104 Andreassen (n 97) 131.

105 *UN News Center* 'Annan Urges Chinese Companies to Embrace Global Compact' reported that by the 20 September 2004, only 6 Chinese companies were parts of the global compact at www.un.org/apps/news/story.asp?NewsID=11975&Cr=global&Cr1=compact (Accessed 4 March 2017).

choice. They do not care about companies' reputations and are ready to work long hours without holidays for less money. They usually say 'an empty stomach has no ears', meaning that when one is hungry, s/he does not check whether laws and regulations protect his/her interests or rights. Customers on their side buy cheap items even if the product is of the worst quality. It is all about survival.

The second reason why the Compact might not reduce or eradicate poverty is that TNCs can join the Compact to clean up their image and establish their legitimacy without applying a single principle from it. This argument is grounded on the fact that there is no real monitoring mechanism of compliance apart from the requirement for participants to communicate annually with all the stakeholders about progress they have made in implementing the Compact. Furthermore, when a company joins the Compact and does not comply with its principles, there is no real sanction. Nevertheless, the UN takes action against 'bad companies' to show that human rights matter. For instance, as of October 2016, it was reported that the UN Global Compact Office had removed or de-listed 336 companies from the Global Compact's online database for not submitting their communication on progress made in implementing the Global Compact.[106] If a company misses two consecutive deadlines for submitting such a report, it is considered 'inactive' and might be removed from the Compact's online database.

Though the Global Compact has its weaknesses, it should be sustained and encouraged because the realisation of human rights is possible away from the courts of law. Lobbying and awareness rising on Corporate Social Responsibility (CSR) is the strength of the Global Compact.[107]

The 2003 UN draft Norms on the Responsibilities of Transnational Corporations and Other Business Enterprises with Regard to Human Rights[108] (the 2003 Norms), developed from 1998 to 2003 by a Sub commission under the auspices of the UN Human Rights Commission, attempted to impose human rights obligations on TNCs. In their preamble, they recognise that

> even though States have the primary responsibilities to promote, secure the fulfillment of, respect, ensure respect of and protect human rights, transnational corporations and other businesses enterprises, as organs of society, are also responsible for promoting and securing the human rights set forth in the Universal Declaration of Human Rights.

Among others TNCs were compelled to protect human rights and such expected to secure the rights to:

1 to equal opportunity and non-discriminatory treatment
2 to security of persons

106 'UN "De-lists" Companies from Global Compact Initiative'. www.worldwatch.org/node/4713 (Accessed 4 March 2017).

107 For more on the Global Compact, see www.unglobalcompact.org/ (Accessed 4 March 2017).

108 The 2003 Norms were unanimously approved by the UN Sub-Commission on the Promotion and Protection of Human Rights 55 session, agenda item 4. UN doc. E/CN/Sub.2/2003/12 Rev.2, 26 August 2003.

3 rights of workers/consumers
4 respect for national sovereignty and human rights and environmental protection

It was argued that the obligatory character of the 2003 Norms 'draw[s] upon the existing web of international obligations which already apply, either directly or indirectly, to business and pull them together into one document which clearly and directly states the human rights standards applicable to business'.[109]

However, the draft Norms adopted without broad consultation of stakeholders created a huge anxiety and rejection by the business sector as well as some governments and was therefore described as 'train wreck'[110] for attempting to impose human rights legal obligations on business. In fact, controversy was so intense that the Human Rights Council (HRC) – then Human Rights Commission – expressly declared that the draft Norms were non-binding.[111] Subsequently, the HRC requested and obtained the appointment of a Special Representative of the Secretary-General (SRSG) on Matters of Human Rights and Transnational Corporations and other Business Enterprises.[112] Then Professor John Ruggie was appointed as the SRSG in April 2005. He was mandated to, among others, 'identify and clarify the standards of corporate responsibility and accountability for business enterprise with regard to human rights; elaborate the role of states in effectively regulating and adjudicating the role of TNCs with regards to human rights; and to explain the implications for TNC of concepts such as "complicity" and "sphere of influence" '.[113]

Building on his 2006 and 2007 Reports, after a broad consultation with various stakeholders, in 2008 Ruggie suggested what is known as the 'protect, respect and remedy' Framework in which he proposed 'a common conceptual and policy framework, a foundation on which thinking and action can be build'[114] to establish the responsibilities of TNCs for human rights. Subsequent to the adoption of the 2008 framework by the HRC, Ruggie reflected on its implementation and produced the Guiding Principles on Business and Human Rights endorsed by the HRC in June 2011.[115]

109 Andreassen (n 97 above) 133.
110 K. Buhmann. 'Navigating From "Train Wreck" to Being "Welcomed": Negotiation Strategies and Argumentative Patterns in the Development of the UN Framework' In S. Deva and D. Bilchitz (eds.) *Human Rights Obligations of Business- Beyond the Corporate Responsibility to Respect* (Cambridge University Press 2013), 29.
111 Commission on Human Rights 'Resolutions 2004/11', E/CN.4/2004/L.73/Rev.1 (20 April 2004).
112 Human Rights and Transnational Corporations and Other Business Enterprises, Commission on Human Rights Resolution 2005/69, adopted on April 20, 2005. The decision to create the position was endorsed by the Economic and Social Council in its decision 2006/273, adopted on 25 July 2005.
113 Ibid., para 1(a),(b),(c).
114 Human Rights Council, 'Protect, Respect and Remedy: A Framework for Business and Human Rights', A/HRC/8/5 (7 April 2008), para 8.
115 Human Rights Council. 'New Guiding Principles on Business and Human Rights Endorsed by the Human Rights Council'. 16 June 2011. www.ohchr.org/Documents/Publications/GuidingPrinciplesBusinessHR_EN.pdf (Accessed 4 March 2017).

The 2008 Framework is based on 3 pillars and the Guiding Principles assist in giving effect to these pillars which comprise:[116]

1 The state duty to protect human rights
2 The corporate responsibility to respect human rights and
3 Access to remedies

The first pillar basically highlights the role of the states as a primary duty bearer of human rights and as such in regulating the activities of TNCs ensure that they comply with human rights standards. This entails that states should take 'appropriate steps to prevent, investigate, punish and redress such abuses through effective policies, legislations, regulations and adjudication'.[117] This requirement originates from the United Nations Charter on Economic Rights and Duties of the States which urge states 'to regulate . . . foreign investment . . . the activities of transnational companies in accordance with its law and regulation in conformity with its national objective and priorities. No state shall be compelled to grant preferential treatment to foreign investment'.[118]

Although this is the traditional approach to human rights, in the context of business and human rights, it shields TNCs from human rights obligations because states are reluctant, unwilling or simply incapable of holding TNCs accountable. Consequently, 'victims can be left without any effective remedies where states are unable or unwilling to perform their duty'[119] to use the words of Bilchitz and Deva. It is submitted that the prescription of the first pillar is not likely to compel companies to advance or achieve the RTD because of the might of these companies which often set rules and policies where they operate.[120] In fact the power of TNCs is so entrenched that it influences international investment law driven by the interest of TNCs. Aguirre explains the situations as follows:[121]

> The jurisprudence emerging from investment disputes seems to indicate an erosion of the government regulatory function. The interpretation of investment law sets out though standards on expropriation and performance requirements in the interest of cooperation. International investment protection is concerned with limiting state interference in economic matters.

However, this erosion of TNCs' responsibility seems to be mitigated by the Guiding Principles as they provide for states extraterritorial obligations or

116 2008 framework, para 9; Guiding Principles, General Principles.

117 SRSG, 'Guiding Principles' principle 1.

118 The United Nations Charter on Economic Rights and Duties of the States, art 2.2; also D. Aguirre. *The Human Right to Development in a Globalized World* (Ashgate 2008), 126.

119 D. Bilchitz and S. Deva. 'The Human Rights Obligations of Business: A Critical Framework for the Future' In *Human Rights Obligations of Business- Beyond the Corporate Responsibility to Respect* (Cambridge University Press 2013), 14.

120 See Kamga and Ajoku (n 96 above) 455.

121 Aguirre (n 118) 124.

duties 'to regulate the conduct of their domestic businesses when they operate internationally'.[122] Unfortunately, the Guiding Principles are ambiguous on extraterritorial obligations by stating that 'states are neither prohibited nor required to regulate the extraterritorial operations of companies domiciled within their territory or jurisdiction'.[123] This is simply in contradiction with the international human rights jurisprudence on the issue, because as correctly demonstrated by Deva, States in which TNCs are domiciled should regulate these companies when the state in which they operate cannot do so.[124] Shielding states from extraterritorial responsibilities in regard of 'their' companies' activities cannot lead to the realisation of the RTD.

As for the second pillar or the corporate *responsibility* to respect human rights obligations, this pillar crafts TNCs' responsibility in the form of negative obligations, away from the duty approach imposed on states.[125] This suggests that the TNC should comply with national laws as not to harm human rights, and importantly acting with 'due diligence' to avoid occurrences of violations of human rights.[126] Using this approach, the Ruggie framework departs from the legal doctrine and well-established legal institutions to design the responsibility of companies in 'social expectation' and 'court of public opinion'.[127] Of course this method does not impose any binding obligation on TNCs which may act positively or not to build its reputation through CSR. According to Bilchitz and Deva, this requirement reduces the expectations of TNCs that have mere '*responsibilities*' and non-binding obligations, to foster human rights[128] and the RTD.

However, in meeting their human rights responsibilities, companies are obliged to adopt policies to that effect. Among others, they should embark on due diligence investigation to 'identify, prevent, mitigate and account for how they address their impacts on human rights', establish mechanisms to ensure the 'remediation of any adverse human rights impacts they cause or to which they contribute'.[129] While this provision is a good development, it all depends on the good will of companies that may or may not follow the instruction. This shows how the second pillar is unlikely to secure the achievement of the RTD.

As a far as the third pillar or access to remedies is concerned, while states are obliged to set up institutional mechanisms and adopt adequate legislative,

122 S. I. Skogly. 'Extra-national Obligations Towards Economic and Social Rights, Background paper (International Council on Human Rights Policy 2002), 7.

123 Deva and Bilchitz (n 119) 14.

124 S. Deva. 'Acting Extraterritorially to Tame Multilateral Corporations for Human Rights Violations: Who Should 'Bell the Cat Out'? (2004) 5 *Melbourne Journal of International Law* 37.

125 SRSG, 2008 Ruggie framework, para 53.

126 SRSG, 2008 Ruggie framework. 2008 Report (as above), para 25.

127 K. Bhumann. 'Navigating From "Train Wreck" to Being "Welcomed": Negotiation Strategies and Argumentative Patterns in the Development of the UN Framework' In Deva, S. and Bilchitz, D. *Human Rights Obligations of Business- Beyond the Corporate Responsibility to Respect* (Cambridge University Press 2013), 53.

128 Bilchitz and Deva (n 119) 15

129 SRSG 'Guiding Principles', Principle 15; also see Principle 17–21.

administrative and judicial measures or any other initiative to secure access to remedies by victims of human rights violations,[130] companies should set up or participate in effective complaint mechanisms for individuals or groups/communities who may be harmfully affected by their activities.[131] Again, while these requirements are appreciated, TNCs seem to be free to act as they wish because there is no accountability mechanism to keep companies on their toes. This is explained by Bilchitz and Deva as follows:[132]

> [I]f companies do not put in place operational-level grievance mechanism, or the established mechanism failed to meet the effectiveness criteria? The GPs [Guiding Principles] do not really indicate the role that the state and the market forces could play in encouraging companies to take this recommendation seriously.

This illustrates how impotent pillar 3 can be in realising the RTD. Even though the Ruggie framework and the Guidelines are good initiatives to compel companies to respect human rights, in their attempt to remedy controversy caused by the 2003 Norms which have the blessings of business and repair the 'wrecked train', too much compromise was made for the sake of consensus. As a result, the international regime on business and human rights remains weak. Kinley and Tadaki write:[133]

> The current scope of what might be loosely called the international human rights law duties of TNCs is wide, but spread thinly and unevenly. It encompasses examples of supposed customary international law, treaty obligations, and so-called soft-law codes of conduct, guidelines, and compacts. The actual legal cover these initiatives provide is meager or non-existent. The legal (or quasi-legal) duties imposed on corporations have some potential authority, but as yet they remain ill-defined and ineffective. In short, the rudiments of an international legal framework may be discernible, but the legal content of the law is almost wholly absent.

Nevertheless, in spite of the weakness of the regime of business and human rights, the emerging view is that business can no longer be indifferent to human rights violations caused by their operations. This in itself is a legal and even moral argument in which the human rights and RTD obligations of TNCs is based. While much work needs to be done to strengthen this regime, it is important to note that holding TNCs accountable will not happen instantly; it will happen through

130 Ibid., Principle 25.

131 Ibid., 29.

132 Bilchitz and Deva (n 119)15.

133 D. Kinley and J. Tadaki. 'From Talk to Walk: The Emergence of Human Rights Responsibilities for Corporations at International Law' (2003–2004) 44(4) *Virginia Journal of International Law* 949.

processes that can, among other things, consider the position of the communities in which companies operate, consider 'a purposive interpretation of international human rights instruments, the implementation of international human rights norms under domestic law, and the declaration of commitment to the International Bill of Rights by cooperation in their voluntary codes', to use Bilchitz and Deva's words.[134]

In addition, ensuring that companies' human rights obligations are derived from philosophical foundations of human rights and not social expectations, and moving beyond mere TNC's respect to more positive obligations to protect[135] will enhance the prospects of TNCs realising the RTD. This approach could be useful in designing, a 'better legal responses to confront challenges and societal threats to people's welfare and freedom caused by powerful business entities in the era of globalisation'.[136]

3.2.2.4. Non-governmental organisations' obligations for the realisation of the right to development

As discussed previously, the state is the primary duty bearer of human rights. It thus has the duty to guarantee and protect human rights. Because it cannot be the player and the referee at the same time, NGOs come into play as observers or watchdogs of the state's actions towards the realisation of human rights including the RTD. NGOs are actually located between the state and the market and should ensure that the state and business activities do not encroach upon human rights and the RTD.[137]

Article 20 (1) of the Universal Declaration provides that 'everyone has the right to freedom of peaceful assembly and association'. Article 22 of the ICCPR puts it this way:

1 Everyone shall have the right to freedom of association with others, including the right to form and join trade unions for the protection of his interest.
2 No restrictions may be placed on the exercise of this right other than those which are prescribed by law and which are necessary in a democratic society in the interest of national security or public safety, public order (*ordre public*), the protection of public health or morals or the protection of the right and freedoms of others. This article shall not prevent the imposition of lawful restrictions on members of the armed forces and of the police in their exercise of this right.

134 Bilchitz and Deva (n 119)25.
135 Ibid.
136 Andreassen (n 97) 139.
137 In general, see J. L. Fernando and A. W. Heston. 'Introduction: NGOs Between States, Markets, and Civil Society' (November 1997) 554 *The Annals of the American Academy of Political and Social Science-The Role of NGOs: Charity and Empowerment* 8; N. Banks, D. Hulme and M. Edwards. 'NGOs, States, and Donors revisited: Still Too Close for Comfort?' (2015) 66 *World Development* 707.

Article 10 of the Banjul Charter reads: '1) every individual shall have the right to free association provided that he abides by the law'. In the same vein, article 16 of the American Convention on Human Rights and article 11 of the European Convention of Human Rights also provide for freedom of association. All these provisions on freedom of association empower people to come together and create institutions such as NGOs to ensure the realisation of human rights through balance of power in the confines of a state and even beyond. At the national level, the argument for NGOs' actions usually lies in the freedom of expression and freedom of association that are provided for in many constitutions. The main role of NGOs is to promote, protect, implement and enforce human rights. Sengupta argues that an NGO has the duty to apply the principle of participation, accountability and transparency in implementing the RTD.[138] This implementation should be overseen by NGOs which are called upon to monitor the programmes, deliver the services and even replace or assist the administration in some cases. In addition, NGOs have the duty to advocate and mobilise the populace to take part in decision-making processes. In South Africa, for instance, 'Lawyers for Human Rights', Section 27 and Equal Education, to name but a few, are NGOs assisting communities in claiming their rights – including the RTD. In the same way, 'The Human Rights Forum' is doing a tremendous job in reporting monthly and annually on human rights violations in Zimbabwe.[139]

NGOs are, however, not always able to perform their duties because some of them lack adequate funding and qualified staff. Others are fly-by-night organisations which, after receiving funding from donors, close their doors and retire. Their efficiency is sometimes nullified by questions related to their accountability or legitimacy. In this perspective, it can be argued that NGOs are not representing the masses and are acting for their own interests. However, this type of argument usually comes from states that are under pressure. In May 2005, when Amnesty International (AI) called the US prison camp in Guantanamo Bay the 'gulag of our time', the US administration, through Vice President Dick Cheney, reacted by saying that it did not take AI seriously and was offended by AI's comment.[140] In other words, in spite of the well-established reputation of AI, the USA did not take the establishment seriously. Similarly, Human Rights Watch (HRW) was said to have lost its credibility when it published 'Fatal Strikes: Israel's Indiscriminate Attacks Against Civilians in Lebanon' which was a 2006 report on Israel's violation of human rights in Lebanon.[141] In any case, NGOs are not there to please national governments or seek legitimacy from them. On the contrary, the best

138 Sengupta (n 11) 17.

139 See the Zimbabwe Human Rights NGO Forum at www.hrforumzim.com/ (Accessed 4 March 2017).

140 H. J. Steiner et al. 'International Non-Governmental Organisations' In *International Human Rights in Context- Law, Politics, Moral* (Oxford University Press 2008), 1422.

141 Ibid.

NGOs are the ones with the ability to put pressure on human rights violators. Hence the argument by R. Brett that:

> NGOs make a major contribution to the standard-setting activities of regional and international bodies. Although the standards are negotiated and adopted by government representatives, NGOs have often been the initiators of new instruments or particulars. . . . The role of NGOs is standard-setting, as with their involvement in implementation procedures, arises from their grounding in the realities of human rights violations in practice. This means that often they are more aware than governments of weaknesses and gaps, thus leading them to push for new standards, or the strengthening of existing ones.[142]

Article 55 of the Banjul Charter reads:

> 1 Before each session, the Secretary of the Commission [African Commission of Human and People Rights] shall make a list of the communications other than those of State parties to the present Charter and transmit them to the members of the Commission, who shall indicate which communication should be considered by the Commission.

This provision clearly empowers the African Commission to take care of communications which are not from state parties to the Banjul Charter. It gives room for NGOs to communicate and take action to protect human rights. In fact, in Africa, NGOs have been instrumental in protecting human rights and the RTD as evidenced earlier by the *SERAC* case.[143] Furthermore, article 5 of the Protocol on the Establishment of the African Court on Human and Peoples' Rights empowers everyone, including NGOs, to access the Court directly. Consequently, NGOs have a critical role to play in turning the RTD into reality.

3.3. The right-holders of the right to development

Usually, individuals are rights holders or beneficiaries of human rights. However, from a RTD perspective, individuals, peoples and even the state (the latter is usually the duty bearer) are all beneficiaries of the right.

3.3.1. Individuals as beneficiaries of the right to development

According to the UNDRTD, 'the right to development is an inalienable human right by virtue of which every human person and all peoples are entitled to

142 R. Brett. 'Non-Governmental Actors in the Field of Human Rights' In R. Hanski and M. Suksi (eds.) *An Introduction to the International Protection of Human Rights* (Turko/Abo: Institute for Human Rights 2000), 408–9.

143 *SERAC & Another v Nigeria*, ACHPR, 2001, Banjul, the Gambia, and www.achpr.org.

participate in.'[144] In this sentence, the beneficiary is an individual right when the provision refers to the entitlement of 'every human person'. Likewise, in portraying development as a process aiming at the improvement of the 'well-being of the entire population and all individuals',[145] it is also clear that the beneficiary of the process is the individual as underlined under the theme 'all individuals'.[146] Additionally, the individual character of the right is also highlighted by article 2(1) of the UNDRTD which provides that 'The human person is the central subject of development and should be the active participant and beneficiary of the right to development'. Even the principal opponent of the RTD –the USA – recognises the RTD if it is accepted as an individual and not a collective right. This view was sustained by US representative Danies at the 61st Commission on Human Rights, as follows:

> [t]he RTD implies that each individual should enjoy the right to develop his or her intellectual capabilities to the maximum extent possible through the exercise of the full range of civil and political rights.[147]

This is in line with the liberalism theory which focused mainly on negative rights, hence the reference to civil and political rights by the US representative whose claim vests the responsibility for RTD on individuals and the state at the local level with the international community at the margin. This view fails to capture the fact that decision or development policies adopted on the international plane can affect the realisation of RTD at the domestic level.

3.3.2. Peoples[148] as beneficiaries of the right to development

The provisions that the RTD is a right in which 'all peoples are entitled to participate in'[149] and that the RTD is a process aiming at the constant development of the 'well-being of the entire population'[150] illustrate the collective nature of the RTD. In this context, peoples are rights holders of the RTD. In other words, communities or groups are beneficiaries of the RTD. In fact, issues related to the beneficiaries of the RTD are controversial. In this respect, while Donnelly interrogates the collective or individual nature of the RTD, Bedjaoui observes that it does not matter whether it is a collective or an individual right, but points out that it is simply

144 Art 1.

145 UNDRTD, Preamble, para 2.

146 The collective aspect of the rights included in these provision will be discussed in the subsection dealing with people as rights holders of the RTD; sec 3.3.2.

147 Explanation of the vote on right to development, 61st Commission on Human Rights' Statement delivered by Joel Danies US Delegation to the 61st Commission on Human Rights, April 12, 2005.

148 The concept of 'peoples' will be covered extensively while looking at the RTD in the African human rights system in the next chapter of this book.

149 Art 1 of the UNDRTD.

150 UNDRTD, Preamble, para 2.

'the right of [the] human race in general'.[151] Similarly, Haocai adds his voice to the debate in arguing that on the one hand, the concept of collective rights is meaningless if individual rights are not guaranteed, and on the other hand, collective rights are the precondition for an effective achievement of individual rights.[152] This means individual and collective rights are complementary. Sharing this view, the Chinese representative, at the twelfth session of the Working Group and the fifth session of the High Level Task Force on the implementation of the RTD,[153] stated that the RTD is a reality and there was no need to waste time and energy pondering on its collective or individual future, but that it was time to move to its implementation.[154] This position was simply echoing the need to enhance human welfare and protect human dignity.

3.3.3. The state as the beneficiary of the right to development

The traditional duty bearer of rights which is the state is also a beneficiary of human rights in RTD discourse. Article 2(3) of the UNDRTD reads:

> States have the *right* and the duty to formulate appropriate national development policies that aim at the constant improvement of the well-being of the entire population and of all individuals, on the basis of their active, free and meaningful participation in development and in the fair distribution of the benefits resulting therefrom.

Even though the provision refers to the duty of the state, the interesting part here is 'States have the right.' In this context, the state is the beneficiary in the sense that it has the right to formulate its development policies without any interference; it is empowered to exercise its sovereignty in defining national development policies independently.

Nevertheless, this interpretation could be misleading because a state is not a human and as such will not enjoy 'human' rights. However, it is important to note that a state can only claim a human right on behalf of its people. The state acts as the representative of its citizens. Crawford notes that the involvement of the state as the main negotiator of the right does not make it the beneficiary, but an instrument or a bridge used for the interest of individuals.[155] In this context, the

151 M. Bedjaoui. 'The Difficult Advance of Human Rights Towards Universality in a Pluralistic World' Proceedings at the Colloquium organised by the Council of Europe in co-operation with the International Institute of Human Rights, Strasbourg (17–19 March 1989), 32.

152 L. Haocai. 'Remarks at the Opening Ceremony of the Beijing Forum on Human Rights' (2008) *China Human Rights* 4.

153 Twelfth session Working Group on the Right to Development, High-level task force on the implementation of the right to development, Fifth session (Geneva, 1–9 April 2009), A/HRC/12/WG.2/TF/2.

154 Twelfth session Working Group on the Right to Development (2009) (as above) para 12.

155 J. Crawford. *The Rights of Peoples* (Crawford 1988), 159.

'state plays the role of the equivalent legal trustee' to quote M'baye.[156] The Working Group on the Right to Development adds more clarification on the notion of states beneficiaries of the RTD as follows:[157]

> States and organizations had rights and obligations as far as the realisation of human rights was concerned and in relation to the right to development as a human right, although that did not mean that they possessed human rights as such.

In the final analysis, a state that claims the RTD for its citizens becomes the beneficiary in claiming the right that will definitely be to the benefit of its populations who are entitled to it.

3.4. Concluding remarks

The aim of this chapter was to examine the implementation mechanisms of the RTD. In doing so, the chapter identified the duty bearers and rights holders of the right. It was found that at the national level, the state is the duty bearer of the right, whereas at international level, based on international solidarity, the international community is the duty bearer, even though this last aspect creates more controversy on the right as it is clear that right is not yet binding at a global level. It was also found that international financial institutions, which are the World Bank and the IMF, as well as the global trade institution known as the WTO have an important role in making sure that their activities do not violate the RTD. Given the multidimensional aspects of the RTD, it was also found that TNCs face similar responsibilities while NGOs who are the checks and balances at the national as well as international levels should also ensure that state and non states actors do not curtail the RTD.

Lastly, the chapter found that the beneficiaries of the right are individuals, peoples as well as the state. However, the state is the beneficiary of the right only when it claims the right to the benefit of and to be enjoyed by its citizens. After a general analysis of the operationalisation of RTD, the next chapter will focus on the right in the African human rights system.

156 K. M'baye. 'Introduction' (part four) 'Human Rights and the Rights of Peoples' In M. Bedjaoui (ed.) *International Law: Achievements and Prospects* (1991), 1041; see also Salomon (n 32) 119.

157 Report of the Working Group of Governmental Experts on the Right to Development (8th session, 24 January 1985) UN Doc E/CN4/1985/11, para 20.

4 The right to development in the African human rights architecture

Its reception at the regional, sub-regional and national levels

4.1. Introduction

At the centre of this chapter is the following question: What is the place of the RTD in the African human rights system? 'The African human rights system' should be understood broadly. It comprises 'the regional' AU-based system, the 'subregional' system and even national laws with its case law.[1] The provisions of this system will be looked at to the extent that they are useful in examining the RTD in the African law. At the outset, it is necessary to note that given the pre-eminence of the African Commission in the 36 years of existence of the African Charter, a full chapter (the next one) will focus on its role in the realisation of the RTD in Africa. Therefore, this chapter is divided into five parts including this introduction. The second part sketches the substantive provisions of the RTD in the African human rights architecture with special attention to African treaties; the third part examines the reception of the RTD at the sub-regional level or in sub-regional treaties; the fourth part assesses how article 22 of the ACHPR is received at the country level. It examines the duty bearer's obligations while focusing on the RTD in selected national laws, namely: Cameroon, Uganda, Malawi, Ethiopia and South Africa. The rationale for focusing on these countries is that firstly, whereas various African countries' constitutions provide for development, Cameroon, Ethiopia, Malawi and Uganda specifically provided for the RTD in their constitutions. These constitutions will be the focus of the study when examining the role of African states in the realisation of the RTD because they expressly provide for the right. Secondly, although the South African Constitution does not mention the RTD, it is known as the most progressive constitution in Africa.[2] The fifth and final section of the chapter provides concluding remarks.

1 For more on this broad definition of the African human rights system, see F. Viljoen. *International Human Rights Law in Africa* (Oxford University Press 2012), 169–170.

2 J. C. Mubangizi. *The Protection of Human Rights in South Africa: A Legal and Practical Guide* (Juta 2004), 71.

4.2. Normative protection of the right to development at the regional level

This section focuses on the substantive provisions on the RTD in the ACHPR, the Protocol on the Rights of Women and the African Children's Charter.

4.2.1. The right to development in the African Charter on Human and Peoples' Rights

Article 22 of the ACHPR reads:

> 1. All peoples shall have the right to their economic, social and cultural development with due regard to their freedom and identity and in the equal enjoyment of the common heritage of mankind. 2. States shall have the duty, individually or collectively, to ensure the exercise of the right to development.

According to the first paragraph, the RTD comprises economic, social and cultural rights as well as freedoms (civil and political rights). It underlines the multifaceted character of the right. During one of the meetings of African Heads of State on the *travaux préparatoires* of the ACHPR, Senghor – the former president of Senegal – highlighted the need to include the RTD in the future African Convention because it entails all economic, social and cultural rights, without neglecting civil and political rights.[3] Furthermore, it could be argued that this view was incorporated in the ACHPR in these terms:[4]

> Convinced that it is henceforth essential to pay particular attention to the right to development and that civil and political rights cannot be dissociated from economic, social and cultural rights in their conception as well as universality and that the satisfaction of economic, social and cultural rights is a guarantee for the enjoyment of civil and political rights.

As far as the beneficiary is concerned, the ACHPR presents the RTD as a collective right, as 'peoples' rights'. However, the concept of peoples and the RTD is problematic, hence the need to give more attention to its significance. In clarifying the concept of people, the section will also assess the right to self-determination which is directly linked to the concept of people as well as to the RTD.

The concept of people is grounded in the UN Charter[5] and in the African philosophy claiming that a person is not perceived as an isolated human being, but as part of a community, as 'an integral member of a group animated by a spirit of solidarity',[6] and as a result individual rights could be clarified and validated

3 Address delivered by Leopold Sedar Senghor, President of the Republic of Senegal, OAU DOC CAB/LEG/67/5.

4 The ACHPR, preamble, para 7.

5 The first sentence of the Preamble reads: 'We the people of the United Nations.'.

6 O. B. Okere. 'The Protection of Human Rights in Africa and the African Charter on Human and Peoples' Rights: Comparative Analysis With the European and American System' 6 *Human Rights*

only by the rights of the community.[7] Following this reasoning, peoples' rights were enshrined in the African instrument from articles 19 to 24: right of people to equality,[8] to existence and self-determination,[9] to dispose freely of wealth and natural resources,[10] to economic, social and cultural development,[11] national and international security[12] and to a general satisfactory environment.[13]

The striking feature here is that the African Charter does not define the concept and it is argued that this was done deliberately in order to avoid disagreement.[14] However, it could be argued that this voluntary omission creates more problems than it solves because as will be shown in the following lines, an undefined 'peoples' is misleading from various angles.

The UN Educational, Scientific and Cultural Organisation (UNESCO) Meeting of Experts on the study of the rights of peoples, held in Paris in 1989, defined peoples for purposes of peoples' rights in international law, as a group of individual human beings who enjoy some or all of the following common characteristics: a) a common historical tradition, b) racial or ethnic identity; c) cultural homogeneity, d) linguistic unity, e) religion or ideology affinity; f) territorial connection; and g) a common economic life.[15] A people should have a peculiar or 'distinct character'.[16] In this regard, Brownlie is of the view that

> [T]he concept of distinct character depends on a number of criteria which may appear in combination. Race or nationality is one of the more important of the relevant criteria, but the concept of race can only be expressed scientifically in terms of more specific features, in which matters of culture, language, religion and group psychology predominance.[17]

However, in the ACHPR, there is no specific criterion to identify people or peoples. In fact, the doctrine is always trying to interpret the provisions related to

---

Quarterly (1984) 148 as quoted by R. Kiwanuka. 'The Meaning of "People" in the African Charter on Human and Peoples Rights' *The American Journal of International Law* (1988) 82.

7 Ibid., 82.

8 ACHPR art 19.

9 Art 20.

10 Art 21.

11 Art 22.

12 Art 23.

13 Art 24.

14 Report of the Draft African Charter presented by the Secretary-General at the 37th ordinary session of the OAU Council of Minister, Kenya, 15–21 June 1981, OAU Doc CM/1149 (XXXVII), Annex II: Rapporteur's Report OAU Doc CAB/LEG/67/Draft.Rept (II) Rev.4 (Rapporteur's Report), also F. Viljoen. *International Human Rights Law in Africa* (1st ed) (Oxford: Oxford University Press 2007), 243.

15 UNESCO. 'New Reflections on the Concepts of Peoples' Rights' (1990) 11(3–4) *Human Rights Law Journal* 441, 446.

16 I. Brownlie. 'The Right of People in Modern International Law' (1995) 9 *Bulletin of Association of Legal Philosophy* 108, 110.

17 Ibid. For more on the clarification of 'peoples,' see The Universal Declaration of the Rights of peoples, Algiers, 4 July 1976; also A. Cassese and E. Jouve (eds.) *Pour un Droit des Peoples Essaie sur la Declaration d'Alger* (Levrault 1978).

'peoples'. Article 19 of the ACHPR reads: 'All peoples shall be equal: they shall enjoy the same respect and shall have the same rights. Nothing shall justify the domination of a people by another'.

This suggests that 'people' is subject to various interpretations: It includes minorities within the state, or the entire population of a state,[18] where no group prevails or discriminates against another.[19] In this context, 'people' applies to all collective rights in the ACHPR.[20] It also implies the protection of minorities against both internal and external forms of colonialism;[21] internally, against the state which could be understood as the right to internal self-determination from an indigenous peoples' rights perspective.[22] This also goes hand in hand with article 20 of the ACHPR which provides for the right of existence and the right to self-determination of all peoples.[23] Indeed the concept of 'people' is vague, unclear and keeps changing, hence the correctness of Ougergouz's argument in which he claims that the concept of 'people in the African Charter is a Chameleon-like concept'.[24]

This vagueness does not assist in claiming the RTD as the state, the duty bearer, can easily twist the concept into whatever can enable it to forgo its responsibilities. For instance, if 'people' is taken to mean the state itself, it is almost impossible for the state to claim a right against itself, but only against the international community as several African countries would like to do.

Nevertheless, saying the RTD is a peoples' right does not negate the fact that it is also an individual right. In this regard, M'baye argues that 'development is a right for all [individuals and people]'.[25] He points out that associating the RTD with collective rights is a 'hasty conclusion' which he opposes.[26] This view is supported by Ougergouz who argues that the RTD is a human and a right of people; an individual and collective right.[27] To drive the point home, Ouguergouz writes:

> [t]he right to development inevitably has an individual dimension, yet this stems rather from the purpose of the right rather than from the way it is

18 P. Kunig. 'The Role of "Peoples" Rights in the African Charter of Human and Peoples Rights' in K. Ginther and W. Benedek (eds.) *New Perspectives and Conceptions of International Law: An Afro-European Dialogue* (Springer 1983), 169.

19 F. Ougergouz. *La Charte Africaine des Droits de l'Homme et des Peuples: Hostorique, Portée juridique et Contribution à la Protection International des Droits de l'Homme en Afrique* (PUF 1993), 140.

20 Ibid.

21 Kiwanuka (n 6) 93.

22 UN General Assembly (GA) Res of 13 September 2007, art 3.

23 More light will be shed on the concept of peoples' rights in the ACHPR under the section allocated to the *Endorois* case ('The right to self-determination and natural resources').

24 F. Ougergouz. *African Charter on Human and Peoples' Rights – A Comprehensive Agenda for Human Dignity and Sustainable Democracy in Africa* (Kluwer Law International 2003), 204.

25 K. M'baye. 'Le Droit au Développement Comme un Droit de l'Homme' 5 *Revue des Droits L'Homme* (1972) 515.

26 K. M'baye. 'Le Droit au Developpement en Droit International' In J. Makarczk (ed.) *Essays in International Law in Honour of Judge Manfred Lachs* (Martinus Nijhoff 1984), 173.

27 Ouguergouz (n 24) 299.

> exercised. Failing any proof of the contrary, the view enshrined in the Charter is firmly directed towards the ultimate goal of the full development of the human person. To deny this would be to fail to recognise that each type of rights, *individual rights and rights of peoples*, in its way strive towards the same goal: respect for human dignity in its two expressions – *that of human beings and of human communities*.[28]

The second paragraph of the article under study clearly identifies states as the duty bearers of the right. They shall act 'individually or collectively to ensure the exercise of the right to development'. While acting individually, the state takes action in the line of the Maastricht Guidelines discussed earlier.[29] It must take action to promote, respect and protect the RTD. This will be further addressed in the subsequent section dealing with the implementation of the right in African countries.

Though the duty of the state at the national level is clear, acting 'collectively' to ensure the RTD implies acting through international cooperation. In this regard, the cooperation should take place amongst African states that are parties to the ACHPR. According to article 26 of the Vienna Convention on the Law of Treaties, the *pacta sunt servanda* rule must be respected by state parties to treaties. In other words, a treaty is binding only on its parties. Before the codification of this rule in 1969, it was emphasised by the Permanent Court of International Justice (PCIJ) in its 1928 consultative opinion through the *Dantzig* case.[30] The Court said that an international law agreement was binding only on parties to the agreement unless the parties had expressed their will or intention to do otherwise.

This rule of international law can constrain African states' ability to provide the RTD because most of them are cash trapped and cannot assist each other financially and turn to the wealthy countries or IFIs that are not parties to the ACHPR. The wealthy countries and IFIs can only assist as they please, on the ground of charity or humanitarian assistance discussed earlier. In fact, this concern will be further analysed when addressing the role of partnership in NEPAD's attempts to realise the RTD.[31]

4.2.2. The right to development in the Protocol to the ACHPR on the Rights of Women in Africa

In addressing one of the shortcomings of the ACHPR, which did not explicitly cater for women's rights, the Protocol on the Rights of Women was adopted in Maputo, Mozambique on 11 July 2003, and entered into force on 25 November 2005. It protects women's rights in general. Nonetheless, interestingly, it addresses women's rights to sustainable development in its article 19, which calls upon state parties to mainstream gender in national development plans. Accordingly, women

28 Ibid., 306. My emphasis.
29 See Chapter 3 above, section 3.2.1.
30 *Jurisdiction of the Court of Dantzig* case, consultative opinion 1928, PCIJ. Ser B, No 15.
31 See Chapter 6 of this book.

should be involved at all levels of development endeavours;[32] women's right to land,[33] to credit and other resources should be promoted to enhance women's quality of life.[34] In addition, women should be protected against the negative effects of globalisation in order to ensure their right to sustainable development.[35]

Furthermore, article 10(3) of the same instrument urges state parties that generally allocate more money to military expenditure to shift the focus and assign more funding for women's development. Indeed, the allocation of more resources to women's education, training and empowerment in general can only enhance women's RTD. In this context, the duty bearer of the right is the state and the beneficiaries are women. The Protocol on the Rights of Women specifically underlines what the duty bearer should do to ensure women's rights to sustainable development. In fact, the state should adopt gender responsive legislations to ensure women's right to sustainable development.

4.2.3. The right to development in the African Charter on the rights and welfare of the child

The African Children's Charter guarantees children's rights in the African context. In this perspective it addresses the African children's 'cultural heritage, historical background and the value of African civilization'.[36] It aims to secure the happiness and dignity of the child within a family environment conducive to his/her development.[37]

It is on this backdrop that article 5 of the African Children's Charter provides for the right to 'survival and development' of the child. Accordingly, the state, the duty bearer, shall amongst others ensure the 'development'[38] of the child who is the beneficiary of the right. In this context, it could be argued that the state shall take appropriate measures to ensure that the child's right to food, health care and education, among others, are respected. The achievement of these rights to the benefit of the child will lead to his or her survival and development.

In the final analysis, at the regional level, the main African treaties offer a normative protection of the RTD which in principle should flow down to the sub-regional and national level.

4.3. The right to development in the African sub-regional instruments

4.3.1. Background of regional integration

The idea of regional integration in Africa originated from the pan-Africanism ideology spearheaded by Henry Sylvester-Williams, W.E.B DuBois, Marcus Garvey

32 Art 19(b).
33 Art 19(c); also 2001 SADC Treaty, art 5(1)(j).
34 Art 19(d).
35 Art 19(f).
36 A. Lloyd. 'The African Regional System for the Protection of Children's Rights' In Sloth-Nielsen (ed.) *Children's Rights in Africa: A Legal Perspective* (Juta 2008) 33.
37 Ibid.
38 African Children's Charter, art 5 (2).

and Frans Fanon from the diaspora and Obafemi Awolowo, and Jomo Kenyatta Nkwame Nkrumah and Juluis Nyerere from the continent to name but a few who called for African Unity. This ideology was informed by the need to liberate Africa from the shackles of colonialism. For this to happen there was a need for the Unity of the African continent.

However, while Pan-Africanists such as Nyerere and Nkrumah agreed to destroy imperialism through the unity of the continent, they disagreed on the way to achieve such unity.[39] On the one hand, Nyerere called for regional integration or federalism at the sub-regional level. Accordingly, the process of a direct African unity would be prolonged and the best way would be to rely on regional building blocks.[40] On the other hand, Nkrumah was of the view that it was imperative to form the union of African governments directly without going through federalism or regional grouping or else imperial powers would use neo-colonial tactics to divide and rule.[41] Nkrumah was also concerned that regional groupings or federalism was going to fuel ultra-nationalism which would be detrimental to the unity of the continent. Echoing this view, proponents of Nkruma's approach write:

> We are committed to the idea of Pan-African unity and we are afraid that our economic interest in federation will clash with our ideological interest in African unity. There will be no federation because it would prevent African unity. We must come together all at once.[42]

Nonetheless, the African leaders established the Organisation of African Unity (OAU),[43] and identified Regional Economic Communities (RECs) as vehicles for the unity of the continent. The OAU – now the African Union (AU) since 2002 – seeks both unity of Africa and regional integration as one of its pillars. It is on this backdrop that the AU recognises the following RECs:

> The Treaties of the Southern African Development Community (SADC), the Economic Community of West African States (ECOWAS), Common Market for Eastern and Southern Africa (COMESA), the Economic Community of Central African states (ECCAS), the Arab Maghreb Union or Union du Maghreb Arabe (UMA), the Community of Sahel-Saharan States (CEN – SAD), the East African Community (EAC), the Economic and Monetary Community of Central Africa (CEMAC) and the Intergovernmental Authority for Development (IGAD) were adopted. Without focusing on the institutional

39 I. G. Shivji. 'Pan-Africanism and the Challenge of East African Community Integration' paper to be presented at the EAC 10th Anniversary Symposium, 13–14 November 2009, Arusha, Tanzania (2009) 5. www.danquahinstitute.org/docs/ChallengeofEACIntegration.pdf (Accessed 14 August 2017).

40 J. K. Nyerere. 'Freedom and Unity/ *uhuru na umoja* (a selection from writings and speeches 1952–65) (Oxford University Press 1966), 204–208.

41 In general, see K. Nkruma. *Africa Must Unite* (Fredericka Praeger Publisher 1963).

42 J. S. Nye. *Pan-Africanism and East African Integration* (Harvard University Press 1966), 196; also Shivji (n 39) 5.

43 Adopted in 1963.

structures of these RECs which are generally similar,[44] the following subsection shows that economic mandates of the RECs cannot be detached to human rights and the realisation of the RTD. So, far from describing the structure of RECs, this subsection explores their role in advancing the RTD.

4.3.2. Regional Economic Communities, human rights and the right to development

Originally the aim of 'regional integration' was to achieve economic development; hence the concept is often synonymous with 'regional economic integration'.[45] The latter has been described as 'the situation where two or more countries come together to discuss common provisions to create a Regional Trade Agreement in the WTO sense' in order to 'regulate or encourage cross-border trade, investment and migration'.[46] In this vein, regional integration has also been described as 'a voluntary pooling of resources for a common purpose by two or more sets of partners belonging to different states' in order to strengthening 'structural interdependencies of a technical and economic sort, with positive effects on economic welfare'.[47] In essence regional integration was more about economic development.

However, achieving economic integration cannot be divorced from realising human rights and the RTD in particular. The RTD is one of the core commitments of the RECs. This is perceptible through objectives and principles that underpinned the RECs and the explicit provisions on human rights by REC treaties as well the judiciarisation of human rights and the RTD in REC.[48]

4.3.2.1. The right to develpment in the objectives of RECs

The RECs objectives revolve around insuring development on the continent. In this context, development should be understood as ensuring a better standard of living for all in RECs. In fact, RECs' primary objective is to ensure access to basic rights such as education, health, food housing, freedom of movement and association especially in the framework of integration which encompasses not only free circulation of goods, but also of persons.[49] This objective is at the centre of

44 For more on the structure of RECs, see S. Ebobrah and A. Tanoh (eds.) *Compendium of African Sub-regional Human Rights Documents* (PULP 2010).

45 S. T. Ebobrah. 'Legitimacy and Feasibility of Human Rights Realisation Through Regional Economic Communities in Africa: The Case of the Economic Community of West African States'. Thesis submitted in partial fulfilment of the requirements for the degree of Doctor of Laws (LLD) at the University of Pretoria (2009) 53.

46 Ibid.

47 N. Bourenane. 'Theoretical and Strategic Approaches' In R. Lavergne (ed.) *Regional Integration and Cooperation in West Africa: A Multidimensional Perspective* (Africa World Press 1997), 50.

48 Viljoen (n 1) 481.

49 W. Willem Maas. 'Trade, Regional Integration, and Free Movement of People' In J. Roy (ed.) *A New Atlantic Community: The European Union, the US and Latin America* (European Union Center of Excellence/Jean Monnet Chair, University of Miami 2015), 111–121.

the RTD discourse. The rights seeking to improve people welfare are composite elements of the RTD. According to Vieljoen, 'improving the welfare of people in the participating countries' is paramount in RECs objectives.[50] Sharing this view, the UNDP argues that regional integration aims to enhance human development which is 'about creating the conditions that allow men, women and children to live lives they value by expanding their freedoms and building their capabilities'.[51]

In addition, the fight against poverty which is at the centre for the RTD discourse is well echoed by the RECs that have the obligation to eradicate poverty while addressing human welfare. In this regard, at its inception, SADC aimed among other things, to 'achieve development and economic growth, alleviate poverty, enhance the standard and quality of life of the people of Southern Africa and support the socially disadvantaged through regional integration'.[52] This was clarified by the 2001 amendment of the SADC treaty which was unequivocal in calling for the incorporation of poverty eradication as key objective of SADC undertakings and programmes.[53] In the same vein, the SADC Protocol on Gender and Development was adopted in 2008. In substance, the content of this protocol is similar to article 19 of the Protocol on the rights of women in Africa which provides for women's rights to sustainable development RTD.

In the EAC, in order to achieve the main objective set out in article 5(1) of the 1999 EAC Treaty, the Community aims at ensuring cooperation in agreed fields to facilitate equitable economic development that will 'raise the standard of living and improve the quality of life of their populations'.[54]

In its 1993 revised treaty, ECOWAS emphasises the necessity to work together to address economic and developmental challenges and ensure the 'expansion of the region's productive capacity',[55] with the main goal being to accelerate and sustain economic development of States Parties'.[56] This provision filtered down to the 2007 ECOWAS Vision 2020 which seeks to improve people lives in the subregion by directly speaking to the grassroots. In this vein, the Vision aims to build a 'borderless, prosperous and cohesive region where people have the capacity to access and harness its enormous resources through the creation of opportunities for sustainable development and environmental preservation'.[57]

Similarly, recognising the role of good health in addressing poverty, the ECOWAS has set up the West Africa Health Organisation (WAHO) to co-ordinate the

50 Viljoen (n 1) 481.
51 UNDP 'Regional Integration and Human Development: A Pathway for Africa' (UNDP 2011) 3.
52 Art 5(1)(a) of the 1992 SADC Treaty.
53 2001, SADC Treaty, art 5(1)(j).
54 Art 5(3)(b) of the 1999 EAC Treaty (as amended).
55 1993 ECOWAS Treaty, preamble para 8.
56 Ibid para 11.
57 Hannah Serwaah Tetteh Minister for Foreign Affairs and Regional Integration, Ghana 'Regional Integration as a Tool for Poverty Reduction in West Africa'. www.cuts-international.org/30thanniversarylectures/pdf/Regional_Integration_as_a_Tool_for_Poverty_Reduction_in_West_Africa-Hanna_s_Tetteh.pdf (Accessed 16 March 2017).

efforts of state parties in fighting diseases, and as correctly observed by Tetteh, this is a significant step towards poverty reduction.[58] Analogous initiatives are taken in various RECs to reduce poverty and improve peoples' lives.

4.3.2.2. The incorporation of explicit provisions on human rights in Regional Economic Communities documents

Subsequent to the advent of democracy and constitutionalism in most African countries in the 1990s, most original RECs documents adopted in the 1960s and 1970s, were amended or protocols were adopted to capture the concepts of rule of law, human rights and democracy. In the process, the RTD or 'human rights put together with consideration of their interdependency'[59] were expressly incorporated into the values of RECs. In reality, human rights were mainstreamed in all arrangements of sub-regional cooperation.[60] In this respect, the 2003 SADC Summit adopted a Charter of Fundamental Social Rights in SADC.[61] Although this document focuses on labour and employment issues, it captures relevant international norms of human rights to be found in major global human rights instruments. From equality,[62] to non-discrimination,[63] to rights of women,[64] children,[65] youth,[66] elderly[67] and persons with disabilities,[68] and the necessity to improve living condition,[69] or the RTD, protection of health, safety and environment,[70] amongst others, this instrument is simply a masterpiece for human rights protection.

In ECOWAS, respect for human rights is even more pronounced. This is illustrated by the centrality of freedom of movement of persons, the right to reside and of establishment in the sub-region which are at the centre of the 1979 ECOWAS Protocol Relating to Free Movement of Persons, the right of residence and establishment.[71] In addition, the ECOWAS protocol on democracy and governance

58 Ibid.

59 C. Okafor. '"Righting" the Right to Development: A Socio-Legal Analysis of Article 22 of the African Charter of Human and Peoples Rights' In *Implementing the Right to Development: The Role of International Law* (Friedricht Ebert Stiftung 2008), 52, 55.

60 Viljoen (n 1) 481–482.

61 The Charter of Fundamental Rights in SADC. www.sadc.int/files/6613/5292/8383/Charter_of_the_Fundamental_Social_Rights_in_SADC2003.pdf (Accessed 2 January/May 2017). For more on ensuring social security or human welfare in SADC, see B. Jordaan, E. Kalula and E. Strydom (eds.) *Understanding Social Security Law* (Juta 2009), 45.

62 Art 6.

63 Art 6.

64 Art 6.

65 Art 7.

66 Art 7.

67 Art 8.

68 Art 9.

69 Art 11.

70 Art 12.

71 ECOWAS Protocol A/P.1/5/79.

repeatedly uses the terms human rights including reference to the African Charter.[72] Similarly, the ECOWAS Protocol on conflict prevention also establishes the link between human rights, governance and conflicts[73] and underlines the significance of 'protection of fundamental human rights and freedoms and the rules of international humanitarian laws' as principles for the realisation of the objectives of the protocol.[74]

The emphasis on human rights and good governance has also found its way in the fundamental principles of the amended EAC Treaty of 1999.[75] In addition, it is expressly provided that a state will not be admitted in the EAC Treaty unless it adheres to 'universally acceptable principles of good governance, democracy, the rule of law, observance of human rights and social justice'.[76]

These freedoms – especially freedom of movement, residence and establishment – are found in most RECs treaties. Besides the treaties mentioned above, these freedoms are equally essential in ECCAS[77] and UEMOA.[78] It is needless to underline that these freedoms and liberties are essential for the realisation of the RTD.

As a result of this emphasis on human rights in RECs instruments, it can be argued that the RTD is secured in various projects of regional integration which ultimately seek to improve peoples' lives or standard of living as posit by the RTD discourse. After all, the need to better peoples' lives had informed the creation of these RECs initially. In the final analysis, the economic tenets of RECs cannot be separated from the poverty eradication objective, and human rights as understood under the RTD discourse. Viljoen writes:

> In so far as the right to development is a conglomerate consisting of numerous rights to basic necessities of life, the developmentalist imperative that drives the project of regional integration closely [seeks its realisation].[79]

4.3.2.3. The judicialisation of human rights in RECs

Originally the approach in RECs was to rely on arbitration and other non-judicial mechanisms to solving disagreements and established courts to deal with issues related to economic and political integration or cooperation.[80] However, the shift from economic to human rights issues in RECs is illustrated by the establishment of courts or tribunals with a human rights mandate, especially in ECOWAS, EAC and COMESA. Human rights protection is informed by the fact that these judicial

72 Protocol A/SP1/12/01 on Democracy and Good Governance.
73 Paras 8, 11 and 13 of the Protocol relating to the Mechanism for Conflict Prevention.
74 Art 2 of the Conflict Prevention Protocol.
75 EAC Treaty, art 6(d), 7(2).
76 EAC Treaty, art 3(3)(b).
77 ECCAS, art 40.
78 UEMOA Treaty, art 91,
79 Viljoen (n 1) 481.
80 Ibid., 489.

institutions accept individual access and not only states'. In ECOWAS, individual access to the ECOWAS Court of Justice to 'seek relief for violation of human rights' is regulated by the supplementary Protocol to the 2005 Protocol relating to ECOWAS.[81] It provides: 'The court has jurisdiction to determine cases of violations of human rights that occur in any member State', and importantly, access to court is open to 'individuals on application for relief for violation of their human rights'.[82] In accessing the court, individuals and corporate bodies may demonstrate that an act or omission of a Community Representative encroached upon their rights. In the EAC[83] and COMESA,[84] the rule is similar.

However, individual's access to court was also the rule in SADC.[85] Nevertheless, in the *Campbell* case[86] Mike Campbell brought the Zimbabwe government to the SADC Tribunal and alleged to have been discriminated against on the ground of race, in violation of article 6(2) of the SADC Treaty. The Tribunal found for the applicants. Unfortunately, the Tribunal was later disbanded as a result of mobilisation against its human rights mandate by Zimbabwe that obviously disagreed with its decision. As result, the current Protocol[87] on the re-instauration of the SADC tribunal does not enable individual access.

However, this negative development at the SADC level cannot lead to a claim that the protection of human rights through RECs' courts or tribunals is generally a failure. This will be overlooking the great work that is done by the ECOWAS Court that relies on the ACHPR to compel states to comply with human rights and also acts as court of first instance. The position of the ECOWAS Court of Justice is unequivocal:

> Under the ECOWAS model, as demonstrated by the [ECOWAS Community Court of Justice] ECCJ's application of the African Charter in its case law, the Charter is perceived as a catalogue of rights for ECOWAS and its substantive provisions are directly invoked in actions before the Court.[88]

Following this approach, the ECOWAS Court of justice protected the right to education,[89] an important element of the RTD which is located in Directives Princi-

81 Protocol on the Community Court of Justice, amended by the Supplementary Protocol Amending the Protocol relating to the Community Court of Justice, ECOWAS Doc A/SP.1/01/05, 19 January 2005; 10(c) of the Protocol (Supplementary Protocol, art 4).

82 Art 9(4) and 10(d).

83 EAC Treaty, art 30.

84 COMESA, art 26.

85 SADC Tribunal Protocol, art 18.

86 *Campbell and 78 others v Zimbabwe* (Campbell case) SADC (T) Case No.2/2007 in which judgement was delivered on 28 November 2008. The *Campbell* case was filed in 2007 and became famous with an interim ruling by the Tribunal in December 2007.

87 See Outcome of the SADC Council of Ministers meeting held on 14 and 15 August 2014 at Victoria Falls, Zimbabwe. www.sadc.int/files/2314/0821/8588/Outcome_of_the_Council_of_Ministers_meeting_of_August_14_and_15_2014L.pdf (Accessed 7 March 2017).

88 See ECCJ decisions *Essien v The Gambia*, Unreported Suit No ECW/CCJ/APP/05/05; also *Koraou v Niger*, Unreported Suit No: ECW/CCJ/APP/08/08 (27 October 2008). *Niger slavery* case.

89 *Registered Trustees of SERAP v Nigeria*, Judgement ECW/CCJ/APP/08/08, 27 October 2009.

ples of State Policy and not the Constitution of Nigeria and therefore non-binding. The Court was of the view that the location of the right to education in the Directives Principles of State Policy does not affect the justiciability.

In addition, in *Karaou v Niger*,[90] the ECOWAS Court of Justice found that Niger was de facto perpetuating the practice of slavery. It also found that the prolonged arrest and detention of a journalist without trial was a violation of the African Charter by the Gambia.[91] The ECOWAS court had been to some extent at the forefront of protecting economic, social and cultural rights and civil and political rights which are all essential for the achievement of the RTD.

Unlike in ECOWAS, in the EAC, the EAC Court of Justice does not have an express human rights mandate. However, the EAC Treaty already contains human rights obligations including the African Charter, and this enables the Court to receive complains based on individual human rights violations. This was the position of the Court in *Katabazi and others v Secretary General of the EAC and another*.[92] In this case, the accused together with one other individual were arrested and detained in Uganda for treason. After 14 of the accused were granted bail by the High Court, they were re-arrested and the Constitutional found the re-arrest to be in violation of the Constitution. Therefore, the proceedings reached the EAC Court that indicated its jurisdiction on human rights matters based on the EAC treaty which underlined human rights and respect for rule of law.[93] The Court went ahead and found for the accused on the ground that the Uganda government's action violates the independence of the judiciary and as such encroaches upon a 'cornerstone' of the rule of law[94] which is provided for in the EAC treaty.[95]

As for the individual access to the EAC court, it was illustrated by the fact that the exhaustion of local remedies is not a pre-requisite to take a case of human rights violation to court. This was emphasised by the East African Court in *Kenyan EALA Nominees*[96] case in which the Court was unequivocal in pointing out that the silence of the rule on local remedies rule was an indication that individuals of the Community have 'the right of direct access to court'.[97] This enables victims of human rights violation to approach the Court directly and this is essential in seeking human rights protection.

In sum, although the RECs were established to repair the divisions caused by colonialism, to foster Africa's unity through economic blocs to achieve economic

90 *Karaou v Niger*, judgement ECW/CCJ/JJD/06/08.

91 *Manneh v the Gambia*, Judgement ECW/CCJ/JJD/03/08, ECOWAS court of justice.

92 *Katabazi and others v Secretary General of the EAC and Another* (Reference 1 of 2007, EAC Court (1 November 2007), 2007 AHLR 119.

93 *Katabazi*, para 36.

94 *Katabazi*, para 35.

95 EAC Treaty, arts 6(d) and 7(2).

96 *Anyang' Nyongo and others v Attoney General of Kenya and Others*, Reference No 1 of 2006, 27 November 2006 (Known as *Kenyan EALA Nominees* case).

97 H. Onoria. 'Locus Standi of Individuals and Non-State Entities Before Regional Economic Integration Judicial Bodies in Africa' (2010) 18 *African Journal of International and Comparative Law* 161; also Vieljoen (n 1) 489.

development, they have evolved to capture human rights as it cannot be denied that one of their core objectives is to 'improving the welfare of the people in the participating countries and the realisation of socio economic rights [and the RTD]'.[98] In reaching this target, numerous RECs treaties clearly aim at reducing poverty; they explicitly include human rights in their objectives, clearly guarantee human rights and ensure the judicialisation of human rights through the establishment of judicial bodies such as the courts in RECs.

4.4. The right to development in selected national laws

After looking at the reception of the RTD in African treaties and sub-regional treaties, the following section focuses on its reception at the national level.[99]

4.4.1. Rationale to examine the reception of the right to development at the national level

Not only national laws are parts and parcels of the African human rights system understood broadly, it is important to see how countries are giving effect to their international and regional human rights commitments. In fact, the successful implementation of human rights can only happen within the confines of a local context. During the drafting of the Universal Declaration of Human Rights, Eleanor Roosevelt explains as follows:

> Where, after all, do universal human rights begin? In small places, close to homes so close and so small that they cannot be seen on any maps of the world. Yet they are the world of individual persons, the neighbourhood they live in, the school they attend, the factory, farm or office they work in. Such are the places where every man, *woman* or child seeks equal justice, equal opportunities, and equal dignity without discrimination. Unless these rights have meaning there, they have little meaning anywhere.[100]

This is a call to ensure that human rights are given effect at the local level. Reiterating this view, Olowu underlines that 'the struggle for human rights will be won or lost at the national level'.[101] In other words, human rights are meaningless if actions are not taken at the local level to turn them into reality.

This suggests that if the ratification of instruments is not followed by its implementation at the local level, these instruments will be meaningless. It is on this backdrop

98 Vieljoen (n 1) 481.

99 This section builds on 'The right to development in the African Human Rights system' discussed in S. D. Kamga. 'Human Rights in Africa: Prospects for the Realisation of the Right to Development under the New Partnership for Africa's Development'. LLD Thesis (University of Pretoria 2011), Chapter 4

100 UNFPA, *Supra* note 37, 9. My emphasis.

101 D. Olowu. *An Integrative Rights-Based Approach to Human Development in Africa* (PULP 2009), 73.

that this section assesses how article 22 of the ACHPR is received at the country level. It explores the duty bearer's obligations while focusing on the RTD in selected national laws, namely: Cameroon, Uganda, Malawi, Ethiopia and South Africa. As indicated earlier, the criteria used for the case studies are the consideration of the African Constitution that goes beyond providing for development to clearly provide for the RTD. Cameroon, Ethiopia, Malawi and Uganda meet this criterion. In addition, the South African Constitution will also be examined because even though it does not expressly mention the RTD, it has a solid reputation for being one the most progressive Constitutions on the continent,[102] with a solid pro-poor jurisprudence.[103] As indicated earlier, the state is the primary duty bearer of the right at the national level. Therefore, this section assesses the extent to which African states listed above comply with the law of development of the African human rights system.

4.4.2. Cameroon

Paragraph 3 of the Preamble of the 1996 Cameroonian Constitution recognises the RTD in these terms:

> [We are] resolved to harness our natural resources in order to ensure the well-being of every citizen without discrimination, by raising living standards, proclaim our right to development as well as our determination to devote all our efforts to that end and declare our readiness to co-operate with all States desirous of participating in this national endeavour with due respect for our sovereignty and the independence of the Cameroonian State.

According to this provision, Cameroon recognises itself as the duty bearer of the RTD and counts on its natural resources to deliver its people from the claws of poverty. It also highlights that all Cameroonians without discrimination will enjoy the right. In addition, it also emphasises the role of international co-operation, by declaring its readiness to work with other states with due respect to the principle of sovereignty in view of achieving the RTD. By the look of things, in providing for the RTD, Cameroon was inspired by the 1986 UNDRTD[104] and the ACHPR which highlights the role of the state and international community in providing the RTD without discrimination. The government of Cameroon takes the RTD very seriously. This was underlined by President Biya's speech at the UN in 2001, when he questioned 'how can we speak of human rights without the right to development?'[105]

102 Mubangizi (n 2) 71.

103 S. Alain, D. Kamga and S. Heleba. 'Can Economic Growth Translate into Access to Rights? Challenges Faced by Institutions in South Africa in Ensuring that Growth Leads to Better Living Standards' (2012) 9(17) *Sur International Journal on Human Rights* 91.

104 See art 1(2), 2(3), 3 to list some of them.

105 'Biya emphasises on the right to development as the main human right' *Afrol News* 8 September 2000 (on file with author).

As far as the justiciability of the RTD is concerned, although the RTD is included in the preambular paragraph of the Constitution, it is justiciable because article 65 of the Cameroonian Constitution underlines that 'the Preamble shall be part and parcel of this Constitution'. Nevertheless, the Cameroonian Supreme Court unambiguously pronounced that the Preamble only offers contextual guidance and comprises mere principles of and as such is not justiciable.[106]

The other challenge facing the enforceability of the RTD in Cameroon is the lack of constitutional remedies for human rights violations. This means that there is no judicial measures to ensure that human rights and the RTD are enforced when violated. This shortcoming does not apply to the RTD only but human rights in general. In his appraisal of the human rights protection in Cameroon, Chofor Che writes: 'Cameroon should clearly and unequivocally integrate socio-economic and political rights in its Constitution, as well as adopt definite measures for their enforcement by state organs'.[107]

It could therefore be argued that to increase the prospect of the RTD, it is imperative to revise the Constitution with a view 'to include a bill of rights, and the provision of remedies in cases of human rights violations'.[108] In this perspective, Cameroon should take action to institutionalise the justiciability of human rights in general and the RTD in particular. In a similar vein, it should foster the separation of powers in which the judiciary shall be fully independent and capacitated to read the law without fear or favour.

The 2016 human development report on Cameroon is not flattering. Human development index shows that Cameroon is not on the pathway to development and to achieve the RTD. In this respect, although as a result of the increase of the oil price, the growth rate was 5.6 percent and anticipated to 5.0 percent in 2013 and 2014 respectively,[109] the country is not committed to reducing poverty as corruption has become endemic in spite of various arrests and sentencing of former Ministers for corruption.[110] It was reported that the only Millennium Development Goal (MDG) achieved by Cameroon was 'fighting HIV, Malaria and other transmissible diseases'.[111] Moreover, data are not encouraging as Cameroon is classified 152nd on the human development index, and only qualifies as a country with 'low human development' with around 30 percent of the population living below 2 dollars per day, and poverty rate nearing 40 percent.[112] Furthermore, as far as

106 Rapport de la Cour Suprême du Cameroun (2000), as quoted by G. Z. Sebenzile. 'The Treatment Action Campaign (TAC) Case as a Model for the Protection of the Right to Health in Africa, With Particular Reference to South Africa and Cameroon'. LLM Dissertation, Centre for Human Rights, University of Pretoria (2005), 41; also S. D. Kamga. 'Realising the Right to Primary Education in Cameroon' (2011) 11 *African Human Rights Law Journal* 187.

107 C. A. Chofor Che. 'Challenges of Incorporating and Enforcing a Bill of Rights in the Cameroonian Constitution' (2008) *Cameroon Journal of Democracy and Human Rights* 1.

108 Kamga (n 105) 189.

109 BTI 2016 | Cameroon Country Report, (2016) 3. www.bti-project.org/fileadmin/files/BTI/Downloads/Reports/2016/pdf/BTI_2016_Cameroon.pdf (Accessed 2 January 2017).

110 Ibid., 3.

111 Ibid., 12.

112 Ibid.

mainstreaming gender in development is concerned, Cameroon is not doing well as only 13 countries are classified worse than Cameroon in the Gender Development Index with an index of 0.622.[113]

In addition, official data on unemployment rate reveals that, in 2011 67 percent of youth of 16 years were unemployed and it got worse in 2012 where 68 percent of the same age group were without employment.[114] These figures led the Economist Intelligence Unit to claim that 'Cameroon's economic growth remains far below potential', and not enough to achieve the country's objective of becoming an emerging-market economy by 2035.[115] These data suggest that Cameroon is doing little for the realisation of the RTD. Nevertheless, to validate this assertion, it is important to check the content of Cameroon reports to the African Commission, with special attention to article 22 of the Charter.

Under article 62 of the ACHPR, state parties shall commit to submit every two years reports on the legislative and other measures they have taken with a view to giving effect to the rights and freedoms recognised and guaranteed by the Charter. It is this context that Cameroon has reported to the African Commission on measures taken to implement art 22 of the ACHPR. Firstly, in its Periodic Report on its implementation of the ACHPR's provisions presented at the 31st Ordinary Session of the African Commission in 2002, Cameroon did not present measures undertaken to protect the RTD. In fact, the Report did not even mention the right in question. This gap showed that the Cameroonian government was not doing enough in achieving the RTD.

Interestingly, in its Concluding Observations on this Report,[116] except from observing that 'poverty hinders the implementation of human rights in Cameroon',[117] the African Commission did not address the issues or rather overlooked the lack of report on article 22 of the ACHPR. There was no recommendation whatsoever on the question. Such reporting and monitoring mistakes do not enhance the prospects of realisation of the RTD in Africa and in Cameroon in particular. It was in fact a missed opportunity by the Commission to raise this as a concern and recommend detailed remedial actions.

However, in its 3rd Periodic Report,[118] to its credit Cameroon reported on measures taken to secure the RTD.[119] Essentially, Cameroon demonstrated its commitments to the rights guaranteed in the ACHPR, civil and political as well

113 Ibid.

114 Ibid., 17. Also Concluding Observations of the African Commission on the 3rd Periodic Report of the Republic of Cameroon, adopted at its 15th Extraordinary Session held from 7 to 14 March 2014 in Banjul, *The Gambia*.

115 The Economist Intelligence Unit. http://country.eiu.com/article.aspx?articleid=718743856&Country=Cameroon&topic=Economy&subtopic=Recent+developments&subsubtopic=Economic+performance:+Economic+growth+in+2011+is+higher+than+expected (Accessed 3 January 2017); also BRI 2016, Cameroon report (2016) 17.

116 Presented at the 39th Ordinary Session of the African Commission on Human and Peoples' Rights held in Banjul, Gambia from 11 to 25 May 2005.

117 Para 12 of the Concluding Observations.

118 Presented at 53rd Session of the African Commission on Human and Peoples' Rights of the African Union, in Banjul, *The Gambia* on 09 to 24 April 2013.

119 Para 579–590.

as socio-economic rights by reporting on their implementation. In addition, it reported on measures such as improvement of the business environment, fighting corruption and financial embezzlement and infrastructural developments as measures to secure the RTD.

Although Cameroon should be commended for these attempts, the statistics on human development index discussed earlier showed that the initiatives undertaken are yet to translate into access to the RTD on the ground. In fact, much more needs to be done for this right to become reality.

Interestingly, in its Concluding Observations, the African Commission did not have a concern with the report on article 22. It however focused on indigenous people rights as an area of concern with specific attention to the fact that:

> The expansion of agriculture and extractive industries in Cameroon which continues to threaten the rights of indigenous populations to their ancestral lands, in particular through the granting, *without their prior, free and informed consent*, of land concessions for development project.[120] It then proceeds to recommend or urge Cameroon to:[121]
>
> Prepare and enact – in a *participatory manner* involving indigenous peoples – a specific law recognizing their rights of ownership over their ancestral lands, as recommended by the Commission in its concluding observations of May 2010 and by the UN Committee on the Elimination of Racial Discrimination in its concluding observations of March 2010, [and]
>
> Ensure *the effective participation* of indigenous populations in the process of reforming the forest law and all other ongoing and future legislative and political reforms having an impact on the rights of indigenous peoples, in particular the land code, the mining code, the national plan to implement the law on regional development and the pastoral code.

This was a missed opportunity by the Commission to cement the meaning and content of the RTD as defined by the *Endorois* case[122] where the RTD was defined to include a meaningful participation of the population in projects in their communities, to include accountability and transparency, equity and choices as well as capabilities to the benefit of populations. Although the measures taken by Cameroon on the RTD were in line with the RTD discourse as defined through the Charter, the Commission could have linked its concern on the 'expansion of agriculture and extractive industries in Cameroon which continues to threaten the rights of indigenous populations' to their RTD as to capture the spirit of its *Endorois* decision. Subsequently, its recommendation would have also made similar remarks to ensure consistency on the nature RTD. So it is imperative that the

120 Concluding Observation, adopted by the African Commission on Human and Peoples' Rights at its 15th Extraordinary Session held from 7 to 14 March 2014 in Banjul, *The Gambia*, para 74 (my emphasis).

121 As above, paras xxiv and xxv, my emphasis.

122 To be discussed in the next chapter

Commission makes these links as much as possible to frame, explain and reinforce the content of the RTD on the continent. In sum, although Cameroon has a normative provision and institutional mechanisms to realise the RTD, much more needs to be done for the right to become reality in the country.

4.4.3. Uganda

The 1995 Ugandan Constitution recognises the RTD. In the draft constitution, the RTD was a significant part of Chapter 3. However, in the final constitution, the RTD finds its place in the midst of the National Objectives and Directive Principles of State Policy as Objective number 9 which reads: 'The right to development' and provides that 'in order to facilitate rapid and equitable development, the State shall encourage private initiative and self-reliance'. In addition, objective number 10 calls upon the state to undertake needed measures to involve the people in the formulation and implementation of development plans and programmes which affect them. In addition, the principles stress the role of the state in development.

Nevertheless, locating the RTD in the National Objectives and Directive Principles of State policy casts serious doubt on the justiciability of the provision. Putting the RTD away from Chapter 4 of the Constitution which deals with the bill of rights shows that the drafters had no intention to ensure its justiciability. However, the amendment of the 1995 Constitution through its article 8 (a) 1 turned the RTD into a justiciable right. It states that 'Uganda shall be governed based on principles of national interest and common good enshrined in the national objectives and directive principles of State policy'.[123] It can be argued that the RTD is now part of the Ugandan bill of rights as provided by Chapter 4 of the Constitution.

Nevertheless, the human development report in Uganda in 2016 shows that notwithstanding the average growth of 6.3 percent,[124] the country remains in the low income category with a human development index of only 0.483, ranked 163 out of 188 countries and territories, with 24.5 percent of the population below the poverty line and cumulated with a Gender Inequality Index of 0.54 percent.[125] In addition, the unemployment rate in Uganda averaged 3.63 percent from 2003 until 2013.[126]

Although, the employment rate is encouraging, the fact that the human development index remains very low is an important indicator showing the RTD is far from being achieved.

In reporting to the African Commission in 2006, Uganda also used the opportunity to submit overdue reports of 2002, 2004 and 2006 in its amalgamated report.[127] The latter did not mention measures taken to operationalise article 22

123 1995 Constitution of Uganda as amended in February 2006.

124 UNDP 'About Uganda'. www.ug.undp.org/content/uganda/en/home/countryinfo/ (Accessed 3 January 2017).

125 Ibid; also UNDP Human Development Report 2015 'Uganda'. http://hdr.undp.org/sites/all/themes/hdr_theme/country-notes/UGA.pdf (Accessed 3 January 2017).

126 Uganda Unemployment Rate 2003–2017. www.tradingeconomics.com/uganda/unemployment-rate.

127 Amalgamated report of 2002, 2004 and 2006 presented at 39th Ordinary Session of the African Commission on Human and Peoples' Rights, Banjul, The Gambia, May 2006, which was a cumulated report of 2002, 2004 and 2006.

of the African instrument dealing with the right under study,[128] and unfortunately this insufficiency was not question by the Concluding Observations and Recommendations of the Commission.

However, in its 4th periodic Report submitted to the African Commission[129] Uganda reported on the RTD. It basically registered its hosting of a NEPAD Summit in Kampala in 2010 and its participation in the African Peer Review Mechanism (APRM) process with the involvement of numerous stakeholders in the country.

In addition, the government highlighted its April 2010 the 5-Year National Development Plan (NDP) 2010/11–2014/15, a successor to the Poverty Eradication Action Plan (PEAP), with the theme: 'Growth, Employment and Socio-economic Transformation for Prosperity' as a means to release the RTD. In this perspective, the NDP maintains the poverty eradication vision, but with a major focus on economic growth and wealth creation. The report also mentioned that the Constitution of Uganda, in articles 32(3), (4) provides for the establishment of an Equal Opportunities Commission (EOC) to safeguard the rights of the marginalised groups.[130]

Although these measures are important, they are not indicative of the implementation of the RTD. For instance, although NEPAD and APRM are the latest responses to Africa's development ills, hosting a NEPAD summit is not enough to claim that such action will lead to the achievement or the actual realisation of the RTD. Similar reasoning can apply to the APRM which does not automatically mean that a participatory country is securing the RTD of its people, especially when on the ground people are poor and miserable. Besides the Constitutional provision on the RTD and the National Development Plan which are likely to make a difference, very little was done to implement the RTD.

However, the Concluding Observations and Recommendations of the African Commission[131] were silent on this. Nevertheless, the Commission offered the following recommendation related to indigenous peoples' rights by calling on Uganda to adopt 'measures to ensure the effective protection of the rights of indigenous populations as guaranteed under the African Charter by establishing laws that protect land rights and natural resources of indigenous populations.[132] Nonetheless, the Commission missed the opportunity to build on this to address

128 Amalgamated report of 2002, 2004 and 2006 presented at 39th Ordinary Session of the African Commission on Human and Peoples' Rights, Banjul, The Gambia, May 2006, which was a cumulated report of 2002, 2004 and 2006.

129 2008–2010 cumulated periodic report by the government of Uganda to the African Commission on Human and Peoples' Rights presented at the 49th Ordinary Session Banjul, the Gambia 28 April to 12 May 2011, pp. 24 and 25; 4th periodic report.

130 Ibid.

131 Concluding Observations of the African Commission on Human and Peoples' Rights on the 4th periodic report of the republic of Uganda (Presented at the 49th Ordinary Session of the African Commission on Human and Peoples' Rights held in Banjul, the Gambia from 28 April to 12 May 2011), this Concluding Observation was adopted on November 2011in Banjul.

132 Ibid., 7, para xiv.

the RTD as per the *Endorois* case; it was a good opportunity to emphasise the right to participation and other elements of the RTD as underlined in the *Endorois* case.

In its 5th Periodic Report, Uganda claimed that the right to property, the protection of freedom of conscience, expression, movement, religion, assembly and association, the right to education, to family, right to culture and similar rights and economic rights are provided for by articles 26, 29, 30, 31, 37 and 40 of the Constitution respectively to give effect to the African Charter. Nevertheless, it failed to mention 'the right to development' provided in Objective 9 of the Constitution, and perhaps this is an indication of the insignificancy of this Objective.

Furthermore, policy measures such as the 5-Year National Development Plan (NDP) 2010/11–2014/15 were adopted in 2010. Ultimately, this policy should contribute to Uganda's Vision of 'a transformed Ugandan society from a peasant to a modern and prosperous country within 30 years'. In addition, on 18 April 2013, Uganda launched its vision 2040 plan to transform the country from a mainly low income to a reasonable upper middle income country within 30 years with a per capita income of USD 9,500.[133]

In its Concluding Observations,[134] the African Commission commended Uganda for its 2040 Vision,[135] but criticised the country for not taking enough steps to implement economic, social and cultural rights as set out in the Principles and Guidelines on the Implementation of Economic, Social and Cultural Rights in the African Charter on Human and Peoples' Rights (ECOSOCC Guidelines).[136]

The Commission could have used this opportunity to also call on Uganda to take additional measures for the implementation of the RTD, or at least link its remarks on the implementation of Economic, Social and Cultural Rights to the realisation of the RTD and show how the execution the former will impact positively on the latter.

4.4.4. Malawi

Section 30 of chapter 4 of the 1994 Malawian Constitution reads:

1 All persons and people shall have a right to development and therefore to enjoyment of economic, social, cultural and political development and women, children and the disabled in particular shall be given special consideration in the application of this right.

2 The state shall take all necessary measures for the realisation of the right to development. Such measures shall include, amongst other things, equality of

133 5th Periodic Report by the Government of the Republic of Uganda to the African Commission on Human and Peoples' Rights presented at the 54rd ordinary session held in Banjul, the Gambia 22nd October–5 November (2013) 28.

134 57th Ordinary Session 04–18 November 2015, Banjul, The Gambia Concluding Observations and Recommendations on the 5th Periodic State Report of the Republic of Uganda (2010–2012).

135 Ibid., para 16.

136 ECOSOCC Guidelines (2010) 8 and 9, para 50 (iii).

opportunity for all in their access to basic resources, education, health services, food, shelter, employment and infrastructure.

3 The state shall take measures to introduce reforms aimed at eradicating social injustices and inequalities.

4 The state has the responsibility to respect the right to development and to justify its policies in accordance with this responsibility.

From this section, different features of the RTD can be drawn: Just like in the first article of the UNDRTD, the RTD is an individual and collective right to be enjoyed without discrimination in Malawi. The content of the right, enjoyment of 'economic, social, cultural and political development' is also similar to the content at the regional as well international levels.

In Malawi, the RTD is justiciable and the state is clearly the primary entity responsible to deliver its people from poverty. In enjoying the RTD, not only should the vulnerable people not be forgotten, they should be given special attention. In fact, the RTD provision in the Malawian Constitution sounds like article 8(1) of the UNDRTD which highlights the most important role of the state in providing the RTD.

However, as far as the human development on the country is concerned, Malawi is the 18th least developed country in the world with a poverty rate of 50.7 percent.[137] Its human development index is 0.414 which ranked the country at 174 out of 187 countries and territories.[138] Although the national poverty rate has declined to 50.7 percent, indicating that almost half of the population is poor, most female-headed households are among the poor.[139] Furthermore, the society is unequal and those in dire need are in the rural area.[140] This state of affairs is due to the fact that, as correctly argued by Kamchedzera and Banda, 'Malawi's era of multiparty politics has been characterised by the use of legislation not based on this right [RTD]'.[141] Furthermore, the paramountcy of the executive in the separation of powers, the widespread corruption and cronyism rooted in the central and local governance structures[142] also foster inequality in the country and hinder the RTD.

In its initial and combined report, 1995–2013 to the African Commission, Malawi clearly highlighted article 29 of its Constitution on the right to economic activity as well as article 30 on the RTD and underlined its membership to the ICESCR which are instrumental to give effect to the RTD.

137 UNDP. 'About Malawi'. www.mw.undp.org/content/malawi/en/home/countryinfo/ (Accessed 3 January 2017).

138 BTI 2016 | Malawi Country Report, (2016) 2. www.bti-project.org/fileadmin/files/BTI/Downloads/Reports/2016/pdf/BTI_2016_Malawi.pdf (Accessed 3 January 2017).

139 Ibid.

140 G. Kamchedzera and C. U Banda. 'Dignified Rural Living, the Right to Development, Multiparty Politics and Legislation in Malawi' (2009) 25 *South African Journal on Human Rights* 73–101.

141 Ibid.

142 BTI 2016 | Malawi Country Report (n 137).

In addition, policy measures including Malawi Growth and Development Strategy I and II (MGDS) and Vision 2020 ideals were presented as the roadmap towards the achievement of the RTD in the country.[143] The African Commission was satisfied with the report and therefore issued no Concluding Observations and Recommendations.[144]

4.4.5. Ethiopia

In its Chapter 3 on Fundamental Rights and Freedoms, the 1994 Ethiopian Constitution provides for the RTD in its article 43 which reads:

The Right to Development

1 The right of the peoples of Ethiopia collectively, or the nations, nationalities and peoples in Ethiopia, individually, to improve their standard of living and sustainable development is guaranteed.
2 Citizens shall have the right to participate in national development, and in particular, to demand that their opinions be heard on matters of policies and of projects pertaining to the community of which they are members.
3 International agreements entered into or relations formed by the State shall be such as to guarantee the right to the sustainable development of Ethiopia.
4 The main objectives of development activities shall be the citizens' development and the fulfilment of their basic needs.

Similar to the Malawian Constitution, the Ethiopian one secures a justiciable RTD in its text. The Ethiopian text addresses all the elements of the RTD as included in the 1986 UNDRTD and the 1993 Vienna Declaration. The individual and collective aspect of the right are mentioned,[145] the right to participation is raised,[146] the international community's duties through international agreements signed by Ethiopia are referred to,[147] and finally the fact that the whole process of development conducted by the state should aim to ensure basic needs or human dignity is highlighted.[148]

Unfortunately, just like Malawi, Ethiopia is one of the poorest countries on earth. In spite of its economic growth of 7 percent to 10 percent annually, its human development index is 0.435 and the country ranks at 173th out 187

143 Initial and combined reports, 1995–2013. Report to the African Commission on Human and Peoples' Rights implementation of the African Charter on Human and Peoples' Rights, 1995–2013 (56th ordinary session of the Commission) 57, 58 and 59.

144 Concluding Observations and Recommendations on the Initial and Combined Periodic Report of the Republic of Malawi on the Implementation of the African Charter on Human and Peoples' Rights (1995–2013), 57th Ordinary Session 04–18 November 2015, Banjul, *The Gambia*.

145 1994 Ethiopian Constitution, art 43(1).

146 1994 Ethiopian Constitution, art 43(1), art 4(2).

147 1994 Ethiopian Constitution, art 43(1), art 43(3).

148 1994 Ethiopian Constitution, art 43(1), art 43(4).

countries and territories.[149] A third of its population lives below the poverty line,[150] with high unemployment rates at between 15 percent and 25 percent of the labour force, with young people extremely affected.[151] The situation is exacerbated by the authoritarian regime running the country, which ultimately got Ethiopia to the 124th place out of 167 countries on the 2014 Democracy index.[152]

In its 1st to 4th periodic Report to the African Commission, the government clearly underlines its constitutional provision on the RTD, as well as article 89(5) which compels the government to hold land and other natural resources on behalf of the people and deploy for their benefit and development. In addition, at all times the government has to promote the participation of the people in the formulation of national development policies and programmes and shall support the initiatives of the people in their development endeavours.[153] The African Commission was happy with the report and did not issue Concluding Observations and Recommendations.[154]

Subsequently in its 5th and 6th Periodic report for 2009–2013, the government of Ethiopia repeated the constitutional dispositions for the RTD. In addition it highlighted administrative, legislative and policy measures taken for the realisation of the RTD. Amongst them, the Public Servants 'Pension Proclamation, the Private Organization Employees' Pension Proclamation and the Social Health Insurance Proclamation and the Sustainable Development and Poverty Reduction Program as well as the Poverty Eradication and Accelerated Sustainable Development Plan are important to improve people's socio-economic condition and have had some success.[155]

In response to this report, the Commission commended Ethiopia 'for its continuous efforts towards the development of the living conditions and environment of its populations through the implementation of diverse development projects and programmes'.[156]

4.4.6. South Africa

Although the South African 1996 Constitution does not mention the RTD specifically, its Chapter 2 or Bill of Rights guaranteeing fundamental rights including socio-economic rights is significant for the protection of the RTD.

149 BTI 2016 | Ethiopia Country Report (n 137).

150 Ibid., 2.

151 Ibid., 20.

152 The Economist Intelligence Unit's 2014; also BTI 2016 | Ethiopia Country Report(n 137) 2.

153 1st to 4th periodic report 1998–2007, para 423, pp. 125–126.

154 See Forty-Seventh Ordinary Session 12–26 May 2010, Banjul, The Gambia Consideration of Reports Submitted by States Parties under Article 62 of the African Charter on Human and Peoples' Rights Concluding Observations and Recommendations on the Initial, 1st, 2nd, 3rd and 4th Periodic Report of the Federal Democratic Republic of Ethiopia.

155 The 5th and 6th Periodic report 2009–2013 on the implementation of the African Charter on Human and Peoples' Rights in Ethiopia (2014) 115–120.

156 The Commission at its 56th Ordinary Session 21 April to 7 May 2015, Banjul, *The Gambia* Concluding Observations and Recommendations on the 5th and 6th Periodic Report of the Federal Democratic Republic of Ethiopia, para 24 of Concluding Observations.

The legislature, the Human Rights Commission,[157] the Commission for Gender Equality, the Public Protector,[158] the Auditor-General[159] and the courts ensure that the RTD is respected. Despite the fact that these institutions do not address the RTD *per se*, they protect socio-economic rights which are the correlative rights to the RTD. The South African Chief Justice Pius Langa stresses that at the national level there cannot be development if socio-economic rights are not realised.[160] In this respect, the South African Constitution has a good reputation for the protection of these rights and as such was characterised as 'transformative'.[161] This transformative attribute goes beyond the text of the Constitution and is embraced by the Constitutional Court that ordered the State to ensure access to the right to housing,[162] health care,[163] education[164] and even clean environment[165] that are all significant for the achievement of the RTD. Gutto has correctly claimed that RTD is undeniably implicit in the South African constitution and constitutional practices.[166]

157 Sec 184(3) of the South African Constitution empowers the Human Rights Commission to demand from all organs of the State 'information on the measures taken towards the realisation of the rights in the Bill of Rights concerning housing, health care, food, water, social security, education and the environment'.

158 Established under Sec 182 of South African Constitution, the Public Protector has the power to 'investigate any conduct in state affairs or in the public administration in any sphere of government, that is alleged or suspected to be improper or to result in any impropriety or prejudice'.

159 Sec 188(1) of the Constitution empowers the Auditor-General to: 'audit and report on the accounts, financial statements and financial management of :

a) all national and provincial state departments and administration;
b) all municipalities; and
c) any other institution or accounting entity required by national or provincial legislation to be audited by the Auditor-General'.

160 Justice Pius N. Langa. 'Human Rights, the Rule of Law, and the Right to Development' speech presented at the Birchwood Conference Center in Johannesburg, 24 November 2006 (on file with author).

161 K. Klare. 'Legal Culture and Transformative Constitutionalism' (1998)14 *South African Journal on Human Rights* (1998) 146–188.

162 *Government of Republic of South Africa and Others v Grootboom and Others* (2000) 11 BCLR 1169 (CC).

163 *Minister of Health and Others v Treatment Action Campaign and* Others (*TAC* case) (No 2) 2002 5 SA 721 (CC).

164 *The Governing Body of the Juma Musjid Primary School and Another v Essay NO and Others* [2011] 7 BCLR 651 (CC); *Section27 v Minister of Education* 2013 (3) SA 40 (GNP); *Basic Education for All and Others v Minister of Basic Education and Others* (23949/14) [2014] ZAGPPHC 251; 2014 (4) SA 274 (GP); [2014] 3 All SA 56 (GP); 2014 (9) BCLR 1039 (GP) (5 May 2014) *The Minister of Basic Education v Basic Education for All* (20793/2014) [2015] ZASCA 198 (2 December 2015).

165 *Fuel Retailers Association of South Africa v Director-General Environmental Management, Department of Agriculture, Conservation and Environment, Mpumalanga Province and others* Case No. CCT67/06. See also *Fuel Retailers Association of South Africa v Director-General Environmental Management, Department of Agriculture, Conservation and Environment, Mpumalanga Province and others* 2007 2 SA 163 (SCA).

166 S. Gutto. 'The Right to Development: An Implied Right in South Africa's Constitutional Order' In SAHRC (ed.) *Reflections on Democracy and Human Rights: A Decade of the South African Constitution (Act 108 of 1996)* (2006) 109–118.

However, the human development of the country is still not satisfactory. Its recent growth of around 3 percent did little in addressing unemployment which is edges 30 percent with youth unemployment of about 70 percent.[167] Some development challenges are created by governance deficit characterised by unethical behaviour from the executive through the President of the Republic who used public funds to upgrade his private residence,[168] and corruption at the provincial and the local government levels.[169] This happens in a context of strong separation of powers, valuable independent monitoring institutions and well-established anti-corruption bodies that are yet to find the panacea to the problem.

The First Periodic Report of South Africa clearly underlines measures taken to give effect to the RTD. The report reads:[170]

> Although the Constitution does not provide for the right to development, this right is implied since the Constitution provides social, economic and cultural rights, including political rights, which are features of the right to development defined in article 1 of the UN Declaration as comprehensive economic, social, cultural and political processes which aim at the constant improvement of the well-being of the entire population and of all individuals, in which human rights and fundamental freedoms can be realised. The above mentioned rights enshrined in the Constitution provide a framework for comprehensive economic, social, cultural and political processes aimed at constant improvement of the well-being of the entire population and all individuals, in which human rights and fundamental freedoms can be realised.

In other words, elements of the RTD as defined by international and regional instruments are parts and parcels of the Constitution. More importantly, aware that the achievement of the right is a continuing process,[171] the government undertook various measures for its achievement: Legislation and Policy,[172] Peoples Housing Process Policy,[173] National Savings Programme,[174] Policy on Joint Ventures,[175] Housing Consumer Protection Measures Act, 1998 (Act of 1998),[176] The Rental Housing Act of 1999,[177] the Local Government: Municipal System Act of 2000[178] and numerous case law discussed below show South African's commitment to the RTD.

167 BTI 2016 South Africa (2016) 3.

168 *Economic Freedom Fighters v Speaker of the National Assembly Others: Democratic Alliance v Speaker of the National Assembly and others* [2016] ZACC 11(the *Nkandla* case).

169 BTI 2016 South Africa (n 166).

170 First Periodic Report of South Africa to the African Commission, 38th Ordinary, para 325.

171 Ibid.

172 Ibid., para 326.

173 Ibid., para 327.

174 Ibid.

175 Ibid., para 328.

176 Ibid., para 329.

177 Ibid., para 330.

178 Ibid., para 331.

In response, the African Commission was only concerned by the lack of participation of states, institutions and of civil society in the preparation of the report.[179] In fact, it can be argued that the African Commission had no problem with South Africa's commitment to the RTD, except that there was a need to involve the civil society and other stakeholders on human rights in the preparation of the Report.[180]

In its combined second periodic report under the African Charter and initial report under the protocol to the African Charter on the rights of women in Africa, South Africa also presented measures taken to implement the RTD. Essentially, emphasis was on policies measures including the 2009 Medium Term Strategic Framework (MTSF, 2009–2014) aiming to increase resource in all levels of government, the institutionalisation of the 2010 National Planning Commission (NPC) to draft vision and national development plans for consideration, which ultimately produced the country Vision for 2030 after a broad consultation.[181]

The discussion above focuses on the implementation of the RTD at the national level where the government is the primary duty bearer of the RTD. It is responsible for the creation of the climate needed to operationalise the right in question. This can be done through the establishment of democratic institutions, respect for the rule of law, good governance and appropriate poverty alleviation policies. Such a framework is indeed important to give effect to article 22 of the ACHPR as well as its Protocol on Women's rights. In other words, before looking outwards for assistance, African governments must first look inwards. They should create a stable legal framework, informed by supreme national constitutions and establish good governance before turning to development partners. In this perspective, Mbazira argues that Africa should begin to get rid of its problems by utilising the locally available resources and avoid relying on external solutions.[182]

In sum, the four African countries discussed have a normative protection of the RTD and strive to ensure its realisation through legal and policy measures. However, these countries face challenges such as poverty and bad governance, weak separation of powers and corruption which hinder the implementation of the right.

4.5. Concluding remarks

From the forgoing, the chapter found that at the regional level, the main African treaties which are the African Charter, the African Women's Protocol and

179 38th Ordinary Session of the African Commission, Concluding Observations and Recommendations on the First Periodic Report of the Republic of South Africa; para 16. (Thirty-Eighth Ordinary Session 21 November–5 December 2005). Consideration of Reports submitted by State Parties under Article 62 of the African Charter on Human and Peoples' Rights Concluding Observations and Recommendations on the First Periodic Report of the Republic of South Africa.

180 Recommendation of the African Commission, para 26.

181 58th ordinary session, combined Second Periodic Report under the African Charter on Human and People's Rights and Initial Report under the Protocol to the African Charter on the Rights of Women in Africa, (August 2015) 485–487.

182 C. Mbazira. 'A Path to Realising Economic, Social and Cultural Right in Africa? A Critique of the New Partnership for Africa Development' (2004) 4 *African Human Rights Law Journal* 47.

the African Children's Charter offer a normative protection of the RTD which cascades down to the sub-regional and national levels.

At the sub-regional level, it was found that although originally the RECs were established to foster regional integration through trade and enhance Africa's economic development, they evolved to protect human rights and the RTD. This development could be seen through the objectives of the RECs aiming to address poverty and improve people's welfare as well as achieving socio-economic rights. In addition, the RECs treaties also adopted or included explicit provisions on human rights in their dispositions and proceed to judicialise these rights through the setting up of courts/tribunal to ensure their justiciability, even though the current SADC Tribunal is no longer open to individuals.

Lastly, the normative provisions on the RTD are also recognised in countries such as Cameroon, Uganda, Malawi, Ethiopia and South Africa. In these countries, including where there is no express recognition of the right like in South Africa, there is a valuable legal protection, normative and legislative measures to turn the right from rhetoric to reality. However, the right unfortunately does not translate into reality as a result of poverty, weak separation of powers and endemic corruption or generalised bad governance, even where institutions have been established to address the governance challenge.

5 The African Commission, the African Court on Human Rights and the realisation of the right to development

5.1. Introduction

The continental legal framework for the protection of human rights and the RTD comprises the African Commission, African Committee of Experts on the Rights and Welfare of the Child (African Children's Committee); and the African Court on Human and Peoples' Rights (African Court). However, the chapter focuses exclusively on two of these institutions: Firstly,the African Commission because as the oldest body for the protection of human rights in Africa, it 'has fully asserted its mandate and entrenched its operations'[1] in advancing human rights in general and specifically the RTD. Secondly, the African Court that has recently (26 May 2017) rendered its first judgement on the RTD in the Ogiek case. The African Commission and the Court are the focus of this chapter as they are the only two bodies that have made a significant difference in addressing the RTD, at least in terms of standard setting.[2]

5.2. The African Commission and the realisation of the right to development

Established under article 30 of the African Charter, the African Commission comprises of 11 members selected amongst African personalities of the highest reputation and known for their morality and integrity credentials;[3] it holds two ordinary sessions and two extra-ordinary sessions per year, and has the mandate to protect and promote human and peoples' rights in Africa.[4] Therefore, the aim of this chapter is to examine the extent to which the African Commission protects and promotes the RTD in Africa, and if so how?

1 F. Viljoen and J. Biegon. 'The Architecture for an African Disability Rights Mechanism' (2013). www.panusp.org/wp-content/uploads/2013/04/Architecture-for-an-African-Disability-Rights-Mechanism.pdf (Accessed 10 March 2017).

2 It is important to note that prior to the Ogiek case, the African Court had adjudicated only one human rights case relating to the right to stand for elections.

3 ACHPR, art 31.

4 ACHPR, art 45.

The chapter is divided into four parts including this introduction. The second part of the chapter focuses on the protective mandate of the Commission with special attention to the RTD. The third part of the chapter assesses the promotional mandate of the Commission in respect of the RTD, the fourth and final part of the chapter provides concluding remarks.

5.2.1. The protective mandate of the African Commission and the right to development

Under article 45(2) of the African Charter, the Commission is mandated to '[e]nsure the protection of human and peoples' Rights.' To deliver this mandate, the Commission relies on the communication procedure[5] and on the on-site protective missions.

5.2.1.1. The communication procedure and the right to development

The communication procedure can be defined as the mechanism which enables individuals, NGOs and the States (through inter-state communications) to bring matters pertaining to the violation of the African Charter by member states to the attention of the African Commission. In order to foster the protection of the rights provided for by the African Charter, the African Commission has developed 'a generous standing and admissibility criteria'[6] or a liberal approach which opens its doors to the stakeholders mentioned above and issues its decisions in the forms of findings and recommendations. It is on this backdrop that the African Commission has received numerous Communications on the RTD. These communications are the following: *William Courson v Zimbabwe*,[7] the *Bakweri Land Claims Committee v Cameroon*[8] (*Bakweri* case), the first ever inter-state complaint brought before the African Commission, *Democratic Republic of the Congo v Burundi, Rwanda, and Uganda*,[9] *SERAC v Nigeri*[10] (*SERAC* case) where the African Commission failed to take a strong stand on the RTD,[11] the

5 Articles 44–49 and 55–56 of the African Charter relate to communication by state and non-state actors respectively.

6 Ibid., 30.

7 Communication 136/94 *William A Courson v Zimbabwe*; for more on this communication, see E. A. Ankuma. *The African Commission on Human and Peoples Rights: Practice and Procedures* (Martinus Nijhoff 1996), 166.

8 *Bakweri Land Claims Committee v Cameroon*, Communication No 260/2002, AHRLR (2004) 43.

9 Communication 227/99, *Democratic Republic of the Congo v Burundi, Rwanda, and Uganda* Annex IV, 20th Annual Activity Report of the African Commission, 111.

10 *SERAC & Another v Nigeria*, ACHPR, 2001, Banjul, the Gambia, and www.achpr.org.

11 It is worth noting that apart from observing that the right to food (violated by the defendant) is implicit in several provisions of the ACHPR such as art 4 on right to life, art 16 on right to health article 22 on the RTD, the African Commission doesn't find a violation of the RTD per se in this case (see *SERAC & Another v Nigeria* para 64). For a critical analysis of this case, see S. D. Kamga and C. M. Fombad. 'A Critical Review of the Jurisprudence of the African Commission on the Right to Development' (2013) 57(2) *Journal of African Law* 196–214.

Kevin Mgwanga Gumne et al v Cameroon[12] *Centre for Minority Rights Development (CEMIRIDE) (on behalf of the Endorois) v Kenya*[13] (*Endorois* case).

William Courson v Zimbabwe

The first ever Communication in which the RTD was explicitly mentioned was in *William Courson v Zimbabwe*.[14] The applicant approached the African Commission on the legal status of homosexuals in Zimbabwe. This was triggered by the criminalisation of homosexuality in Zimbabwe. According to the complainant, outlawing homosexuality was a violation of gay people's right to economic, social and cultural development with due regard to their identity as a people and their equal enjoyment of the common heritage of mankind as provided by article 22 of the African Charter. Unfortunately, the human rights community did not benefit from this case for the communication was withdrawn before any decision of the Commission.

However, it would have been interesting to see and examine the extent to which the violation of the right to equality[15] affects the RTD. Not only may this case have helped in addressing homophobia which is rampant on the continent, it may have also assisted in linking the right not to be discriminated against to the achievement of the RTD. Nevertheless, although the Commission did not finalise the *Courson* communication, the value of this case cannot be undermined as it was the first time that the RTD was raised and recorded in front of the Commission, and it was an indication that article 22 of the Charter was to be taken seriously.[16] It set a precedent on bringing a communication on the RTD to the African Commission.

The Bakweri Land Claims Committee v Cameroon

In the *Bakweri* case,[17] the *Bakweri* people located in the South West province of Cameroon sent a communication to the commission claiming that they have been dispossessed from their land by non-native people. They based their communication on the violation of their right to have their cause heard,[18] their rights to property,[19] wealth and natural resources[20] as well as the violation of their RTD.[21] Regrettably this case did not pass the admissibility stage because the applicants failed to exhaust local remedies before taking the matter to the Commission.[22] As a result of this inadmissibility, the human rights fraternity did not benefit from the

12 Communication 266/2003: 26th Annual Activity Report of the African Commission, annex IV.
13 Communication 276/2003: 27th Annual Activity Report of the African Commission, annex 5.
14 Communication 136/94 (n 7).
15 The African Charter, art 2 and 3.
16 Ankuma (n 7).
17 *Bakweri Land Claims Committee v Cameroon,* (n 8).
18 Art 7(1)(a) of the ACHPR.
19 Art 14 of the ACHPR.
20 Art 21 of the ACHPR.
21 Art 22 of the ACHPR.
22 Art 50 of the ACHPR reads: 'The Commission can only deal with a matter submitted to it after making sure that all local remedies, if they exist, have been exhausted, unless it is obvious to the commission that the procedure of achieving these remedies would be unduly prolonged'.

communication and its implication for the RTD, besides observing that the African Commission can attend to a communication on the RTD if all the conditions to approach it are met.[23]

Democratic Republic of the Congo v Burundi, Rwanda and Uganda

The *Democratic Republic of Congo (DRC)*[24] case is the first inter-state communication filed before the African Commission. As a matter of fact, on 9 March 1999, the DRC sent a communication to the Commission claiming that Burundi, Rwanda and Uganda have invaded its borders in the East of the country. In the process they committed massive massacres that constituted violations of human rights law. These violations included the mass killing of civilians, the invasion of a hydroelectric dam that led to disruption of electricity supply to houses, schools and hospitals which caused the death of patients relying on life support.

Moreover, the DRC alleged that the respondent States committed rape, mass looting of civilian property and national resources, forced people into 'concentration camps' in Rwanda to set up Tutsi land. Furthermore, DRC also underlined that besides violating the rights in the African Charter, the respondents also violated international law with special focus on the Geneva Convention relative to the Protection of Civilian Persons in Time of War 1949 and its additional protocol 1, the UN Charter and the UN Declaration on Friendly Relations between Nations.

In reaction, while Burundi stayed away from the proceedings, Rwanda participated but not beyond the admissibility stage and Uganda simply denied the allegation against it. However, the African Commission found for the DRC. In reaching its decision, the Commission noted that as provided by article 23 of the Charter, all people are entitled to national and international peace and security. In addition, empowered by 60 and 61 which enable the Commission to draw inspiration from international and regional laws in reaching its decision, the respondents were found guilty of violating international law as well as the African Charter.

23 According to article 56, communications relating to human and peoples' rights referred to in Article 55 received by the Commission, shall be considered if they:

1 Indicate their authors even if the latter requests anonymity,
2 Are compatible with the Charter of the Organisation of African Unity (AU Constitutive Act currently) or with the present Charter,
3 Are not written in disparaging or insulting language directed against the State concerned and its institutions or to the Organisation of African Unity,
4 Are not based exclusively on news disseminated through the mass media,
5 Are sent after exhausting local remedies, if any, unless it is obvious that this procedure is unduly prolonged,
6 Are submitted within a reasonable period from the time local remedies are exhausted or from the date the Commission is seized with the matter, and
7 Do not deal with cases which have been settled by those States involved in accordance with the principles of the 8.Charter of the United Nations, or the Charter of the Or- ganisation of African Unity or the provisions of the present Charter.

24 Communication 227/99, (n 9).

With special attention to the RTD, the African Commission was of the view that the respondents violated the right for two reasons: firstly, killing the people of the Eastern province in DRC and placing them in mass graves was disgusting and violated their RTD. The commission explained as follows:[25]

> The Commission further finds these acts barbaric and in reckless violation of Congolese peoples' rights to cultural development guaranteed by Article 22 of the African Charter, and an affront on the noble virtues of the African tradition and values enunciated in the preamble to the African Charter.

While indeed there is a clear violation of the right to life, the Commission equated such violation to encroachment on the RTD, without exactly making the link between the right to life and the right to cultural development.

In addition, the Commission pointed out that the right to wealth and national resources and the RTD are closely linked, and that violating the former as the respondent States did will hinder the DRC's ability to achieve the latter. The Commission clarifies in these terms:[26]

> [the] deprivation of the right of the people of the Democratic Republic of Congo, in this case, to freely dispose of their wealth and natural resources, has also occasioned another violation – their right to their economic, social and cultural development and of the general duty of States to individually or collectively ensure the exercise of the right to development, guaranteed under Article 22 of the African Charter.

In other words, in the *DRC* case the African Commission clearly established that the realisation of the RTD is intrinsically linked to the achievement of the right to wealth and natural resources. This approach which takes into account the interconnectedness of human rights should be welcomed because as demonstrated earlier, the RTD is a multifaceted human right and should be addressed as such.

SERAC v Nigeria

In the *SERAC*[27] case, although the core issues revolve around the protection of socio-economic rights, the case is important as it shows the interconnectedness of rights composites of the RTD and illustrates how the African Commission failed to interpret the law and to define the scope and advance the RTD.

The facts of the communication are as follows: In mining oil in the Niger Delta in Nigeria, Shell Company was alleged to have violated numerous human rights provided for by the African Charter. These violations include encroachment on

25 Ibid., para 87.
26 Ibid., para 95.
27 *SERAC & Another v Nigeria* (n 10).

the right not to be discriminated against,[28] the right to life,[29] to property,[30] health,[31] a family,[32] wealth and natural resources[33] and to satisfactory environment.[34] These were allegations brought to the attention of the African Commission by two NGOs who did not mention the violation of RTD.

The NGOs also highlighted the lack of participation of Ogoni people (indigenous community on the ground) in the conclusion of the contracts (depriving them of their land and natural resources) between the Nigerian government and Shell Company. Not only these people were overlooked in the sharing of profit related to the exploitation of their land, they were also forcibly removed from their ancestral land without compensation, and this resulted in the violation of their right to wealth and natural resources.

In highlighting the effect of mining on the environment, it was also claimed that the oil production caused environmental degradation and poor health as a consequence of the contamination of the environment in the Ogoni community. The exploitation disposed toxic wastes into the environment and local waterways in violation of applicable international environmental standards. The subsequent pollution of water, soil and air had serious health impacts, including skin infections, gastrointestinal and respiratory diseases, and increased risk of cancers, neurological and reproductive problems.

All human rights, elements of the RTD, were at stake. However, the African Commission did not mention the RTD in its final decision. Although it was of the view that the RTD was indeed violated, it referred to the violation of the RTD while emphasising the violation of 'the right to food implicit' in several violated provisions.[35] The Commission affirmed that:

> The Communication argues that the right to food is implicit in the African Charter, in such provisions as the right to life (article 4), the right to health, and the right to economic, social and cultural development (article 22). By its violation of these rights, the Nigerian government trampled upon not only the explicitly protected rights, but also upon the right to food implicitly guaranteed.[36]

As correctly observed by Kamga and Fombad, 'the African Commission missed the opportunity to provide a dynamic reading of the law to clarify the scope and protect the RTD'.[37] The Commission could have simply relied on the interrelatedness of human rights violated to pronounce on the RTD. Moreover, recognising

28 African Charter, art 2.
29 Ibid., art 4.
30 Ibid., art 14.
31 Ibid., art 16.
32 Ibid., art 18.
33 Ibid., art 21.
34 Ibid., art 24.
35 Para 64 of the decision.
36 Ibid.
37 Kamga and Fombad (n 11) 213.

that article 21 of the African Charter aimed to ensure 'cooperative economic development'[38] as it did was enough for the Commission to validate the 'participatory development imperative'[39] and subsequently pronounce on the violation of the RTD.

The other disturbing part of this decision is that the African Commission found that the violation of the right to health and family put together was equivalent to the violation of the right to shelter, not provided for in the Charter.[40] While this approach appropriately considers the 'interconnectedness and seamlessness of the rights contained in the African Charter',[41] it is surprising that the same logic was not followed to find the violation of the RTD by the Commission that apparently did not analyse the communication beyond the applicants' claims.

The additional problem with the decision of the Commission was its silence on the question of 'peoples' in article 21 of the African Charter. The silence of the Commission on the concept of people was equated to playing 'the ostrich game' by Olowu[42] who is of the view that the Commission was unable to establish whether the 'Ogoni communities' could qualify as a specific group to be identified as 'peoples'[43] likely to be rights holders of the RTD. Nevertheless, as will be discussed later, various omissions which led to overlooking the RTD were corrected in the *Endorois* case.[44]

The other lesson from this case is its illustration of the weakness of international law to hold business/investors accountable for human rights. Although Shell was the perpetrator of violations of human rights through its activities, Nigeria (unlike Shell) is party to the African Charter and was held accountable for failing to regulate its space as to ensure that the TNC does not violate peoples' rights. This gap in international law is unfortunate because investors are extremely powerful and do not hesitate to use their influence to 'force changes in domestic law, constitutions and pressure policy making'[45] to enrich themselves. In this context, the prospect for the realisation of the RTD is thin.

Kevin Mgwanga Gumne et al v Cameroon

In the *Gumne*[46] case, the complainants are 14 individuals who brought the communication to the Commission on their behalf and on behalf of the people of Southern Cameroon against the Republic of Cameroon. The complainants alleged

38 *SERAC & Another v Nigeria* (n 10) para 56.

39 O. C. Okafor. '"Righting" the Right to Development: A Socio-Legal Analysis of Article 22 of the African Charter of Human and Peoples Rights' In S. Marks (ed.) *Implementing the Right to Development – The Role of International Law* (Friedricht Ebert Stiftung 2008), 55.

40 *SERAC & Another v Nigeria* (n 10) para 60.

41 Okafor (n 39) 55.

42 D. Olowu. *An Integrative Rights-Based Approach to Human Development in Africa* (PULP 2009), 155.

43 Ibid.

44 Communication 276/2003 (n 13).

45 D. Aguirre. *The Human Right to Development in a Globalized World* (Ashgate 2008),124.

46 Communication 266/2003 (n 12).

the widespread marginalisation and systemic exclusion of Anglophones which results in the violation of most of their individual rights as well as collective or peoples' rights including their RTD provided for by the African Charter.[47] Importantly, the complainants also noted the violation of their collective rights to self-determination as a people to which they linked their RTD.

In this communication, the Commission was called upon to perform a very difficult dance in recognising a people and at the same time in violation of the objectives of the AU allow a specific group/people to secede from a sovereign country. Unlike in the *SERAC* case where the Commission was silent on the concept of people, in *Gumne* the Commission recognised that Southern Cameroon was a people. It was of the view that the people of Southern Cameroon were recognised as such for 'they manifest numerous characteristics and affinities, which include a common history, linguistic tradition, territorial connection and political outlook. More importantly they identify themselves as a people with a separate and distinct identity, [bearing in mind that] [i]dentity is an innate characteristic within a people'.[48] To use Ngang's words, they 'self-proclaim a collective identity that is distinct from the rest of society'.[49]

However, in light of the need to preserve territorial sovereignty as intended by the AU constitutive Act, and as held in the Katangese case, the African Commission refused 'to condone secession, as a form of self-determination for the Southern Cameroons, [as] that will jeopardise the territorial integrity of the Republic of Cameroon'.[50] To make itself clear the African Commission held as follows:[51]

> [S]ecession is not the sole avenue open to Southern Cameroonians to exercise the right to self-determination. The African Charter cannot be invoked by a complainant to threaten the sovereignty and territorial integrity of a State party.

This is an interpretation of self-determination from a post-colonial perspective which distances itself from territorial possession within a state, but more about accessing 'statehood' by an entire country.[52] As will be demonstrated in the *Endorois* case where the Commission thoroughly engaged with the concept of people,

47 The Complainants allege that: 1) Articles 2, 3, 4, 5, 6, 7.1, 9, 10, 11, 12, 13, 17.1, 19, 20, 21, 22, 23.1, 24 of the African Charter have been violated. 2) the Republic of Cameroon has violated its general duty under in Article 26 of the African Charter to guarantee the independence of the judiciary; see para 19 of the Communication.

48 *Gumne* (n 12) para 179. Communication 266/2003: 26th Annual Activity Report of the African Commission, annex IV, para 179.

49 C. Ngang. 'Indigenous Peoples' Right to Sustainable Development and the Green Economy Agenda' (2015) 44(4) *Africa Insight* 32.

50 Ibid.

51 *Gumne* (n 12) para 190.

52 J. Gilbert. *Indigenous Peoples' Land Rights under International Law From Victims to Actors* (Brill 2016), 219. Also J. Gilbert. 'The Right to Freely Dispose of Natural Resources: Utopia or Forgotten Right?' (2013) 31(2) *Netherlands Quarterly of Human Rights* 318–320.

the need to preserve the territorial integrity of African countries is paramount at the African Commission which generally remains very reluctant in deciding for secession.

As far as the violation of human rights was concerned, the Commission agreed with the complainant that most human rights violated were civil and political rights also known as first generation human rights.[53] Consequently, unlike in the *SERAC* case where the interconnectedness of all rights at issues was clearly established, in the *Gumne* case no socio-economic right was found to have been violated and only one collective right, the right to equality of all peoples[54] was violated. As a result the Commission did not have to rely on the interpretation of various rights at issues, and perhaps more importantly because the applicants had actually addressed the RTD independently.

As far as reference to the RTD is concerned, highlighting the extent to which their RTD was encroached upon, the complainants underlined their 'economic marginalization, and lack of economic infrastructure'[55] as constitutive elements of the violation of the RTD. However, data and statistics on allocation of development resources in various socio-economic sectors in Cameroon in front the Commission showed that Southern Cameroon was not particularly underfunded and underdeveloped, and this persuaded the Commission that the RTD was not violated.

It is understandable that the right to participation of Anglophones in the governance of the country was not an issue as many of them are members of the National Assembly and Ministers. This state of affairs reduced the RTD to access to resources and economic infrastructure, but also their equitable sharing. This approach also reiterates the composite feature of the RTD. However, the disquieting part is the Commission's agreement with Cameroon's that the RTD can be achieved progressively considering the availability of resources.[56] This is a misreading of the African Charter which does not submit human rights to progressive realisation as even economic social and cultural rights should be achieved immediately.

Nevertheless, empowered by articles 60 and 61 of the Charter, the Commission can rely on international law to interpret the Charter.[57] In this case, the Commission relied on the General Comment in making its decision. Although this can be problematic in terms of standard setting as not all African countries including Botswana and Comores are parties to the ICESCR,[58] it could be argued that infusing the concept of progressive realisation of economic socio-economic and cultural rights

53 Art 1, 2 4, 5, 6 and 7(1) were found to have been violated.

54 Article 19 of the Charter.

55 *Gumne* (n 12) para 206.

56 Ibid.

57 African Commission on Human and Peoples' Rights, 'Principles and guidelines on the implementation of economic, social and cultural rights in the African Charter on Human and Peoples' Rights'. www.achpr.org/files/instruments/economic-social-cultural/achpr_instr_guide_draft_esc_rights_eng.pdf

58 Kamga and Fombad (n 11).

into the African Commission's Principles and Guidelines on the Implementation of Economic, Social and Cultural Rights in the African Charter as it is currently the case,[59] clearly turns the concept into an African rule to be complied with by all state parties to the Charter including those that are not parties to the ICESCR. It could therefore be argued that the African Commission was pragmatic in agreeing that the RTD could be realised progressively considering the availability of resources, for it does not help to issue decisions that are almost impossible for States to implement or else such decisions can only do a disservice to the authority of the Commission.

Centre for Minority Rights Development (CEMIRIDE) (on behalf of the Endorois) v Kenya

The 46th Ordinary Session of the African Commission[60] will forever be remembered in Africa for it afforded the opportunity to the Commission to deliver a historic decision in the *Endorois* case.[61] The uniqueness of this communication cannot be overemphasised. Indeed for the first time, the African Commission was able to address the RTD in a substantive manner and affirm its justiciability.

On 22 May 2003, the Centre for Minority Rights Development (CEMIRIDE) with the assistance of Minority Rights Group International (MRGI) and the Centre for Housing Rights and Evictions approached the African Commission with a Communication on behalf of the *Endorois* community. Amongst other things, the complainants claimed the eviction of the *Endorois* (a pastoralist group) from their ancestral land at Lake Bogoria in central Kenya in the 1970s to set up a national game reserve and tourist facilities. The communication addressed numerous human rights violations of the *Endorois* community.

The complainants claimed that the eviction was a violation of the *Endorois* peoples' human rights due to the displacement from their ancestral lands (upon which their sustainable way of life was based) without adequate compensation. In addition, they alleged that their removal from their land led to the disruption of their pastoral activities and violated their rights to practice their religions and culture as well as their 'overall process of development'.[62] Furthermore, the complainants claimed that the *Endorois* people were dispossessed from their land, their property without expressing their views and that all decisions affecting their land were taken without their effective participation; they protested that this was a violation of their RTD.

59 African Commission on Human and Peoples' Rights, 'Principles and guidelines on the implementation of economic, social and cultural rights in the African Charter on Human and Peoples' Rights'. www.achpr.org/files/instruments/economic-social-cultural/achpr_instr_guide_draft_esc_rights_eng.pdfpara, 13, 14 and 15 for examples. www.achpr.org/files/instruments/economic-social-cultural/achpr_instr_guide_draft_esc_rights_eng.pdf (Accessed 2 September 2017).

60 Held in Banjul, *The Gambia* from 11–25 November 2009.

61 Communication no 276 / 2003 (n 13).

62 Ibid., para 1.

After exhausting local remedies, the complainants took the matter to the African Commission and they alleged that the *Endorois*' freedom of conscience and religion,[63] right to property,[64] right to culture,[65] to free disposition of natural resources[66] and RTD[67] of the African Charter have been violated by the Republic of Kenya.[68] Although many other provisions of the African Charter were alleged to have been violated, the focus of the discussion will be on the RTD which is at centre of this book.

The applicants based their claim for the RTD on two fundamental arguments:

1 The violation of their right to participation in decisions affecting their land and development and
2 The violation of their right to self-determination and natural resources attached to their right to be a distinct 'people'.

These two elements deserve special attention as they were significant in determining the content of the RTD.

THE RIGHT TO PARTICIPATION OF INDIGENOUS COMMUNITIES

The right to participation or the right not to be excluded is secured in several human rights instruments. The ICCPR provides for the right to participation as follows:[69]

> In those States in which ethnic, religious or linguistic minorities exist, persons belonging to such minorities shall not be denied the right, in community with the other members of their group, to enjoy their own culture, to profess and practise their own religion, or to use their own language.

It could be argued that this provision guarantees the right to participation of indigenous people under the concept of ethnic or linguistic minorities. The right to participation is also located in the 1986 UNDRTD, which sees the human being at the centre of development and should therefore be the 'participant and beneficiary',[70] or rather the beginning and the end of any development initiative. Furthermore, not only should individuals and groups participate in development,[71] their participation should 'be active, free and meaningful' and they should also benefit from the result of development.[72] In other words, the involvement of indigenous people

63 African Charter, art 8.
64 Ibid., art 14.
65 Ibid., art 17.
66 Ibid., art 21.
67 Ibid art 22.
68 Communication 276/2003 (n 13) para 2.
69 ICCPR, art 27.
70 UNDRTD, art 2(1).
71 Ibid., art 2(2).
72 Ibid., art 2(3).

should entail a 'process undertaken free of coercion or manipulation, involving self-selected decision-making processes undertaken with sufficient time for effective choices to be understood and made, with all relevant information provided and in an atmosphere of good faith and trust'.[73]

Besides the ICCPR and UNDRTD, the Rio Declaration,[74] the 1990 African Charter for Popular Participation in Development and Transformation,[75] the ACHPR[76] and the Declaration on the Rights of Indigenous People[77] also provide for the right to participation. From the reading of these instruments, participation could be defined as:[78]

> A process by which the government and civil society open dialogue, establish partnerships, share information and otherwise interact to design, implement and evaluate development policies, project and programs . . . that requires the involvement and commitment of all interested parties, including, among others, the poor and traditionally marginalized groups, especially racial and ethnic minorities.

According to this definition, all stakeholders of development including 'traditionally marginalised groups especially racial and ethnic minorities' shall be involved in the development process. This is in line with article 23 of the 2007 UN Declaration on the Rights of Indigenous Peoples which provides:

> Indigenous Peoples have the right to determine and develop priorities and strategies for exercising their right to development. In particular, indigenous peoples have the right to be actively involved in determining health, housing and other economic and social programmes affecting them and, as far as possible, to administer such programme through their own institutions.

As observed earlier, the African Commission's pronouncement on the right to participation was heard when in the *SERAC* case the commission noted that the

73 H. Tugendhat, V Couillard, J Gilbert and C Doyle 'Business and Human Rights- The Right to Free, Prior and Informed Consent'. paper submitted to the UK Joint Committee on Human Rights Committee Office, House of Commons (2009). www.researchgate.net/publication/228184480_Business_Human_Rights_and_Indigenous_Peoples_The_Right_to_Free_Prior_and_Informed_Consent (Accessed 2 April 2017).

74 Adopted at the Rio Conference on Environment and Development in Rio de Janeiro, Brazil, 3–4 June 1992, para 21 and 22 clearly underline the right to participation of indigenous people in development.

75 Adopted at the International Conference on Popular Participation in Development and Transformation in Arusha, Tanzania UN doc. E/ECA/CM.16/11,1990. Addis Ababa, UN Economic Commission for Africa.

76 Art 13.

77 UN Res GA/10612 of 13 September 2007, art 11 and 12 for example.

78 This definition is the fruit of the 1996 Santa Cruz Summit on Sustainable Development. It was subsequently adopted by the Inter-American Council for Development in 2000; also K. Mynnti. 'The Right of Indigenous Peoples to Participate in Development Projects' In M. Scheinen and M. Suksi (eds.) *Human Rights in Development Year Book 2002- Empowerment, Participation, Accountability and Non-discrimination: Operationalising a Human Rights Based Approach to Development* (Martinus Nijhoff 2005), 235.

Ogoni people were marginalised by the government while dealing with the Dutch oil company, Shell.

In the *Endorois* case under discussion, on the one hand, the *Endorois* people complain that their right to participation was violated as they were not involved in decisions concerning the development and the expropriation of their land.[79] They sustained that their consent was not requested in arguing that an adequate assent to a proposal unequivocally 'requires at minimum that all of the members of the community are fully and accurately informed of the nature and consequences of the process with an effective opportunity to participate individually or collective'.[80]

On the other hand, the Kenyan government dismissed these allegations on the ground that the right to participation of all Kenyans is guaranteed through a democratic process informed by free and fair elections involving representatives.[81] It is clear that the African Commission was requested to clarify the link between the right to participation and the RTD and whether this right is significant for the realisation the RTD.

The African Commission found that the consultations undertaken with the community were inadequate and cannot be considered effective participation. The conditions of the consultation failed to fulfil the African Commission's benchmark of consultations in a form appropriate to the circumstance. The African Commission observed that 'community members were informed of the impending project as a *fait accompli* and not given an opportunity to shape the policies or their role in the Game Reserve',[82] hence its decision to urge the state to warrant the right to effective participation of the *Endorois* community in development issues.

In calling upon the state to ensure an 'active, free and meaningful participation in development',[83] by the beneficiaries of development, it could be argued that the African Commission underscored the point that even if the beneficiaries ignore their right to participate, they should be educated and informed timeously to ensure their inclusion in development projects. This was a call to move from 'development aggression' to 'self-determined development'[84] which is central for the RTD of indigenous community.

The African Commission should be commended for its approach which is conductive to the realisation of human rights and the RTD in particular, because as noted through the Maastricht guidelines,[85] the state has the obligation to promote, protect and fulfil human rights. In this respect, it should take all necessary

79 Communication 276/2003 (n 13) para 125.

80 Ibid., para 133; also *Mary and Carrie Dann v USA* (2002), para 136.

81 Communication 276/2003 (n 13) para 270.

82 Para 281.

83 UNDRTD, art 2(3).

84 C. Doyle and J. Gilbert. 'Indigenous Peoples and Globalization: From "Development Aggression" to "Self-Determined Development"' (2008/9) 7 *European Yearbook of Minority Issues* 223.Also Gilbert (n 52) 249.

85 The Maastricht principles describe the duty of the state in terms of human rights realisation. Accordingly, the state has the duty to promote, respect and fulfilled human rights. See section 3.4.1.1 of this book.

measures to involve the beneficiaries of rights in the process of development. Consequently, the African Commission correctly observed:

> The State has a duty to *actively consult with the said community according to their customs and traditions*. This duty requires the State to both accept and disseminate information, and entails constant communication between the parties.[86]

State's compliance with this recommendation will certainly be a good step towards ensuring the RTD.

THE RIGHT TO SELF-DETERMINATION OF INDIGENOUS PEOPLE

As indicated in Chapter 2 of this book, the right to self-determination is provided in major human rights instruments.[87] These instruments provide for national self-determination in the realisation of development with an authoritative language. In general, they give instructions to states by using 'shall' in various instances; the state 'shall' take steps to.[88] For most of these instruments, self-determination is a group right or 'peoples' right'. This suggests that in the international arena, self-determination refers to sovereign entities like states and not 'indigenous peoples' approaches to territorial rights' within the state.[89]

However, back in 1999, in its Concluding Observation on Canada, the Human Rights Committee recognised that numerous 'peoples' may exist within a state.[90] It stated that

> The right to self-determination requires, *inter alia* that all people must be able to freely dispose of their natural wealth and resources and that they may not be deprived of their own means of subsistence. The Committee recommends that decisive and urgent action be taken towards the full implementation of the recommendations on land and resource allocation. [Recommendations made by the Royal Commission on aboriginal Peoples in view to protect indigenous peoples' rights in Canada].[91]

Similarly, the Committee on Human Rights used common article 1 on self-determination to protect indigenous peoples' rights within the confine of countries like Mexico,[92] Norway[93] and Australia,[94] amongst others.

86 Communication 276/2003 (n 13) para 289; my emphasis.

87 ICESCR and the ICCPR in their common article 1(1); the African Charter, art 20; the Vienna Declaration, part 1 para 1, art 4; the NIEO Declaration, 26(k) and 14(e) of Copenhagen Declaration; The UNESCO Convention Protection and Promotion of the Diversity of Cultural Expressions, art 2; and UN Declaration on the Rights of Indigenous Peoples, art 5.

88 Art 5 UNDRTD for example, also CERDS, art 1(3) The States Parties to the present Covenant, . . ., shall promote the realization of the right of self-determination, and shall respect that right, in conformity with the provisions of the Charter of the United Nations.

89 Gilbert (n 52) 219.

90 Concluding Observations on Canada, UN Doc. CCPR/C/79/Add.105 (1999), para 8.

91 Ibid.

92 Concluding Observations on Mexico, UN Doc. CCPR/C/79/Add.109 (1999).

93 Concluding Observations on Norway, UN Doc. CCPR/C/79/Add.112 (1999).

94 Concluding Observations on Australia, UN Doc. CCPR/CO/69/AUS (2000).

However, emphasising the need to use an interconnectedness approach to human rights interpretation, Scheinin observes that the interdependence-based interpretation of the ICCPR's provisions reveals that article 1 and article 27[95] are linked. Following this approach, article 27 on minority rights reveals that self-determination is also an individual human right.[96] In *Makuika et al v New Zealand*,[97] which dealt with national fisheries settlement in New Zealand and the share of the indigenous peoples known as Maori, the Human Rights Committee realised that minorities rights included in article 27 incorporate various elements of self-determination as provided for by article 1 of the Covenant.

Beside the Human Rights Committee's Concluding Observations which view peoples' rights to self-determination within the boundaries of a state as a reality, the only international instrument which provides clearly for self-determination of 'people' in a midst of a state is the 2007 UN Declaration on the Rights of Indigenous Peoples. It reads in articles 3 and 6 respectively:

> Indigenous peoples have the right to self-determination. By virtue of that right they freely determine their political status and freely pursue *their economic social and cultural development.*
>
> Every indigenous individual has the right to a nationality.

These provisions not only shed more light on the legal source of the RTD, they also showcase that the right to self-determination can be enjoyed by groups within the confines of a state. Again, the composite aspect of the RTD appears. More importantly, the right to self-determination of an indigenous individual does not deprive him or her of his or her nationality. His or her right to self-determination is actually to be exercised within his or her country of origin.

The right to self-determination of people under colonial rule is at the centre of the Copenhagen Declaration.[98] In the same vein, article 20 of the ACHPR reads:

1 All people shall have the right to existence. They shall have the unquestionable and inalienable right to self-determination. They shall freely determine their political status and shall pursue their economic and social development according to the policy they have freely chosen.
2 Colonised or oppressed peoples shall have the right to free themselves from the bond of domination by resorting to any means recognized by the international community.

95 Art 27 of the ICCPR reads: 'In those States in which ethnic, religious or linguistic minorities exist, person belonging to such minorities shall not be denied the right, in community with the other members of their groups, to enjoy their own culture, to profess and practice their own religion, or to use their own language'.

96 M. Scheinin. 'Advocating the Right to Development Through Complaint Procedures Under Human Rights Treaties' In B. Andreassen and S. Marks (Harvard School of Public Health, Francois Xavier Bagnoud Center For Health and Human Rights 2006), 276.

97 Communication No 547/1993 *Makuika et al v New Zealand* (27 October 2000). See 2000 Report of the Human Rights Committee, vol. II, UN Doc. A/56/40 (vol. II), 11–29.

98 Art 26(k) reads: 'Reaffirm the right of self-determination of all peoples, in particular of peoples under colonial or other forms of alien domination or foreign occupation, and the importance of the effective realization of this right, as enunciated, *inter alia*, in the Vienna Declaration'.

3 All peoples shall have the right to the assistance of the States parties to the present Charter in their liberation struggle against foreign domination, be it political, economic or cultural.

According to this provision, all people shall enjoy the right to self-determination. People here might include sovereign states or groups within a state. In any case, the article is self-explanatory; colonised peoples are also entitled to self-determination. This underscores the colonial domination of Africa and the need for freedom from colonial power. From a decolonisation perspective, self-determination is the national sense of self-esteem without which all societies cannot develop.[99] It is based on the assertion that all people have an equal right to liberty, to free themselves from any foreign intrusion, to choose their own regime and fight for their freedom, and to benefit from other people's help in their fight if it is necessary.[100]

More importantly, article 20(2) underlines the right to self-determination of 'oppressed people'. This provision also empowers peoples or groups inside a sovereign state to claim their rights to secede if they are oppressed. This is very much in line with the UN Declaration on the Right of Indigenous Peoples. In this perspective, the African Commission protected the right to self-determination and to natural resources of the Ogoni people through *SERAC v Nigeria*[101] discussed earlier.

Unfortunately, the practice of the right to self-determination does not always comply with the law. Nmehielle argues that, 'African States have individually and under the auspices of the OAU [now AU], taken the position that self-determination does not apply outside the colonial context, because such post-colonial application of the concept will undermine African unity'.[102] This approach was applied to the *Gumne* case discussed earlier. Prior to that, it was also observed during the Biafra struggle when the late Julius Nyerere, former President of Tanzania opposed Biafra's attempt to secede from Nigeria on the ground that it was an attempt to destroy African unity.[103] Similarly, Emperor Selassie of Ethiopia acting as Head of the Consultative Committee on the Nigeria-Biafra crisis was of the opinion that national unity of individual African states was a key factor in uniting the continent and therefore the territorial integrity of OAU member states was not negotiable.[104] The refusal to apply the provision on self-determination to groups

99 F. Viljoen. 'Introduction to the African Commission and the Regional Human Rights System' In C. Heyns (ed.) *Human Rights in Africa* (Mantinus Nijhoff 2004), 387; C. Heyns. 'The African Regional Human Rights System: The African Charter' (2004) 108 *Pennsylvenia State Law Review* 691–692.

100 Ibid.

101 *SERAC* (n 10).

102 V. O. Nmehielle. *The African Human Rights System, Its Law, Practice, and Institutions* (Martinus Nijhoff 2001), 143.

103 Ibid.

104 Ibid.

within Africa was also applied by the ICJ in the case between *Burkina Faso and Mali.*[105] The ICJ declared as follows:

> The maintenance of territorial status quo in Africa is often seen as the wisest course, to preserve what has been achieved by the peoples who have struggled for their independence, and to avoid a disruption which would deprive the continent of the gains achieved by much sacrifice.

In the same vein, in the *Katangese* case[106] where the Katangese People Congress requested that the African Commission recognise the peoples' right of the 'Katangese people' to independence, thus allowing them to split from the state of DRC, then Zaire, the African Commission refused to recognise them as a 'people' and held that it had an obligation to uphold the territorial integrity and sovereignty of all member states of the OAU and those state parties to the African Charter.[107] The African Commission also held that:

> In the absence of concrete evidence of violations of human rights to the point that the territorial integrity of Zaire should be called to question and in the absence of evidence that the people of Katanga are denied the right to participate in Government as guaranteed by article 13(1) of the African Charter, the African Commission holds the view that Katanga is obliged to exercise a variant of self-determination that is compatible with the sovereignty and territorial integrity of Zaire.[108]

Through the same communication, the African Commission clarifies that self-determination may be exercised through

> [i]ndependence, self-government, local government, federalism, confederalism, unitarism or any other form of relations that accords with the wishes of the people but fully cognisant of other recognised principles such as sovereignty and territorial integrity.[109]

Surprisingly, applicants for self-determination did not claim their RTD which is connected to self-determination. They could have based their claim on article 22 of the ACHPR as well, but they did not.

Another instance where the African Commission was called upon to clarify the right to self-determination was the *Gambian Coup* case.[110] In this case, a *coup d'etat* was planned by a military force, which later came into power by force. The

105 *Burkina Faso v Republic Mali,* ICJ (22 December 1986) ICJ Reports 554, 566–567.
106 *Katangese Peoples' Congress v Zaire* (2000) AHRLR *72* (ACHPR 1995).
107 The *Katangese* case, para 5.
108 The *Katangese* case, para 6.
109 Ibid., para 4.
110 *Jawara v The Gambia* (2000) AHRLR 107 (ACHPR 2000).

African Commission held that the military *coup d'état* was a grave violation of the right of the Gambian people to freely choose their government as entrenched in article 20(1) of the African Charter.[111] It was the violation of the right to vote of Gambians which amounts to the violation of their right to self-determination.

As noted above, the rationale behind the refusal of right to self-determination at the national level has to do with African unity which was fundamental for the decolonisation of the continent. However, such policy seems to be very detrimental to the protection of indigenous peoples' rights in general and their RTD in particular. In Namibia as in many parts of the world, indigenous peoples are discriminated against; they have no rights to land, access to justice, culture, education and healthcare.[112] In fact, they are oppressed and should be given a right to claim their self-determination not in theory, but in practice because their RTD is at stake. The successful protection of their RTD calls for the implementation of a right to self-determination involving external as well as internal self-determination.[113] In other words, externally, a group should be free to set up its own political institutions, to have its own economic resources and to be in charge of its culture;[114] internally, a group should not have its freedoms taken by other groups, states or by an oppressor.[115]

In the *Endorois* case, claiming their RTD, the complainants underlined that their eviction from their land negated their right to self-determination over their land and their natural resources. In other terms, their territorial and economic self-determination were violated;[116] in this instance, the complainants combined the right to self-determination (art 20 of the ACHPR) and the right to natural resources (article 21 of the ACHPR) to claim their RTD. They also argued that encroachment upon these two rights abolished their choices and capabilities in terms of 'liberty in their action',[117] and therefore hinders their RTD. They also contended that the eviction demolished their way of life, sources of income and as a result, hindered their ability to pay their taxes which led to the impounding of their cattle by the government.[118]

In response to these allegations, Kenya argued that the complainants' contention was untrue as a tax is charged in income and that if the *Endorois* had no income, they were not taxed at all.[119] In resolving this question, the African Com-

111 Ibid para 73.

112 S. A. Djoyou Kamga. 'Promotion of indigenous and tribal peoples' rights through the implementation of the principles of ILO Convention No.169 and the African Charter on Human and Peoples' Rights: Namibia desk review'. ILO Project prepared under the auspices of the Centre for Human Rights, University of Pretoria (2009) 5 (on file with author).

113 L. B. Sohn. 'The New International Law: Protection of the Rights of Individuals Rather Than States' (1982) 32 *American University Law Review* 1, 50.

114 Ibid.

115 Ibid.

116 Communication 276/2003 (n 13) para 129.

117 Ibid., para 128.

118 Ibid., para 126.

119 Ibid., para 273.

mission had to address the right to territorial and economic self-determination as an important element of the RTD.

In the present case (*Endorois*), the African Commission underlined freedom of choice as a core element of the RTD as highlighted by Sengupta, the former Independent Expert on the RTD.[120] Accordingly, people should be given the choice to develop their potentials and this cannot be done without territorial and economic self-determination. Development should be understood in terms of freedom where people are free to choose their way of life. In this context, 'freedom is the primary end and the principal means of development'.[121] Therefore, without freedom, development and the RTD become a pipe dream, hence the correctness of the African Commission's decision in ruling that the eviction of the *Endorois* people hinders their right to self-determination and reduced their freedom of action to empower themselves. It could be argued that the African Commission's decision was a good move towards the 'legal empowerment of the poor'.[122] In other words, this decision set a precedent that will inspire and allow the poor to claim their human rights.

In reaching its decision, the African Commission was not only guided by the Report produced by the UN Working Group on Indigenous Populations requiring that 'indigenous peoples are not coerced, pressured or intimidated in their choices of development',[123] but also by the decision of the court in the *Yakye Axa community* case[124] where it was argued that the

> [d]isplacement of the members of the community from [their] lands has caused special and grave difficulties to obtain food, primarily because the area where their temporary settlement is located does not have appropriate conditions for cultivation or to practice their traditional subsistence activities, such as hunting, fishing, and gathering.

In other words, the mere fact that the *Endorois* people were removed from their land and deprived of their self-determination hindered their ability to realise their RTD. It is observed that the concept of 'peoples' and self-determination are

120 A. Sengupta. 'The Right to Development as a Human Right' (Francois-Xavier Bagnoud Centre Working Paper No. 8, (2000) (on file with author).

121 A. Sen. *Development as Freedom* (Knopf 1999), 35, also H. J. Steiner, P. Alston, and R. Goodman. *International Human Rights in Context Law, Politics, Morals – Text and Materials* (Oxford University Press 2007), 1434.

122 D. Banik. 'Introduction' In D. Banik (ed.) *Rights and Legal Empowerment in Eradicating Poverty* (Ashgate 2008), 1.

123 Antoanella-Iulia Motoc and the Tebtebba Foundation, Preliminary working paper on the principle of free, prior and informed consent of indigenous peoples in relation to development affecting their lands and natural resources that they would serve as a framework for the drafting of a legal commentary by the Working Group on this concept. UN Doc. E/CN.4/Sub.2/AC.4/2004/4 (2004), para. 14(a).

124 *Indigenous Community Yakye Axa v Paraguay* 17 June 2005, Inter American Court of Human Rights.

linked. Unlike in its previous decision where the African Commission was silent on the issue, it elaborated extensively and clearly defined 'peoples'.[125] Relying on the Report of the Working Group on Indigenous Peoples,[126] the Commission highlighted the identification criteria of indigenous people to be:

a) the occupation and use of a specific territory;
b) the voluntary perpetuation of cultural distinctiveness;
c) self-identification as a distinct collectivity, as well as recognition by other groups;
   and
d) an experience of subjugation, marginalisation, dispossession, exclusion or discrimination[127]

Essentially, the central element that characterises indigenous people is that they are 'communities who live in a non-dominant situation' to use the words of Gilbert.[128] Based on this feature, the African Commission just like in the *Gumne* case went on to identify the *Endorois* as specific group in these words:

> The alleged violation of the African Charter by the respondent state are those that go to the heart of indigenous rights – the right to preserve one's identity through identification with ancestral lands, cultural patterns, social institution and religious systems. The African Commission therefore accepts that self-identification for the Endorois as indigenous individuals and acceptance as such by the group is an essential component of their sense of identity.[129]

Following the pattern set in the *Gumne* case, the African Commission explained the notion of 'peoples' and its new approach was vital in finding the violation of the RTD by Kenya. Nevertheless, unlike in *Gumne*, the *Endorois* people did not seek to secede from Kenya, and this eased the task of the Commission which is reluctant to undermine or jeopardise African Unity.

THE SIGNIFICANCE ON THE *ENDOROIS* DECISION

The significance of this decision cannot be underestimated. This case does not only define the concept of indigenous people that have been quite controversial in Africa, it also emphasises the need to protect their right and not without providing adequate compensation when they are disposed of their land.

125 Para 156–157 of the decision.

126 Report of the Working Group 'Report of the African Commission's Working Group of Experts on Indigenous Populations/Communities submitted in accordance with 'Resolution on the Rights of Indigenous Populations/Communities in Africa adopted by the African Commission on Human and Peoples' Rights at its 28th ordinary session (2005), Chapter 4.

127 *Endorois* case (n 13 para) 150.

128 J. Gilbert. 'Nomadic Territories: A Human Rights Approach to Nomadic Peoples' Land Rights' (2007) 7(4) *Human Rights Law Review* (2007) 694.

129 Para 157 of the decision.

Moreover, through this decision, unlike in the *SERAC* case, the African Commission seized the opportunity to clarify the substance of the RTD. It clearly stated the 'constitutive and instrumental'[130] features of the right. In other words, it is a process or a tool through which all human rights are realised in order to reach the end product which is the RTD. Furthermore, the *Endorois* decision is the first case which affirms the justiciability of the RTD. Human Rights Watch observes: '[I]t is the first time that any international tribunal has found a violation of the RTD'.[131]

Another benefit of the *Endorois* decision is that the African Commission unambiguously explained the holistic feature of the RTD which comprises elements of non-discrimination, participation, accountability and transparency, equity and choices.[132] The African Commission's ruling is important as it calls upon state parties to the ACHPR to respect human rights in general. In fact, this decision 'spells the beginning of a brighter future'[133] for the realisation of the RTD, even though the implementation of this decision remains to be seen.

In the final analysis, considering the amount of communications and activities for the development of the content and legality of RTD through the African Commission's communication procedure, it could be concluded that this procedure has been the key in shaping the RTD at least at the normative level in Africa.

5.2.1.2. On-site protective mandate and the right to development

Also known as 'fact finding', 'protective', 'on-site investigative' or 'high level' missions,[134] the on-site protective mission is generally triggered by a Communication against a State. In this context, based on article 46 of the Charter which empowers the Commission to use any 'appropriate method of investigation' to establish the facts in its protective mandate, the Commission undertakes the high-level mission to investigate and seeks ways to resolve the problem amicably between the parties.[135]

However, sometimes the link between the mission and the initial communication is not always established. For instance, a mission to Senegal from 1 to 7 June 1996, focused specifically on the crisis in Casamance Province. The mission was triggered by a communication received in 1992 when it was alleged that Casamance insurgent forces were clashing with the Senegalese army.[136] Neverthe-

130 Communication 276/2003 (n 13) para 277.

131 Human Rights Watch 'Kenya: Landmark Ruling on Indigenous Land Rights African Human Rights Commission Condemns Expulsion of Endorois People for Tourism Development' www.hrw.org/news/2010/02/04/kenya-landmark-ruling-indigenous-land-rights (Accessed 10 March 2017).

132 Communication 276/2003 (n 13) para 277.

133 Human Rights Watch 'Kenya: Landmark Ruling on Indigenous Land Rights African Human Rights Commission Condemns Expulsion of Endorois People for Tourism Development (n 131).

134 For more on this, see T. Mutangui. 'Fact-Finding Mission or Omission? A Critical Analysis of the African Commission on Human and Peoples' Rights'(2006) 12 *East African Journal of Peace and Human Rights* 1.

135 F. Viljoen. *International Human Rights Law in Africa* (Oxford University Press 2012), 344.

136 For more, see the Country Report, Annex VIII to the 10th Annual Activity Report.

less, at the end of the mission, the latter recommended 'constructive dialogue'. However the the mission's report did not link the site visit or the mission to the communication decided against Senegal which triggered it in the first place.[137] This approach casts a doubt on the 'protective' character of the mission which in reality could be qualified as fact findings without any link to a communication.[138]

Nonetheless, the confusion caused by the characterisation of the missions as 'fact finding', 'investigative', 'protective' or other is not the most important limit to the effectiveness of these missions which after all are useful in finding solutions to human rights violations. The challenge is rather the fact that none of these missions can take place without the consent of the State to be visited. For instance, in 1994, although the mission prepared and sent delegates for a protective mission in Zaire, now DRC, the visit did not materialise as the government did not consent to it.[139]

Notwithstanding the flagrant poverty in Africa, none of these missions focuses on the RTD, but rather on cases of massive violations of human rights.[140] While these cases are important, the Commission should also consider fact-finding missions in case of extreme poverty as this can assist to protect the RTD. Of course this can be very challenging because of the multifaceted and multidimensional features of the RTD and even more difficult if the visit must be activated by a communication on the matter. Consequently, the Commission's promotional mandate to be discussed below could be more useful in advancing the RTD during site visits.

5.2.2. Promotional mandate and the right to development

Under article 45(1) of the African Charter, the African Commission is empowered to promote 'human and peoples' rights'. In discharging this mandate, the commission relies on numerous approaches including the State reporting procedure, special mechanisms, promotional visits, resolutions, seminars and conferences.

5.2.2.1. The state reporting procedure and the right to development

Established under article 62 of the African Charter, the state reporting procedure provides an avenue to monitor the implementation of the Charter by members States. According to Viljoen and Biegon, it is a 'forum for constructive dialogue between the treaty bodies and state parties on the extent to which the latter have

137 Viljoen (n 135) 345.

138 Similar confusion was caused in the outcome to a mission to Mauritania from 19–27 June 1996; see the Commission Report, Annex IX to the 10th Annual activity Report.

139 Communications, 25/89, 47/90,100/93; *Free Legal Assistance v Zaire* (2000) AHRLR 74, (ACHPR 1995) 9th Annual Activity Report), see para 36 of the Communication.

140 S. D. Kamga. 'The Effectiveness of the African Commission on Human and Peoples Rights in Addressing Human Rights in Situation of Emergency' (2014) 39 *South African Yearbook of International Law* 114–132.

guaranteed and afforded human rights'.[141] Consequently, it is an opportunity that enables the Commission to follow up on what state parties are doing to give effect to the RTD.

To kick start the process, in 1988 the African Commission adopted the initial set of guidelines for Periodic National Reports[142] revised later[143] to reduce their length and ensure their comprehensiveness.

Essentially, upon joining the African Charter, member states have two years to present their initial report on the human rights situation, background and legal system in their territory. Subsequently, every two years, they should submit reports on legislative and other measures taken to give effect to the rights provided for in the Charter.

Even though the efficiency of the State reporting process is often limited by challenges including budgetary constraints[144] and delayed reports or no submission of reports, it could be argued that the state reporting process has enabled States to present what they have done to implement the Charter, but especially the RTD. This was observed in the previous chapter with specific attention to some countries that explicitly provide for the RTD in their constitution and for South Africa which has a progressive constitution. On a positive note, Concluding Observations provide guidance on what is missing and what needs to be done to improve the implementation of the Charter. Although sometimes the Commission misses the point or some opportunities to advance a specific right as seen previously with the RTD, in general its intervention through Concluding Observations and Recommendations is welcomed as it has the potential to guide the policy makers and implementers at the country level. In enhancing the potential of Concluding Observations and Recommendations, the Commission should highlight the difference between the State's obligations and the progress achieved without overlooking the challenges faced by the State and probably how to overcome such challenges.[145] This approach could be key in monitoring the implementation of the RTD. However, the Commission should also follow up on the implementation of its recommendations and do so consistently.[146]

141 Viljoen and Biegon (n 1) 28.

142 The African Commission fourth Ordinary Session held in Cairo, Egypt; See Promotion, Protection and Restoration of Human Rights, Guidelines for National Periodic Reports, ACHPR Doc. AFR/COM/HPR. 5(IV) (October 1988).

143 At the African Commission 23rd Ordinary Session.

144 The 32nd Session of the African Commission, held in October 2002 in Banjul, The Gambia, was shortened to a mere seven days due to budgetary constraints that could not be met by the host country. As a result, the examination of the State report of the Democratic Republic of Congo was delayed until the following session. At the following session, held in Niamey, Niger, the consideration of the report had to be delayed again, as even though there was full attendance of both civil society and government representatives at the previous session, no one could afford to attend this session. The report was finally considered in November 2003 at the 34th Ordinary Session held in Banjul, The Gambia.

145 C. Heyns and F. Viljoen. *The Impact of the United Nations Human Rights Treaties in the Domestic Level* (Kluwer Law International 2002), 350, 639.

146 Viljoen (n 135) 367.

5.2.2.2. Special mechanisms

Empowered by article 46 of the African Charter and article 23 of the Rules of Procedures of the African Commission, the latter has established special mechanisms to address human rights violations and ensure the protection of rights through some thematic areas. Special mechanisms of the African Commission include Special Rapporteurs, Working Groups and Committees. These mechanisms include:

- Special Rapporteur on Prisons and Conditions of Detention in Africa;
- Special Rapporteur on the Rights of Women in Africa;
- Special Rapporteur on Human Rights Defenders in Africa;
- Special Rapporteur on Freedom of Expression and Access to Information in Africa;
- Special Rapporteur on Refugees, Asylum Seekers, Internally Displaced Persons and Migrants in Africa;
- Committee for the Prevention of Torture in Africa;
- Working Group on Indigenous Populations/Communities in Africa;
- Working Group on Economic, Social and Cultural Rights in Africa;
- Working Group on the Death Penalty;
- Working Group on the Rights of Older Persons and People with Disabilities in Africa;
- Committee on the Protection of the Rights of People Living with HIV (PLHIV) and those at Risk, Vulnerable to and Affected by HIV;
- Working Group on Extractive Industries, Environment and Human Rights Violations in Africa.

While all these mechanisms are important for the realisation of human rights, those that have directly advanced the RTD are the Working Group on Indigenous Populations/Communities in Africa; the Working Group on Economic, Social and Cultural Rights in Africa and the Working Group on Extractive Industries, Environment and Human Rights Violations in Africa. The first one has assisted in defining indigenous people and this definition was important in crafting the *Endorois* decision which enabled the Commission to clarify the content and the justiciability of the RTD. The second one was equally instrumental in securing the justiciability of socio-economic rights which is essential for the realisation of the RTD, and finally the Working Group on Economic, Social and Cultural Rights in Africa and the Working Group on Extractive Industries, Environment and Human Rights Violations in Africa produced a joint Interim Report on 'Human Rights Impact of and Human Rights Based Solutions to Illicit Financial Flows from Africa' with a strong emphasis on the RTD and the impact of illicit financial flows on its realisation.[147]

147 A. Ramgobin et al. 'The Human Rights Impact of and Human Rights-Based Solutions to Illicit Financial Flows From Africa' A study by the Human Rights Development Initiative (2015) 10 and 11. www.hrdi.org.za/publications/i%20Human%20Rights%20Impact%20of%20and%20

This is to say that notwithstanding challenges such as the lack of resources and insufficient visibility of the special mechanisms,[148] they are important in promoting human rights and the RTD. They should be funded and capacitated to conduct their work. Furthermore, given that the RTD is an important specific feature of the African human rights system, it should be allocated an explicit theme or special mechanism or at least be mainstreamed in all other special mechanisms.

5.2.2.3. Promotional visits

The promotional visits provide Commissioners with an opportunity to engage with government officials and institutions, as well as civil society of state parties to the African Charter in general. However, it is important to note that the State's consent is needed for such visits.[149] Notwithstanding this constraint, States are likely to open their borders for such visits which are non-confrontational, but rather constructive in advising government representatives on the need and how to comply with the African Charter.

Besides the State's consent needed to conduct a promotional visit, the latter is also hindered by the lack of financial resources which ultimately closes the door to the possibility to undertake the visit. The financial constraints were reported to be a serious barrier to promotional visits.[150]

So far there is no record of a promotional visit centered on the realisation of the RTD. Therefore, the Commission should definitely consider focusing on this question in its future promotional visits, or mainstream the RTD in its visits as achieving this multidimensional right will also help realise many other human rights provided for by the Charter.

5.2.2.4. Resolutions

Article 45 of the Charter empowers the Commission to 'formulate and lay down principles and rules aimed at solving legal problems relating to human and peoples' rights.' Pursuant to this provision, the Commission adopts resolutions to address diverse human rights issues.

Resolutions are tools used by the Commission to explain the content of rights not articulated in the Charter. As correctly observed by Viljoen, similar to General Comments from treaty bodies, they elaborate 'in greater detail on substantive rights' and give clarity on their implementation.[151] Resolutions are not only adopted on specific themes, they can also be country-specific especially in case of

---

Human%20Rights%20Based%20Solutions%20to%20IFF%20in%20Africa.pdf (Accessed 10 March 2017).

148 J. Harrington. 'Special Rapporteurs of the African Commission on Human and Peoples' Rights' (2001) 2 *African Human Rights Law Journal* 248.

149 In 2005, a schedule promotional in visit to Zimbabwe could not take place when the government withdrew its consent. (See 19th activity, Report para 35; also Viljoen (n 135) 379.

150 See the 20th Activity Report, para 22.

151 Viljoen (n 135) 379.

widespread violation of human rights in a country. So, a country-specific resolution focuses exclusively on a particular violation of human rights in that country. In this case, the resolution 'serves a quasi-protective function, especially in the absence of individual communications against' that country.[152] This suggests that the value of the Commission's Resolution cannot be underestimated.

Nevertheless, similar to the promotional visits which are yet to focus on the RTD, the African Commission has thus far failed to adopt a resolution on RTD. It would be suitable to have a thematic resolution on the RTD as to explain its content in line with the *Endoris* decision. This will be useful in advancing the RTD in Africa.

5.2.2.5. Seminars and conferences

In discharging its promotional mandate, the African Commission has also organised numerous seminars and conferences in collaboration with NGOs and National Human Rights Institutions. The focus has been on women's rights, impunity, prison conditions, fair trials as well other human rights issues. Some topics discussed in these conferences and seminars have developed into resolutions aimed at advancing the normative content of the African Charter, including those on the Protocol on the Rights of Women in Africa. The latter led to the adoption of a 'General Comment' on socio-economic rights and guidelines on states reporting related to these rights.[153]

It could be argued that seminars and conferences on the RTD will not only enhance the visibility and understanding of the right, but will go a long way in ensuring that more initiatives are taken to give effect to it. Furthermore, for these seminars and conferences to make a meaningful impact, their outcomes should be publicised and disseminated across the continent and beyond to educate the masses on the African human rights system in general and the RTD in particular.

Overall, although the promotional mandate faces some challenges and does not always focus specifically on the RTD, it is a great initiative set up by the drafters of the African Charter. Its strength is in its flexibility and multiple approaches which can accommodate numerous mechanisms to promote human rights, including the RTD. Bearing this in mind, the Commissioners and other stakeholders must simply consider mainstreaming the RTD in any initiative to promote human rights, or/and to adopt a specific resolution on the RTD.

5.3. The African Court on Human Rights and the right to development

Before examining the extent to which the African Court on Human Rights protects the RTD, this section starts with a brief overview of the establishment of the court.

152 Ibid., 380.
153 Ibid., 382.

5.3.1. *The African Court on Human Rights: an overview of its establishment*

Unlike in other regions where the setting of a court was embedded in the human rights system at the onset, in Africa this institution was an afterthought as the African Commission was the main body in charge of adjudication.[154] In fact the journey to the adoption of a Protocol for the African Charter on the Establishment of an African Court on Human Rights (the Court Protocol) was a lengthy one as it took almost 40 years to have a Court Protocol. In this respect, the wind of democratisation which shook Africa in the 1990's carried with it the idea of a court to advance justice.[155] Consequently lawyers working for their governments gathered in Cape Town, South Africa, to adopt the initial draft Protocol[156] characterised by the direct access of individuals to the court after ratification by their countries.[157] This created an uneasiness from African governments which went back to the drawing board in Nouakchott, Mauritania where another draft known as the 'Nouakchott draft'[158] was adopted. As correctly observed by Viljoen,[159] the Nouakchott draft differed from the Cape Town draft by increasing the number of state parties needed for the Protocol to come into force from 11 to 15[160] and by submitting individual direct access to the court to a Declaration signed by their countries to that effect.[161] Following a subsequent debate of the draft in Addis Ababa, Ethiopia, where no major amendement was made, the OAU Assembly adopted it on 9 June 1998[162] in Ouagadougou, Burkina Faso and it came into force on 25 January 2004 and its Seat located in Arusha, Tanzania.

5.3.2. *The African Court on Human Rights, its mandate and the right to development*

Under Article 2 of the African Court on Human Rights Protocol, the African Court on Human Rights 'complement[s] the protective mandate of the African Commission. . .' This mandate is further reinforced by Article 8 of the Court Protocol which is unequivocal in affirming that the Rules of Procedure of the Court should be cognisant of the 'complementarity between the Commission and the Court'. It is against this backdrop that on 26 May 2017 the African Court on Human Rights rendered an important judgement on the RTD with the Ogiek case.[163]

154 F. Viljoen. International Human Rights Law in Africa (2012) 411 and 412.
155 Ibid, 412.
156 OAU Doc OAU/LEG/EXP/AFC/HPR(I).
157 Article 6 of the draft adopted in Cape Town.
158 OAU Doc OAU/LEGAL/EXP/ACHPR/PRO (2).
159 F Viljoen . . . International Human Rights Law in Africa (2012) 413.
160 See Cape Town Draft, art 31 (3); Nouackchott draft, art 33 (3).
161 See Cape Town Draft, art 6(1); Nouackchott draft, art 6(5).
162 OAUDocOAU/LEG/MIN/AFCHPR/PROT(I).
163 African Commission on Human and Peoples' Right v. Republic of Kenya.judgement in Application 006/2012 (the Ogiek case).

The Ogiek case was related to the eviction notice served against the Ogiek Community and other settlers of the Mau Forest by the Kenya Forestry Service in October 2009. The notice requested the Ogiek Community and other settlers of the Mau Forest to vacate the Mau Forest within 30 days. In response to this request, the Centre for Minority Rights Development (CEMIRIDE) together with Minority Rights Group International (MRGI), both acting on behalf of the Ogiek Community of the Mau Forest, approached the African Commission to remedy the situation. The Commission received the Communication on 14 November 2009.[164] Subsequently, on 23 November 2009, concerned by the possible impact of the eviction on 'the political, social and economic survival of the Ogiek Community and its potential irreparable harm'[165] the eviction would cause, the Commission delivered an Order for Provisional Measures demanding the government of Kenya to suspend implementation of the eviction notice. Nevertheless, on July 2012, it had not received the response from Kenya, hence on July 2012, relying on article 5 (1a) of the Protocol to the African Charter on Human and Peoples' Rights on the Establishment of an African Court on Human and Peoples' Rights (the Court Protocol), it took the matter to the African Court on Human Rights where it claimed that Kenya violated articles 1, 2, 4, 8, 14, 17(2) and (3), 21 and 22 of the African Charter. Given that article 22 on the RTD is the centre of this book, it will be the focus of our analysis.

In making its case and consistent with its own jurisprudence (the *Endorois* case), the Commission demonstrated that the Ogieks were indigenous people not recognized as such by Kenya. It claimed that Kenya failed to ensure Ogiek's right to determine their 'development priorities and strategies' and exercise their right to 'be actively involved in developing economic and social programmes affecting them and, as far as possible', and to administer such programmes through their own institutions.[166] Furthermore, according to the applicant, in line with its jurisprudence which emphasises the importance of 'meaningful participation'[167] of the beneficiaries of the RTD, the failure by Kenya to establish 'a framework which provides for the realisation of this right in its procedural and substantive processes, including consultation and participation' amounts to the violation of the RTD.[168]

In response, Kenya unsuccessfully tried to demonstrate the inadmissibility of the case on various grounds, including the lack of material jurisdiction, by claiming that the AU Assembly of Heads of State and Government is competent and not the Court.[169] It also alleged the lack of personal jurisdiction on the ground that the original complainants have no 'authority to represent the Ogieks, nor were they acting on their behalf',[170] and that due to the fact that the matter is still pending at the Commission, it should not be admissible before the Court. It also relied on the

164 Ibid, para 3.
165 Ibid, para 4.
166 Ibid, para 202.
167 See article 2 (3) UNDRTD; also the *Endorois* case, para 281.
168 African Commission on Human and Peoples' Right v. Republic of Kenya.judgement in Application 006/2012, para 203.
169 Ibid, para 48.
170 Ibid.

exhaustion of a local remedies rule claiming that the original applicants did not exhaust the local remedies in Kenya.[171] All these arguments were set aside by the court, which demonstrated that Kenya's admissibility objections were not legally acceptable and were therefore dismissed.[172]

On the merit, Kenya argued that 'the Ogieks are not a distinct ethnic group, but rather a mixture of various ethnic communities'.[173] However it failed to convince the court which reiterated the features of indigenous people presented by the Commission's Working Group on Indigenous Populations/Communities in Africa, namely self-identification, voluntary perpetuation of cultural distinctiveness, attachment to their ancestral land, and experience of subjugation and exclusion.[174]

In addition and perhaps most importantly, the Court was also inspired by the work of the United Nations Special Rapporteur on Minorities, which describes the criteria to identify indigenous populations as follows:[175]

i. That indigenous people can be appropriately considered as 'Indigenous communities, peoples and nations which having a historical continuity with pre-invasion and pre-colonial societies that developed on their territories, consider themselves distinct from other sectors of societies now prevailing in those territories, or parts of them. They form at present non-dominant sectors of society and are determined to preserve, develop, and transmit to future generations, their ancestral territories, and their ethnic identity, as the basis of their continued existence as peoples, in accordance with their own cultural patterns, social institutions and legal systems';
ii. That an indigenous individual for the same purposes is ". . . one who belongs to these indigenous populations through self-identification as indigenous (group consciousness) and is recognised and accepted by these populations as one of its members (acceptance by the group). This preserves for these communities the sovereign right and power to decide who belongs to them, without external interference".

Based on these criteria, the Court was of the view that important elements to take into account while defining Indigenous people are:

> the presence of priority in time with respect to the occupation and use of a specific territory; a voluntary perpetuation of cultural distinctiveness, which may include aspects of language, social organisation, religion and spiritual values, modes of production, laws and institutions; self-identification as well

171 Ibid, para 81.
172 Ibid, paras 75,80,89 and 98.
173 Ibid, para 104.
174 Ibid, para 105; also Advisory Opinion of The African Commission On Human And Peoples' Rights On The United Nations Declaration On The Rights Of Indigenous Peoples, adopted by The African Commission On Human And Peoples' Rights At Its 41 st Ordinary Session Held In May 2007 In Accra, Ghana, at page 4.
175 The Ogiek case, para 106.

> as recognition by other groups, or by State authorities that they are a distinct collectivity; and an experience of subjugation, marginalisation, dispossession, exclusion or discrimination, whether or not these conditions persist.[176]

The Ogiek populations meet this criteria, hence the weakness of the respondent's claims that the Ogieks were not indigenous. In countering the applicant's argument on the violation of the RTD, Kenya claimed that the African Commission did not demonstrate how the Ogieks are excluded from development processes, or the lack of development or instances of discrimination against the Ogiek in the 'enjoyment of the fruits of development'.[177] On the participation of the Ogieks in the development initiatives, Kenya was of the view that under Article 1(2) of the Constitution of Kenya, 'consultations were held with the Ogieks' democratically elected area representatives and that the State has established several participatory task forces to review the legal framework and reports applicable to the situation while taking into account the views of the public'.[178] Lastly, the respondent argued that its Vision 2030, its various budget statements and Article 10(2) of its Constitution, provide that the fundamental criteria for governance include equity, participation, accountability and transparency.[179]

The Court found for the applicant on the rights alleged to have been violated by the respondent except the right to life (article 4 of the African Charter). Importantly, in finding the violation of the RTD, the Court relied on the Report of the UN Special Rapporteur on Indigenous People and the Working Group to show that the Ogieks were still indigenous and needed protection and their RTD realized.[180] In addition supplementing the *Endorois* communication jurisprudence, the Court interpreted the RTD in the light of the UN Declaration on the Rights of Indigenous People. In this regard, it echoed article 23 of the UN Declaration on the Rights of Indigenous People which reads:

> Indigenous peoples have the right to determine and develop priorities and strategies for exercising their right to development. In particular, indigenous peoples have the right to be actively involved in developing and determining health, housing and other economic and social programmes affecting them and, as far as possible, to administer such programmes through their own institutions.[181]

In other words, failure by Kenya to 'effectively consult'[182] with the Ogiek people as well and the lack of prior engagement with these communities were instrumental in determining that Kenya violated the RTD of the beneficiaries. Even

176 See E/CNA/Sub.2/ACA/1996/2, para 69. Also the Ogiek case, para 107.
177 The Ogiek case, para 205.
178 Ibid, para 206.
179 Ibid.
180 Ibid, para 208.
181 Ibid, para 209.
182 Ibid, para 210.

though the court did not mention the concept or clarified the concept of 'meaningful participation' as the Commission did in the *Endorois* communication, it could be argue that this notion was implicit in the court decision even though it is always important to explicitly rely on previous jurisprudence so as to provide a complete rationale for a judgement.

Analyzing the Ogieks' conditions in light of the quote above, the Court established the violation of their RTD and ordered Kenya to 'to take all appropriate measures within a reasonable timeframe to remedy all the violations established and to inform the Court of the measures taken within six (6) months from the date of this judgment'. This is a strong judgement as it provides an interdict instructing the respondent to report back within six month on what have been done to give effect to the decision. This enables the court to monitor the implementation of its decision.

5.3.3. The significance of the Ogiek case

The Ogiek case shines the light on the justiciability of the RTD. Unlike the decisions of the African Commission on this right which were mere recommendations, the Ogiek decision has a stronger value as it is binding on parties before the Court.

The strength of the decision is not questionable. Unlike the recommendation of the Commission, the court decision is clear, binding and fosters the visibility of the RTD. The decision is complemented with an interdict which to some extent enhances Kenya's accountability for the implementation of the judgement. In this respect, not only does the decision clearly issue a declaratoru order, but it also prescribes a structural interdict[183] to enable the court to monitor the implementation of its decision by the government of Kenya.

Not only that, but the decision also harmonises the African human rights system discourse on the RTD already defined by the African Commission through its jurisprudence. It also demonstrates the effectiveness of the complementarity before the Court and the Commission and how their respective mandate enables the protection of human rights in Africa in general but the RTD in particular. This decision shows that the complementary mandate of the African Court of Human Rights and the African Commission is a good thing for the realisation of justice on the continent.[184] This complementarity of the African Court on Human Rights and the African Commission reinforces the capacity of the continental main human rights bodies to deliver human rights and the RTD in particular. To use the word of the African Commission, the Ogiek decision is:

> a landmark judgement in the operationalization of the complementary relationship between the Commission and the Court as provided for under Article 2 of the Court Protocol. It has served as a test case for identifying the legal,

183 For more on 'interdictory relief', see I Currie and J de Waal The Bill of Rights Handbook (JUTA, 2005) 2016-219.

184 M Mutua 'The African Human Rights Court: A two-legged stool? (1999) 21 Human Rights Quaterly 343.

procedural and technical factors that shape how the complementary relationship of the two institutions in practice plays itself out through referral of cases under Article 5(1)(a) of the Court Protocol.[185]

Therefore, to the question whether the Ogiek case brought anything new,[186] the answer is a positive one as the decision of the court unequivocally shed more light on the justiciability of the RTD. It also shows 'the potential that a strong and well-functioning regional human rights system will have in tackling and redressing major human and peoples' rights violations on the continent'.[187]

5.4. Concluding remarks

The aim of this chapter was to examine the role of the African Commission and the African Court on Human Rights in fostering the RTD on the continent. To this end the chapter unpacked the protective and promotional mandate of the Commission to explore whether anything was done under these mandates to advance the RTD.

It was found that the protective mandate is operationalised through the communication procedure and the on-site protective missions. On the one hand, the communication procedure led to the development of an impressive jurisprudence on the RTD by the Commission. While the *Curson* and the *Bakweri* Communication failed to test the Commission on the issues, the *DRC*, *SERAC*, and more importantly the *Gumne* case were useful for the development of the RTD by the African Commission which underlined the content, nature and justicibility of the right. On the other hand, it was found that while the on-site protective missions are yet to focus on the RTD per se, they have the potential to enhance its achievement.

As far as the promotional mandate is concerned, it is conducted through state reporting, special mechanisms, promotional visits, resolutions, seminars and conferences. The state reporting has been quite efficient for the promotion of the RTD as state parties are compelled to underline steps taken to give effect to the right in the Charter including the RTD. It was observed already from the case studies in the previous chapter, how States reported on the RTD and the responses from the African Commission. So State reporting contributes immensely in the promotion of the RTD, although the process faces some challenges such as the delayed or absent report by some states.

As for special mechanisms, it was found that in spite of the resources and capacity challenges facing the special mechanisms in general, the Working Group

185 Press Statement of the African Commission on Human and Peoples' Rights following the handing down of the judgement in Application 006/2012 by the African Court, 29 May 2017.

186 R Roesch 'The Ogiek Case of the African Court on Human and Peoples' Rights: Not So Much News After All?' available at https://www.ejiltalk.org/the-ogiek-case-of-the-african-court-on-human-and-peoples-rights-not-so-much-news-after-all/ (accessed 22 November 2017).

187 Press Statement of the African Commission on Human and Peoples' Rights following the handing down of the judgement in Application 006/2012 by the African Court, 29 May 2017.

on Indigenous Populations/Communities in Africa, the Working Group on Economic, Social and Cultural Rights in Africa and the Working Group on Extractive Industries, Environment and Human Rights Violations in Africa have promoted the RTD through these different engagements. Promotional visits, resolutions and conferences have a great potential for the promotion of the RTD, but so far this right is yet to be the focus of these promotional initiatives. Therefore, it is important to mainstream the RTD in these initiatives or to adopt a specific resolution on this right.

As far as the African Court on Human Rights is concerned, it was found that its protective mandate complements the African commision's mandate. In this respect, it had adjudicated the RTD through the Ogiek case brought to its attention by the African Commission. It identified the Ogiek community as indigenous people and had found that by the deprivation of these people from their 'right to determine and develop priorities and strategies'[188] for development amounted to the violation of their RTD. Ultimately, failure by Kenya to ensure that the Ogiek people actively get to take part or participate in the design and implementation of numerous development programmes through their own institutions was a violation of their RTD.

Overall, the RTD is not an alien concept to the African Commission and the African Court on Human Rights that have both worked very hard for its development. Notwithstanding its challenges, in its 30 years of existence, the African Commission's jurisprudence on the RTD is an indication of its significance in protecting and promoting human rights in Africa. Similarly, the first decision of the the African Court on Human Rights on the RTD is significant as it further demonstrates the justiciability of the right which now has a stronger legal value due to the binding decision of the Court.

188 The UN Declaration on the Rights of Indigenous People: para 23. Ogiek case, para 209.

6 The African Union governance institutions and the right to development

6.1. Introduction

The vital question in this chapter is whether the political organs[1] of the African Union have a role to play in the realisation of the RTD. Having established that the RTD is a human right in Africa and examined the role of the quasi-judicial body, the African Commission in turning it into reality, the aim of this chapter is to explore the extent to which the continental governance institutions can ensure the realisation of the RTD. The AU institutions that are significant for human rights achievement on the continent are: the AU Assembly, the Executive Council, the PRC, the PSC, the Pan-African Parliament, NEPAD and APRM. They will be examined in respect of their capacity to foster the RTD.

6.2. The African Union Assembly and the realisation of the right to development

An important turning point in the protection of human rights in Africa was the adoption of the AU constitutive Act[2] which gives special attention to human rights by explicitly stating the AU objectives to '[p]romote and protect human and peoples' rights in accordance with the African Charter on Human and Peoples' Rights and other relevant human rights instruments.'[3] This implies that the RTD *as per* the African Charter and the UNDRT are very much at the centre of the AU activities.

Comprising Heads of States and Government, the AU Assembly is the highest organ of the AU. Amongst other tasks, the AU Assembly is mandated to foster the realisation of human rights in Africa. To oversee the continental affairs including the protection of human rights, the AU Assembly meets in ordinary sessions from time to time every year, and during the sessions, the Head of States hosting the meeting is appointed as Chairperson. However, this rule was set aside in

1 For more on the AU political organs, see J. Akokpari, A. Ndingfa-Muvumba and T. Muruthi (eds.) *The African Union and its Institutions* (Fanele 2008).

2 Adopted in Lomé, Togo on 11 July 2000 and entered into force on 26 May 2001. The Assembly of the AU held its inaugural meeting in Durban, South Africa in July 2002.

3 The AU Constitutive Act, Art 3(h).

January 2006 when Sudan hosted the session and its President was not allowed to Chair the session. This was due to human rights concerns in Sudan, especially during the civil conflict in which the government of President Al-Bashir played an important role.[4]

Still, in discharging its human rights mandate, the AU Assembly defines the AU Common policy, which comprises the adoption of treaties on the continent, the provision of financial resources and overseeing the operations of the continental human rights treaties bodies such as the African Commission or the African Charter on Rights and Welfare of the Child for example. In monitoring the activities of these treaties bodies, the AU Assembly is empowered to take appropriate measures based on the reports of these treaty bodies. In fact, the protective measures adopted by treaty bodies cannot be made public until their adoption and authorisation to be publicised by the AU Assembly.

The paramountcy of the AU Assembly provides a huge avenue to foster the RTD. In this regard, this body can ensure that the AU common policy is informed by the need to ensure the RTD. It can also provide more funding to the African Commission to organise seminars and conferences and adopt special resolutions on the RTD to promote this right intensively. The Assembly meeting is also an opportunity for Heads of States and government to thoroughly discussed ways to foster the realisation of the RTD.

However, firstly, the success of these initiatives depends on the political will of African governments. Secondly, African government representatives are not necessarily experts on human rights, and more importantly on the RTD, even though this cannot be an excuse not to deliver on their human rights mandate which includes delivering on the binding RTD in Africa.

The other opportunity provided through the AU Assembly is that the latter elects members of the treaty bodies such as the Commissioners at the African Commission. This gives them the opportunity to scrutinise and choose those that have a pro-poor record in their work and who have some expertise on human rights and the RTD.

Overall, the AU Assembly has the political muscle necessary to foster the realisation of the RTD in Africa. It simply needs to be sensitised on the importance of this specific right and unleash a political will for its impact on the RTD to be felt.

6.3. The AU Executive Council and the realisation of the right to development

The AU Executive Council is made of Ministers of Foreign Affairs or other chosen Ministers of AU Member States. It is very influential as it is in charge of adopting the agenda and resolutions to be tabled at the AU Assembly.

4 F. Viljoen. 'The African Regional Human Rights System' In C. Krause and M. Scheinin (eds.) *International Protection of Human Rights: A Text Book* (2nd revised, Abo Akademi, University Institute for Human Rights 2012), 566.

The latter meets to deliberate and put its stamp on matters. However, most of the work is conducted by the Executive Council which is often mandated by the AU Assembly to examine the African Commission's Reports and offer recommendations.

This provides an avenue for the Council to focus on the RTD while studying States' reports for example or when examining the human rights situation on the continent. In fact, the Executive Council has the power to spearhead the promotion and the protection of the RTD as it can put the much needed pressure on state parties, request the adoption of resolutions on countries and at the same time give more teeth to the African Commission that would have recommended measures to give effect to the rights in the first place.

Nevertheless, most Minsters sitting at the Executive Council basically implement the policy of their governments which may not be informed by the realisation of the RTD or may not even have expertise on this specific right. However, this can be mitigated by the African Commission during its promotive mandate. In this respect, seminars and trainings on human rights and the RTD with the strong participation of the foreign Ministers and high level government officials should be organised whenever financial resources are available. For example, in 2016 the AU Commission on Social Development organised a high level training for the protection on disability rights in Africa.[5] This training was pitched at the level of Directors, and various high level government officers in charge of protecting disability rights participated. Such initiatives should be replicated for the sake of the realisation of the RTD as it will lead to the implementation of numerous human rights interdependently.

6.4. The Permanent Representatives Committee and the realisation of the right to development

The Permanent Representatives Committee (PRC) is in charge of the day-to-day activities of the AU on behalf of the Assembly and Executive Council. Made up of ambassadors or representatives of members States of the AU, the PRC is the platform where negotiations take place before getting to the Executive Council. All Member States are represented on the PRC at the level of Permanent Representative. Similar to the AU Assembly and the Executive Council, the PRC Bureau consists of a chairperson, three vice-chairpersons and a rapporteur. The Bureau positions are held by the same states that form the Assembly and Executive Council Bureaus.[6]

5 Workshops 'on disability mainstreaming and implementation of the Continental Plan of Action on the African Decade of Persons with Disabilities (2010–2019)' for senior government officials of the African Union Member States, 8–12 November 2015 in Pretoria, and from 30 November to 4 December 2015 in Lomé, Togo. The author was one the facilitators in these workshops.

6 The Permanent Representatives' Committee (PRC) www.au.int/en/organs/prc (accessed 10 March 2016).

In terms of mandate, the PRC acts as an advisory body to the AU Executive Council. It reports to the Executive Council, prepares the Council's work and acts on its instructions.[7] It also prepares its Rules of Procedure and submits them to the Executive Council; arranges Executive Council meetings, including the agenda and draft decisions; makes recommendations on areas of common interest to Member States particularly on issues on the Executive Council agenda; facilitates communication between the AU Commission and Member States' capitals; suggests the composition of AU organ bureaus, ad hoc committees and sub-committees and deliberates on matters relating to the AU's programmes and projects, particularly issues relating to the socio-economic development and integration of the continent; and makes recommendations to the Executive Council, among other things.[8]

In other words, the PRC is the tool without which the Executive Council cannot function. Given its broad mandate, the PRC also plays an important role in the protection of human rights. For instance it was involved in the process of 'finalization and submission' of the draft protocol merging the African Court on Human Rights and the AU Court of Justice.[9] In the same vein, the PRC Sub-Committee on Refugees, Returnees and Internally Displaced Persons also led the process of the adoption of a 'legal framework for the protection and assistance of internally displaced persons in Africa'.[10]

The prominent place of the PRC in negotiating what reaches the Executive Council turns it into the great platform to discuss the RTD. The latter having a political dimension, the PRC or the negotiations' forum should be utilised to ensure that diplomats address the question and ensure its inclusion on the agenda of the Executive Council. This is to say that the PRC is the appropriate forum to play the diplomatic game needed to ensure the achievement of RTD. It provides an opportunity to be tapped into by the African Commission and other stakeholders to foster the realisation of the RTD in Africa because, as correctly observed by Viljoen, 'many decisions affecting human rights that are finally taken by the Executive Council or Assembly are initially debated by the PRC'.[11]

6.5. The Peace and Security Council and the realisation of the right to development

The legal status of the Peace and Security Council (PSC) is based on article 5(f) of the AU Constitutive Act which lists the PSC as one of the organs of the Union. Then, the PSC Protocol[12] defines the PSC as the 'standing decision-making organ

7 AU Constitutive Act, art 21.

8 Rule 4 of the PRC Rules of Procedure.

9 AU DOC EX.CL/Dec.237 (VIII)Decision on the merger of the African Court on Human and Peoples' Rights and the African Court of Justice of the African Union; also F. Viljoen. *International Human Rights Law in Africa* (Oxford University Press 2012), 173.

10 AU Doc EX.CL/Dec.284(IX) para 9. Also Viljoen (n 9).

11 Viljoen (n 9) 191.

12 Adopted by 1st Extraordinary Session of the Assembly of the AU in Addis Ababa, Ethiopia on 3 February 2003; see art 21(1).

for the prevention, management and resolution of conflicts' in Africa. It promotes peace and security on the continent.[13]

The connection between peace, security and human rights cannot be overemphasised. The PSC unambiguously stresses its attachment to human rights, especially the standards covered by the UDHR.[14] It also emphasises the need to be guided by fundamental human rights and freedoms[15] which implies those covered by global human rights standards, but more importantly those covered by the African Charter, although it would have been better to explicitly refer to the African Charter.[16]

In spite of this shortcoming, the PSC Protocol compels the PSC to *seek close cooperation* with the African Commission on Human Peoples' Rights in all matters relevant to its objectives and mandate.[17] In addition, it urges the African Commission to 'bring to the attention of the [PSC] any information relevant to the objectives and mandate of the [PSC]'. The explicit link between the two institutions shows that peace, security and human rights are extrinsically connected. This is more so because the African Charter clearly provides for the right of all peoples to national and international peace and security.[18] Interestingly, the right to peace and the RTD are both third-generation human rights and as such are also connected by their classification.

The 'prevention, management and resolution of conflicts' at the centre of the PSC's mission are necessary for the realisation of the RTD which cannot thrive in time of conflict. Central to the PSC's objectives is the protection of human rights and fundamental freedoms and respect for human life,[19] which are core components of the RTD. This suggests that the PSC works to achieve the RTD while addressing peace and security issues.

As part of the prevention of conflict, it is important to create conditions for peace which goes through socio-economic development, infrastructure building, respect for rule of law and respect for human rights without which the possibility of war remains a reality as people have no hope. Similarly, after the eruption of a conflict, peace building also requests the implementation of conflicts prevention measures mentioned previously. According to Gawanas, the promotion of peace and security is an essential element of the RTD 'because conflicts exacerbate social issues such as the lack to food, water, health care, sanitation and education'[20] without which the RTD cannot be realised. This means that an effective PSC council is vital for the attainment of the RTD.

13 S. Gumedze. *The Peace and Security Council of the African Union- Its Relationship with the United Nations, the African Union and Sub-Regional Mechanisms* (Abo Akademi University Press 2011), 27.

14 The PSC Protocol, art 4.

15 Ibid., art 4(c).

16 Gumedze (n 13) 36.

17 PSC Protocol, art 19. My emphasis. For more on 'close cooperation' between the two organs, see Gumeze (n 13) 157–158.

18 African Charter, art 23.

19 Art 3(f) and 4(c) of the PSC Protocol.

20 B. Gawanas. ' The African Union: Concepts and Implementation Mechanisms Relating to Human Rights' In A. Bosl and J. Diesco (eds.) *Human Rights in Africa – Legal Perspectives on Their Protection and Promotion* (Konrad-Adenauer-Stiftung 2009), 144 and 157.

The African system provides an enabling environment at least normatively to ensure that the PSC succeeds in fostering human rights in its mandate to prevent, resolve and manage conflicts. In this respect, as provided for by the PSC protocol,[21] the PSC should work hand in hand with the African Commission. This means that these two bodies should cooperate closely and feed each other information.

Nevertheless, as correctly alluded to by Viljoen,[22] the PSC and the African Commission are yet to tap into their potential to work together to achieve peace and fulfil the RTD on the continent. In this respect, regrettably, in 2006 the PSC rejected the request of the Commission to take part in the Council meeting in which the situation in Sudan was considered. The request was rejected despite the fact that the Africa Commission focus was to be essentially human rights related.[23]

It is therefore imperative that the PSC and the African Commission explore the possibilities of close collaboration for their mutual success which will trickle down in the form of RTD. Amongst other means, through its promotional mandate, the African Commission can reach out not only to countries, but also to other AU institutions including the PSC with whom it is important to collaborate to enhance their chances to succeed. Importantly, during this meeting the Commission can inform the PSC on the RTD and its determinants which include peace. Similarly the PSC can use the opportunity to discuss its human rights mandate which is vital for peace and security, and get some guidance/expertise from the Commission.

6.6. The Pan-African Parliament and the realisation of the right to development

Established under the African Economic Community (AEC) Protocol,[24] and reiterated in the AU Constitutive Act,[25] the Pan-African Parliament (PAP) is the platform for people from all African states to take part in discussions and decision making on challenges facing the continent. It plays an oversight role for the AU Executive. Its ultimate objective is to ensure the effective 'participation of the African peoples in the economic development and integration of the continent'.[26]

As far as its human rights mandate is concerned, the treaty establishing the PAP is unequivocal in stressing its aim to strengthen good governance, democracy and

21 Art 19.

22 Viljoen in Crause and Scheinin (eds.) (2012) F. Viljoen 'The African Regional Human Rights System' In C. Krause and M. Scheinin (eds.) *International Protection of Human Rights: A Text Book* (2nd revised, Abo Akademi, University Institute for Human Rights 2012), 568.

23 The AU Audit Review, para 195; also Gumedze (n 13) 159.

24 Protocol to the Treaty Establishing the African Economic Community Relating to the Pan-African Parliament, AU Doc CM/2198 (LXXIII) (PAP Protocol Annex I).

25 See the AU Constitutive Act, art 5(1)(c).

26 Preamble of the PAP Protocol to the EAC treaty.

human rights in 'accordance with the African Charter' as well as 'other human rights instruments'.[27] This is an avenue to promote the RTD in line with article of 22 of the African Charter and the UN Declaration on the RTD. One way could be to rely on the promotional mandate of the African Commission to inform and capacitate representatives of other AU institutions in matters related to human rights and the RTD. As State representatives, capacitated members of the PAP can ensure the accomplishment of the RTD at the national level by pushing for adoption of legislative and other measures to achieve this right.

The PAP is also empowered to examine and express its views on 'any matter' including democracy, good governance, human rights and respect of the rule law in Africa.[28] When the world was shocked by the magnitude of the human rights crisis in Darfur, Sudan, relying on its power to examine 'any matter', in 2004 the PAP organised a fact-finding mission in the region to assess the causes and impact of the conflict and made recommendations.[29] In line with this precedent, the PAP also organised peace missions to Cote d'Ivoire, DRC and Mauritania. Moreover, in discharging its human rights mandate, the PAP adopted numerous human rights resolutions including the 2005 request that the detained Uganda opposition leader Dr Kizza Besigye to be released from prison.[30]

The human rights mandate as well as the PAP's power to look into 'any matter' is clearly enabling it to discuss issues of human rights including the RTD and advise States on ensuring its recommendations in order to achieve the AU's objectives. However, so far besides the initiatives enumerated above, which are of course valuable, the PAP is yet to address matters related to the RTD. On the contrary many opportunities seem to be missed by the PAP which 'has not been able to become more than a forum for discussion'[31] with little or no impact. For this to change, the PAP needs to collaborate with other continental bodies.

Ultimately, it is important to reiterate the need for collaborative efforts between AU institutions for effectiveness in discharging their mandate which are as interconnected as the rights composing the RTD. An effective collaboration between these institutions will go a long way in addressing the RTD in Africa.

6.7. NEPAD, APRM and the realisation of the right to development

This section is divided into two parts: The first part examines the role of New Partnership for Africa's Development (NEPAD) in achieving the RTD and the second one focuses on the role of the African Peer Review Mechanism (APRM) in fulfilling the same right.

27 PAP Protocol, Preamble.
28 PAP Protocol, art 11(1).
29 Viljoen (n 22) 568.
30 Ibid.
31 Ibid.

6.7.1. NEPAD and the right to development

Adopted in 2001 in Lusaka, Zambia by African Head of States, the NEPAD was established to address the continent's development challenges. It came into existence through the Millennium Africa Recovery Plan (MAP), conceived in 2000 by presidents Mbeki of South Africa, Obasanjo of Nigeria and Bouteflika of Algeria. MAP was later merged with Senegal's President Abdoulaye Wade's Omega Plan, resulting in the New African Initiative (NAI) in 2001. NAI was approved by the 37th OAU meeting of Heads of State and Government held in Lusaka, Zambia in July 2001 and its name was changed to NEPAD. According to the NEPAD Declaration of Democracy, Political, Economic and Corporate Governance,[32] the NEPAD was established to

> [e]radicate poverty and to place our countries, individually and collectively, on a path of sustainable growth and development and at the same time, to participate actively in the world economy and body politic on equal footing. We reaffirm this as our most pressing duty.[33]

In other words, NEPAD seeks to improve the standard of living in Africa as per the RTD discourse. This can be explained with reliance on the general rule of treaty interpretation under the 1969 Vienna Convention on the Law of Treaties. Accordingly, 'a treaty shall be interpreted in good faith in accordance with the ordinary meaning to be given to the terms of the treaty in their context and in the light of its object and purpose'.[34] This means that any treaty interpretation shall consider the context and purpose of the agreement. Although NEPAD is not a treaty, to understand its significance, its context and purpose cannot be overlooked. In this respect, NEPAD was established in a context of poverty and its purpose was to remedy the situation. This is explicit in the NEPAD programme which articulates the need to address poverty and foster the continent's socio-economic development[35] which is at the centre of the RTD. Therefore, based on its context and purpose, it could be argued that the NEPAD programme, which was criticised in its early days as being a shopping list because of its length,[36] is actually a tool to capture and address all human rights necessary for the RTD to become reality. According to Sengupta, development programme associated with the RTD should strive 'to remove capability poverty in addition to income poverty through the expansion of education and training, health and nutrition'[37] such as found in the NEPAD Programme.

32 Assembly of Heads of State and Government, 38th Ordinary Session of the OAU, 8 July 2002, Durban South Africa, NEPAD Declaration on Democracy, Political, Economic and Corporate Governance AHG/235 (XXXVIII) Annex I.

33 Assembly of Heads of State and Government, 38th Ordinary Session of the OAU, Preamble, para 2 and 5.

34 Art 31(1).

35 NEPAD, 2001, para 5.

36 In general see, J. O. Adésna et al. *Africa and Development Challenges in the New Millennium-The NEPAD Debate* (Zed book 2006).

37 A. Sengupta. 'Implementing The Right to Development' 8 (on file with author).

Undeniably the NEPAD strategy is to increase human capability (freedoms) through education programmes such as e-school projects (right to education) and to provide better health care (right to health) and nutrition (right to food) through programmes such as NEPAD Comprehensive Africa Agriculture Development Programme (CAADP). It caters for income poverty reduction through a broad creation of employment (right to employment) through its infrastructural and other projects, as well as its policy to increase the gross national product. It is an all-inclusive, wide-ranging and combined strategic framework for the socio-economic development of Africa. Mangu argues that the advent of the AU and NEPAD provides the needed structure for respect of human rights in the African continent;[38] and has actually transformed 'the human rights landscape in Africa'.[39]

As the latest African response to development questions, NEPAD supplements the AU in discharging its human rights obligations.[40] In this respect, it recognises the vital place of respect for human rights in any development initiative[41] and underlines that any endeavour fostering democracy and political governance seeks to advance human rights including the RTD.[42]

However, the NEPAD plan was the subject of numerous criticisms. Most of these criticisms were centred on the neoliberal features of the African plan. An important part of these features is embedded in NEPAD language which emphasises issues of 'capital flows', primarily in the structure of 'investment', within Africa and from outside the continent. Furthermore, NEPAD also emphasises the 'urgent need to create conditions that promote private sector investment by both domestic and foreign investors'; it also provides for 'great opportunities for investment', especially through 'public-private partnerships', as well as 'lowering the risks facing private investors', emphasises 'financial market integration', 'market enlargement', 'urgent need to diversify production', acknowledges 'the new trading opportunities that emerge from the evolving multilateral trading system', highlights 'the unparalleled opportunities that globalisation has offered to some previously poor countries', but that 'pursuit of greater openness of the global economy has created opportunities for lifting millions out of poverty' and calls for the urgent reintegration of Africa into the global economy.

Additionally, key neoliberal concepts such as 'governance', 'transparency', 'accountability', 'anti-corruption', 'trade liberalisation', and 'poverty reduction' characterise neoliberal institutions such as the IFIs entrenched in the NEPAD document. Obi argues that NEPAD is the domestication of 'the macro-economic, macro-political frameworks and market-led growth policies' of the Bretton Woods institutions by African leaders',[43] or rather a 'self-imposed structural adjustment

38 The Changing Human Rights Landscape in Africa: Organisation of African Unity, African Union, New Partnership of Africa's Development and the African Court' (2005) 3 *Netherlands Quarterly of Human Rights* 408.

39 Ibid.

40 Art 3(h) of the AU Constitutive Act.

41 NEPAD 2001, para 43, 49, 71 and 79.

42 Ibid., para 80.

43 C. I. Obi. 'Reconstructing Africa's Development in the New Millennium Through NEPAD: Can African Leaders Deliver the Goods?'(2001) 4 *African Journal of International Affairs* 148.

programme'[44] in Africa, to use Landsberg's words. Based on this neoliberal approach, it could be argued that even though NEPAD mentioned human rights, it cannot foster the achievement of the RTD. In this vein, Mathews writes that the RTD 'had been neatly excised from the key sections in the NEPAD Declaration of Democracy, Political, Economic and Corporate Governance' and argues that this excision is due to the fact that the language of the RTD does not gel well with NEPAD's main donors who sponsor neoliberalism approaches to development.[45]

However, even though donors can influence NEPAD, claiming that the RTD is completely removed from the NEPAD plan could be a wrong assumption because Africa leaders highlighted this important right in the context of globalisation in these terms:

> The new phase of globalisation coincided with . . . the emergence of new concepts of security and self-interest, which encompass *the right to development* and the eradication of poverty. Democracy and state legitimacy have been redefined to include accountable government, a culture of human rights and popular participation as central elements.[46]

This clearly shows that human rights and the RTD is very much at the heart of NEPAD, and the realisation of this right rests on democracy, state legitimacy, accountable government, a culture of human rights and popular participation. As correctly contended by Mangu, NEPAD became necessary because of the lack of accountability of African leaders and the democracy and human rights deficits which are essential for the achievement of the RTD.[47]

Furthermore, from Sengupta's perspective, achieving the RTD not only implies a holistic course of action for the protection of all human rights,[48] but also infers economic growth made of growth of resources, such as Gross Domestic Product (GDP) and advancement in technology and institutions[49] as highlighted by the NEPAD programme. In this regard, Rukato argues that[50]

> [o]ne of the objectives of the NEPAD Programme is the protection of democracy and human rights. The Democracy and Political Initiative of NEPAD is aimed at contributing to the enhancement of political and administrative frameworks in line with the internationally accepted standards and principles

44 C. Landsberg. 'NEPAD: What Is It? What Is Missing?' paper written for NALEDI, 11, www.sarpn.org.za/documents/d0000550/P503_Landsberg.pdf (Accessed 10 March 2017).

45 S. Mathews. 'The Right to Development, Global Partnership and Peer Partner Review'; Submission to the Task Force on the Right to Development, January 26–27 2007.

46 NEPAD 2001, para 43. My emphasis.

47 A. M. Mangu. 'Assessing the Effectiveness of the African Peer Review Mechanism and Its Impact on the Promotion of Democracy and Political Good Governance' (2007) 7 *African Human Rights Law Journal* 397.

48 A. Sen. *Development as Freedoms* (Knopf 1999).

49 Sengupta (n 37) 17.

50 H. Rukato. *Future of Africa – Prospects for Democracy and Development Under NEPAD* (Africa World Press 2010), 51.

> of democracy, transparency, accountability, integrity, respect for human rights and promotion of the rule of law.

Nevertheless, it is important to note that although the continental plan has goals that are essential for human rights realisation, it does not use a human rights angle in addressing its development targets. In this regard, Manby points out that NEPAD should have defined 'the objectives of development in terms of legally enforceable entitlements',[51] which would have empowered human rights advocates to claim people's right not to be poor;[52] since it is necessary to set up appropriate mechanisms to claim the RTD. Another lack of human rights approach is the fact that under NEPAD socio-economic rights are dealt with as mere access to services, and not as human rights, as entitlement or claimable rights.[53]

However a teleological interpretation of the NEPAD pledge reveals its commitments for human rights. In fact, the NEPAD Declaration on Democracy, Political, Economic and Corporate Governance is unambiguous. In this important document, African leaders clearly committed themselves to ensuring peace and security, putting an end to unconstitutional change of government, promoting human rights, respecting the rule of law and good governance.[54] In detail, African leaders pledge to comply with the ACHPR,[55] the 1990 African Charter for Popular Participation in Development and Transformation[56] (right to participation), the African Charter on the Rights and Welfare of the Child[57] that provides for the RTD of the child,[58] the Protocol on the establishment of the African Court on Human and Peoples' Rights,[59] the 1999 (Grand Bay Mauritius) Declaration and Plan of Action for the Promotion and Protection of Human Rights,[60] the Framework for an OAU Response to Unconstitutional Changes Government[61] and the AU Constitutive Act.[62] Murray correctly argues that NEPAD is significant for the promotion of human rights in Africa.[63] Similarly, and with specific attention the RTD, Gawanas observes that 'NEPAD places human rights at the Centre' of development' and together with the AU, they seek to 'reinforce, social

51 B. Manby. 'The African Union, NEPAD, and Human Rights: The Missing Agenda' (2004) 26 *Human Rights Quarterly* 1002.

52 Ibid.

53 E. Baimu. 'Human Rights in NEPAD and Its Implementation for the African Human Rights System' (2002) 2 *African Human Rights Law Journal* 310.

54 AHG/235 (XXXVIII) Annex I, para 3 and AU Constitutive Act: Preamble, para 10; art 3(h) and (g); 4(m), (c), (L) (N) and (p).

55 AHG/235 (XXXVIII) Annex I, para 3(b).

56 Ibid., para 3(c).

57 Ibid.

58 Art 5.

59 AHG/235 (XXXVIII) Annex I, para 3(h).

60 Ibid., para 3(i).

61 Ibid., para 3(j); also OAU 2000 Summit in Lomé, Togo.

62 Ibid., para 3(l).

63 R. Murray. *Human Rights in Africa: From the OAU to the African Union* (Cambridge University Press 2004), 264.

economic and cultural rights, as well as *the right to development'*.[64] Sharing this view, Sengupta describes NEPAD as a 'comprehensive partnership' agenda to give effect to the RTD.[65]

Nevertheless, to enhance NEPAD ability to address human rights on the continent, it is imperative to establish the link between this institution and the African Commission and the African Court on Human and Peoples' Rights and the APRM to be discussed below.

In its early days, the uncertainty of NEPAD's legal status was a hindrance to its ability to deliver. It was autonomous from the AU and this created problems in its operationalisation as it lacked the legal *personae* and was represented by the Development Bank of Southern Africa. However, following the recommendation of the NEPAD Heads of State and Government Implementing Committee (HSGIC) at its 8th session held in Maputo, Mozambique on 9 July 2003, African governments formally integrated NEPAD into the AU structures and processes under the name of NEPAD Planning and Coordinating Authority. This decision was adopted by the 10th AU Assembly in Addis Ababa in January/February 2008,[66] and on 10 June the same year, the African Union Commission inaugurated the NEPAD Coordinating Unit (the Unit) in Addis Ababa. This was done in compliance with the decision of NEPAD HSGIC at its 8th session held in Maputo on 9 July 2003 which decided to mandate the Chairperson of the AU to

> [e]nter into a temporary host agreement with the Government of the Republic of South Africa with a view to providing the NEPAD Secretariat with a legal status of an AU office operating outside the African Union Headquarters for a transitional period of three years as from July 2003, or until such time the relevant structure of the African Union are fully operational, whichever comes first.[67]

The host agreement was signed and the NEPAD Secretariat operates (now legally) from Midrand, South Africa. In fact, the integration of NEPAD in the AU has known positive progress and it would not be wrong to argue that NEPAD is now integrated in the AU. In this respect, the NEPAD Secretariat has been transformed into the NEPAD Planning and Coordinating Agency (NEPAD Agency);[68] the 21st NEPAD Heads of State and Government Implementation Committee Meeting,[69] worked on 'the adoption by the NEPAD Secretariat of AU policies and procedures in finance, administration, human resource (HR) management, auditing, legal,

64 B. Gawanas (n 20) 138, my emphasis.

65 A. Sengupta. 'Development Cooperation and the Right to Development' (2003) 19–20. http://tanzaniagateway.org/docs/Development_cooperation_and_the_Right_to_Development.pdf (Accessed 22 March 2017).

66 Assembly/AU/10(X).

67 The Draft Communiqué issued at the end of the 8th Summit of HSGIC of NEPAD in Maputo, Mozambique, 09 July 2003 (on file with author).

68 T. Pampalone. 'The New NEPAD' *Mail & Guardian*, 19 March 2010.

69 Held in Sirte, Libya, on 30 June 30 2009.

protocol and procurement'.[70] In terms of operation model, the NEPAD Agency has adopted a strategic direction based on six thematic areas:

1 agriculture and food security
2 climate change and natural resource management
3 regional integration and infrastructure
4 human development
5 economic and corporate governance
6 crosscutting issues of gender, capacity development and information communications technology

In terms of financing, the Agency is financed through the statutory budgets of the AU, voluntary contributions from AU Member States and from development partners and the private sector.

This new arrangement has addressed the criticism related to the length of the original document, the financial challenges facing NEPAD is yet to be resolved as like the AU, it still needs foreign assistance for its operations.[71]

In sum, in spite of the imperfection of NEPAD, its ultimate goal of poverty eradication, and its current integration into the AU go a long way in showing that its mere existence and activities constitute a good initiative to achieve the RTD.

6.7.2. The APRM and the right to development

Adopted at the first AU summit in Durban,[72] 'the APRM is the cornerstone of NEPAD'.[73] It is a tool for enhanced collective responsibility within the family of African countries; it is voluntarily acceded to by AU Member States; it is an instrument and criterion for measuring African governments' compliance with their commitments encompassed in the Declaration on Democracy, Political, Economic and Corporate Governance. To join the process a country signs the APRM Memorandum of Understanding (MoU). In terms of practice, the APRM is based on a self-assessment questionnaire divided into four parts: democracy and political governance, economic governance and management, corporate governance and socio-economic development. These questions seek to examine African states' commitments to regional and global standards for the protection of human rights. According to the MoU, the primary purpose of the APRM is to

70 J. Ping. 'Opening Remarks at the 22nd NEPAD Head of State and Government Implementation Committee' 4 (on file with author).

71 GBN Ayittey. 'Can Foreign Aid Reduce Poverty? No' In P. M. Haas and J. A. Hird (eds.) *Controversies in Globalisation: Contending Approaches to International Relations* (CQ Press 2009), 89.

72 Adopted at the 1st Assembly of the AU held in Durban, South Africa, 8–10 July 2002; Declaration on the implementation of NEPAD, Assembly/AU/Decl.1 (I).Assembly /AU/Decl.1 (I).

73 International Federation for Human Rights (FIDH) *A Human Rights Approach to the New Partnership for Africa's Development (NEPAD) and the African Peer Review Mechanism (APRM)* (FIDH 2004), 121.

> [f]oster the adoption of policies, standards and practices that lead to political stability, high economic growth, sustainable development and accelerated subregional and continental economic integration through sharing of experiences and reinforcement of successful and best practice, including identifying deficiencies and assessing the need for capacity building of participating countries.[74]

In other words, the APRM is considered the device of good governance in the NEPAD programme. It emphasises the review of policies and programmes of rule of law, the need to address corruption, alleviate poverty, foster literacy, and health, and enforce corporate governance laws which are all essential for the realisation of the RTD. The commitment of the APRM to human rights is also illustrated by the fact that out of nine objectives under the commitment of democracy and political governance, five directly address human rights. These objectives are the promotion of constitutional democracy, including periodic political competition and opportunity for choice, the rule of law and the inclusion of a Bill of Rights in a supreme constitution;[75] the promotion and protection of economic, social, cultural, civil and political rights enshrined in the African and international human rights instruments;[76] the promotion and protection of the rights of women,[77] of children and young persons,[78] and of vulnerable groups including displaced persons and refugees.[79]

Moreover, the APRM unequivocally urges participating states to promote human rights at the national level[80] and to ratify international human rights instruments and comply with their monitoring mechanisms at regional and global levels. Mangu writes that 'in order to achieve NEPAD's objectives which all revolve around the protection and promotion of human and peoples' rights in Africa',[81] African leaders established the APRM.

Furthermore, aware of the historical exclusion of women from the development agenda, the APRM caters for women's rights through its objective seven, which reiterates the commitment made in NEPAD.[82] This objective urges members States to:

> p]romoting the role of women in social and economic development by reinforcing their capacity in the domain of education and training; by developing

74 MoU para 8; APRM Base Document para 3.
75 Objective 2.
76 Objective 3.
77 Objective 7.
78 Objective 8.
79 Objective 9.
80 Country Review Report, Benin, 58.
81 A. M. Mangu. 'The Changing Human Rights Landscape in Africa: Organisation of African Unity, African Union, New Partnership of Africa's Development and the African Court' (2005) 23 *Netherlands Quarterly of Human Rights* 391.
82 NEPAD 2001 paragraph 49(7) and 67(2).

revenue-generating activities through facilitating accesses to credit; and by assuring their participation in the political and economic life of African countries.

Although this objective emphasises gender mainstreaming in development activities, it does not rely on existing instruments for protection of women's rights such as the Convention on the Elimination of All Forms of Discrimination Against Women (CEDAW)[83] or the Convention on the Political Rights of Women,[84] or the Convention on Consent to Marriage[85] and others. Nevertheless, given that the APRM urges members States to ratify international and regional standards of human rights, it could be argued that the international and regional standards for the protection of human rights are included in the APRM's request.

However, the lack of explicit reference to these instruments does not ensure their visibility. In addition, the fact that women's daily problems such as rape, domestic violence and various other abuses are not specifically mentioned reduces the potential effectiveness of the protection of women in NEPAD and APRM. According to Manby, 'the protection of women's rights by NEPAD is not matched with a pledge to provide effective remedies to address their plight'.[86]

Similarly, the NEPAD and APRM do not cast their protection of children's rights on the 1989 Convention on the Right of the Child (CRC) or/and the African Children's Charter. In the same vein, while referring to the predicament of refugees and displaced persons, the APRM[87] does very little or nothing in prescribing adequate remedies to solve the problem in Africa. It does not even rely on the 1969 OAU Convention Governing Specifics Aspects of Refugees Problems in Africa which is the main continental tool to deal with refugee's crisis on the continent.[88]

Nevertheless, notwithstanding these shortcomings, it cannot be claimed that the APRM has no RTD attributes. Its primary objective is to foster governance without which the RTD will remain rhetorical. In fact, the APRM's economic governance and management commitment encourages macroeconomic policies that support sustainable development;[89] sound public finance management,[90] anti-corruption and money laundering mechanisms and policies,[91] which are all essential for the achievement of the RTD. In general, all APRM arrangements aim to improve the quality of lives on the continent and this is at the centre of the RTD.

83 Adopted in 1979 and entered into force in 1971.
84 193 UNTS 135, adopted 20 December 1952, entered into force 7 July 1954.
85 ILO Convention no 100, 165 UNTS 303, adopted 29 June 1951, entered into force 11 August 1954.
86 Manby (n 51) 1005.
87 Objective 9.
88 Manby (n 51) 1005.
89 Objective 1.
90 Objective 3.
91 Objective 4.

However, the legal status of the APRM is weak for it is non-binding with no consequence for recalcitrant States who accept voluntarily to participate in the process and do not comply with its recommendations. Practically nothing can be done besides unclear 'appropriate measures'[92] to convince unruly Sates to comply with the prescriptions from the process, and generally the process is simply discontinued since there is no follow-up mechanisms. Echoing the view of a NEPAD official, Kebonang and Fombad write.[93]

> A weakness with the current review process is that it does not prescribe sanctions or penalties and as such it runs the risk of being ineffective. Unless there are penalties or sanctions, the review will become a sham and attempts at achieving sustainable development through the adoption of best practices will fail.

In terms of standard setting, this weakness of the APRM does not enhance the prospects of the RTD. Unlike at the global and regional levels where state parties to treaties have to report absolutely to treaties bodies and attend to the recommendations of these bodies, under the APRM, there are no compelling elements on the participating states. Nevertheless, this weakness of the APRM is not unique to the African process, but is inherent to international law in general because even in binding treaties, States do not always report or do not always implement the recommendations from the treaty bodies that can only name and shame non-compliant States.[94]

In spite of the non-binding nature of APRM instruments, in order to advance governance on the continent, participating countries adopt adequate laws, policies and standards and build the necessary human and institutional capacity. They also undertake to adopt specific objectives, standards, criteria and indicators for assessing and monitoring progress in key areas regularly in accordance with the APRM Base Document and the Declaration on Democracy, Political, Economic and Corporate Governance. This comprises the commitment to submit to periodic reviews and be guided by established parameters. If state parties fail to comply with their commitments, the APRM should name, denounce and shame States that are non-compliant with its recommendations.

The other weakness facing the APRM is the broadness of its terms of reference or standards. The latter includes all African instruments, binding and non-binding plus resolutions and declarations of the OAU and AU; it also contains a variety of non-binding instruments originating from the ILO, IMF and commonwealth for

92 APRM Base document, para 24.

93 Z. Kebonang and C. M. Fombad. 'The African Peer Review Mechanism: Challenges and Prospects' In *AU, NEPAD and the APRM: Democratisation Efforts Explored* (The Nordic Institute 2006), 51.

94 For more on naming and shaming, see S. D. Kamga and O. O. Ajoku. 'Reflections on How to Address the Violations of Human Rights by Extractive Industries in Africa: A Comparative Analysis of Nigeria and South Africa' (2014) 17(1) *PER* 498–499.

instance. In addition, all the UN conventions, declarations, resolutions and conference reports are included and all these are tagged together under the heading 'APRM Governance Standards'.[95] Although the broadness of these standards can be counterproductive, it can also be argued that the APRM seeks to relay explicitly on all important documents and ensure the visibility of those protected under these standards. Therefore, there is a need to strike a balance between reducing the scope of the standards and ensuring that all the beneficiaries of these principles are covered. One way of doing this could be to narrow the standards into four thematic areas with special focus on binding instruments as it is easier to measure compliance. But, at the same time no one should be left behind in the thematic areas.

However, for some the APRM – like NEPAD – is unable to fulfil human rights and the RTD in Africa because of its neoliberal attributes. Proponents of this view[96] hold that the good governance and democracy as prescribed under APRM are not likely to advance Africa's development, but will rather obstruct this development. In this respect, Kankwenda argues that the APRM approach will affect Africa's sovereignty in the course of development cooperation negotiations. For Bond, the good governance concept was inserted in NEPAD/APRM to disguise 'the neo-colonial relationship during the period of the 2000s – in the wake of two decades of rampant structural adjustment that demolished living standards except for newly empowered political, financial and commercial elites'.[97] He emphasises that the neo-colonial direction of the [APRM] is similar to that 'imposed by the IMF, the US State Department and Brussels'.[98] Similarly, Amin adds:

> Unquestionably, the NEPAD document lines up with liberal thought on the discourse of "good governance." This is a concept that is useful as a way to dissociate democratic progress from social progress, to deny their equal importance and inextricable connection with one another, and to reduce democracy to good management subjected to the demands of private capital, an "apolitical" management by an anodyne civil society, inspired by the mediocre ideology of the United States.[99]

95 See SAIIA. *APRM Governance Standards* (Salla 2008).

96 M. Kankwenda. 'Forty Years of Development Illusion: Revisiting Development Policies and Practices in Africa' In L. O. C. Agubuzu, B. Onimode and A. Adedeji l (eds.) *African Development and Governance Strategies in the 21st Century. Looking Back to Move Forward- Essays in Honour of Adebayo Adedeji at Seventy* (Zed Books in Association with the African Centre for Development & Strategy Studies 2004) 12.

97 P. Bond. 'Removing Neocolonialism's APRM Mask: A Critique of the African Peer Review Mechanism' (2009) *Review of African Political Economy* 596–597. For dissenting views, see R. Herbert and S. Gruzd. 'Taking Stock of the African Peer Review Mechanism' (2007) 14 *South African Journal of International Affairs* 5–28; also R. Herbert and S. Gruzd. *Le Mecanisme Africain d'evaluation par les pairs*: Lecons des pionniers' (SAIIA 2008).

98 Bond (n 97).

99 S. Amin. 'The Millennium Development Goals: A Critique from the South' *Monthly Review* (2006). www.monthlyreview.org/0306amin2.php (Accessed 10 March 2017).

Sharing this view, Olukoshi argues that NEPAD's democracy and governance arrangement is designed to feed the donor's interest and not the African populace.[100]

In spite of these criticisms, it is contended that before the adoption of NEPAD and APRM, Africa's development questions were no longer discussed, they were simply forgotten as the plans which preceded NEPAD and APRM were the subject of a resounding silence and as such were becoming impotent. Therefore, the architects of the NEPAD and APRM should be credited for resurrecting the debate on Africa's development because, if development, good governance and human rights had been achieved in Africa, the launching of NEPAD would not have been necessary.[101] Therefore, to foster human rights, the NEPAD and APRM were set up. Mangu argues that 'in order to achieve NEPAD's objectives which all revolve around the protection and promotion of human and peoples' rights in Africa',[102] African leaders established the APRM.

Perhaps the missing link in the APRM process and the African human rights system in general is the lack of reliance on local realities or cultures to promote and protect human rights. Yet the African system underlines 'people's rights because African culture is firmly grounded in the age-old traditions of the supremacy of collectivism, sense of belonging to a community, humanism and ubuntu'.[103] For instance the APRM standards reiterate global norms of human rights. While this is fine, these norms should be supplemented by conceptual philosophies embedded in African societies. Put differently, it is hard to find where the APRM and other continental mechanisms for the protection of human rights encourage people to rely on the bottom-up approach for human rights achievements. To be specific, the concept of Ubuntu secure under the notion of 'Peoples' in the African system is not relied upon to foster human rights and the RTD. While the APRM standards are good, they need to be vernacularised to resonate to the grassroots who after all are the humans to whom human rights are applied. Failure to do this may keep the human rights discourse at an esoteric level reserved for a few.

It is important to rely on what Zwart calls 'the receptor approach' to human rights, which basically posits that a better implementation of human rights should tap into local realities, to supplement the global standards of human rights.[104] In this context, it is necessary to explore avenues to tap into African social institutions (such as kingship), custom, indigenous knowledge to foster human rights. For example, the core question here could be to learn from the *Gacaca* which is a form of traditional justice system which was relied on to rebuild the social fabric after the genocide in Rwanda.[105] This is not to reject the current APRM

100 A. Olukoshi. 'Governing the African Political Space for Sustainable Development: A Reflection on NEPAD' In P. Anyang' Nyong'o, A. Ghirmazion and D. Lamba (eds.) *New Partnership for Africa's Development: A New Path*? (Heinrich Boll Foundation 2002), 90.

101 Mangu (n 47) 397.

102 Ibid., 391.

103 Gawanas (n 20) 143.

104 T. Zwart. 'Using Local Culture to Further the Implementation of International Human Rights: The Receptor Approach' (2012) 34 *Human Rights Quarterly* 546–569.

105 For more on the Gacaca, see H. N. Brehm, C. Uggen and J-D. Gasanabo. 'Genocide, Justice, and Rwanda's Gacaca Courts' (2014) 30(3) *Journal of Contemporary Criminal Justice* 333–352.

standards, but to ensure that African indigenous knowledge systems are infused in these standards for a better implementation. During the *Travaux Preparatoires* of the African Charter, the then President of Senegal, Leopold Senghor clarified the need to rely on culture in these words:[106]

> As African, we shall neither copy, nor strive for originality. . . . We could get inspirations from our beautiful and positive traditions. Therefore, you must keep constantly in mind our values of civilisation and the real needs of Africa.

This is to say that while relying on global norms for the protection of human rights, it is imperative not to forget African traditions, especially the positive ones, and this should be infused in the APRM. This approach could be important for the RTD for it to legitimise the human rights discourse in local communities; people identify with the discourse and this is more important in the African context where people not only have rights, but also duties towards their community.[107] In other words, accepting human rights as originating from the community' values will go a long way in their successful realisation. From this perspective people will definitely play their role, discharge their duty and partner with the States to achieve the RTD. So, besides relying on global standards, the APRM should also rely on African wisdom to foster human rights and governance for the achievement of the RTD.

In sum, while acknowledging that the APRM has its challenges, it is equally necessary to recognise its uniqueness because nowhere else in the world do leaders of sovereign states gather to assess each other, for self-examination, accept criticisms from their peers and learn from each other. Furthermore, considering the goal of the APRM which aims to foster governance and respect for human rights, and also taking into account the high number of states that have voluntarily agreed to undergo the review process, it could be claimed that this mechanism has the potential to achieve the RTD, even though the challenges facing the process cannot be ignored. Therefore, African leaders should imperatively address the shortcomings of the process to improve its effectiveness.

6.8. Concluding remarks

The aim of this chapter was to explore the extent to which the AU governance institutions – namely the AU Assembly, the Executive Council, the PRC, the PSC, the PAP, the NEPAD and APRM – could foster the realisation of the RTD in

---

See C. Clapham. 'Gacaca: A Successful Experiment in Restorative Justice?' (2012). www.e-ir.info/2012/07/30/gacaca-a-successful-experiment-in-restorative-justice-2/ (Accessed 10 March 2017).

106 L. Senghor. 'Address to the Legal Meeting Convened to Draft the African Charter on Human People's Rights, in 1979' In C. Heyns and K. Stefisyen (eds.) *Human Rights Peace and Justice in Africa: A Reader* (PULP 2006), 51.

107 The African Charter, art 27, 28 and 29.

Africa. It was found that while the AU Assembly as the supreme organ of the AU has the necessary power to advance the RTD, it needs to be sensitised on the question and shows a strong political will. At the same time, its efficiency and willingness to deal with the RTD depends on the nature of political negotiations conducted at the PRC that will table them to the Executive Council for them to reach the AU Assembly.

The PSC's mandate is intrinsically linked to the achievement of the RTD and it is compelled to work closely with the African Commission in ensuring human rights and the RTD, but so far the PSC is yet to work with the Commission for their mutual success. The PAP has strong potential to achieve the RTD, but needs to work in direct collaboration with African Commission as well as other continental institutions to unleash its potential to realise the RTD.

Finally the NEPAD and APRM, in spite of the critics, are more likely to foster the realisation of the RTD as they resurrected Africa's development debates, proposes a plan (NEPAD) and a process (the APRM) to monitor its implementation. Although imperfect, the ultimate goals of these initiatives centred on poverty eradication are essential for the RTD to thrive. To improve the responsiveness of the APRM standards to African problems, it is imperative to infuse African values and traditions in the process as to strengthen its legitimacy at the grassroots level.

Overall, the AU institutions have a great potential to foster the accomplishment of human rights and the RTD in Africa. In 2006, the former UN Secretary General applauded the AU as follows:[108]

> The [AU] itself is in many ways the most eloquent testimony of progress, in development, in security, in human rights – the three interlinked pillars on which the human family must built its future. [This] institution has established itself as defining voice in each of those areas.

This is a clear endorsement of efforts and progress made by the AU and its institutions towards the realisation of the RTD, even though these institutions have to cooperate with each other to enhance the prospect of success.

108 K. Annan. 2006. Address to the AU Summit in Banjul, the Gambia as quoted by Gwanas (n 20) 161.

7 The way forward for the realisation of the right to development in Africa

7.1. Introduction

The aim of this chapter is to explore the way forward in turning the RTD into reality in Africa. It begins by summarising the discussion in the form of closing remarks and then proceeds with suggestions on what needs to be done to improve people's lives in Africa in giving effect to the RTD.

7.2. Closing remarks

The book has vigorously demonstrated that against the backdrop of the controversy on the RTD at the global level, this right is part and parcel of the African human rights system where it is absolutely binding. In reaching this conclusion, the book defines the African human rights system broadly to include arrangements at the continental, sub-regional, and national levels and assesses the extent to which these arrangements influence the realisation of the RTD or are likely to do so.

In detail, following Chapter 1 which set the scene for the discussion, Chapter 2 examined or unpacked the RTD concept. It found that the right is inalienable, is a composite right encompassing civil and political rights, economic, social and cultural rights, right to participation and right to self-determination with an exceptional emphasis on the interdependence, indivisibility and universality of all its elements. Apart from its multifaceted feature, the right is also a claim for global justice and fairness in sharing the world resources.

The other specificity of the RTD is its controversial feature which cascades down from the UN to the academic arena, via international organisations. Nevertheless, despite the controversy, the RTD has evolved through the years and has been the subject of numerous activities at the global and national levels, and as such has become a '*fait accompli*'[1] with a normative force, despite its non-binding character at the global level.

1 P. Alston. 'Development and the Rule of Law: Prevention Versus Cure as a Human Rights Strategy' In International Commission of Jurists (ed.) *Development, Human Rights and the Rule of Law* (Pergamon Press 1981) 31.

After establishing the existence of the RTD in Chapter 2, the subsequent chapter or Chapter 3 explored its implementation. It found that at the country level, the State is the duty bearer of the right whereas at the international level, based on international solidarity, the international community is the duty bearer, although this last aspect is controversial as the right is not binding at the global level. It was also found that international financial institutions which are the World Bank and the IMF, as well as the global trade institution known as the WTO, have a responsibility in fulfilling the RTD. Similarly, TNCs are not exonerated from ensuring the achievement of the right under discussions while NGOs that are the checks and balances at the national and international levels should also ensure that State and non states actors do not encroach upon the RTD. Lastly, it was found that the beneficiaries of the right are individuals, people, as well as the state. This speaks to the nature of right holders in the African Charter. The latter protects the right of every human or individual. It also covers the right of peoples as groups or collective. In this context, groups would include communities or indigenous peoples with the ultimate objective to ensure the development of everyone in the group and the entire group. The state was also identified as a beneficiary of the RTD. This is the external aspect of the RTD in which the state speaks on behalf of its people. The state is the beneficiary of the RTD only when it claims it for its citizens who are the ultimate right holders.

Subsequent to the analysis of the general principles which inform the RTD, its nature and implementation, Chapter 4 focused on the right where it is binding in the African human rights system. Given the broadness of the system, the chapter dealt specifically with RTD at the regional, sub-regional and national levels.

The chapter unveiled that at the regional level, the key African treaties – namely, the African Charter, the African Women's Protocol and the African Children's Charter – provides for a normative protection of the RTD which flows down to the sub-regional and national levels.

At the sub-regional level, although originally the REC treaties had nothing to do with human rights and the RTD, they evolve and seek to improve the standard of living for all as prescribed by the RTD discourse. In this respect, human rights and the RTD are now embedded in RECs objectives. In addition, explicit provisions on human rights are included in REC treaties and these rights are now generally judicialised with the establishment of courts and tribunal in RECs with clear jurisdiction to address these rights.

Lastly, it was found that at the national level, while countries such as Cameroon, Uganda, Malawi and Ethiopia have provided for the RTD in their constitutions, South Africa through its transformative constitution guarantees the RTD. However, the various measures taken to turn the right from rhetoric to reality are yet to have made a difference as a result of poverty, weak separation of powers and endemic corruption or generalised bad governance.

Given the 30 years' history and significant role of the African Commission as well as the recent case on the RTD at the African Court on Human Rights, Chapter 5 was allocated to these two institutions. It was found that the tools at the disposition of the African Commission are its protective and promotional mandates.

On the one hand, under the protective mandate the communication procedure enables the Commission to oversee the implementation of the RTD in African states and provide recommendations, where necessary. So far this procedure has enabled the Commission to develop an impressive jurisprudence on the RTD. Additionally, still under the protective mandate, the on-site protective missions are yet to be relied upon to foster the RTD.

On the other hand, the promotional mandate is operationalised through state reporting, special mechanisms, promotional visits, resolutions, seminars and conferences. So far, the state reporting has been a good platform for the Commission to address the RTD. However, the Commission has not always been consistent in responding to state reports through its Concluding Observations and Recommendations. The other challenge is that many states do not report timely or do not report at all.

As far as special mechanisms are concerned, notwithstanding the resources and capacity challenges facing the special mechanisms in general, the Working Group on Indigenous Populations/Communities in Africa, the Working Group on Economic, Social and Cultural Rights in Africa and the Working Group on Extractive Industries, Environment and Human Rights Violations in Africa have promoted the RTD through the different activities.

Promotional visits, resolutions and conferences have a great potential for the promotion of the RTD, but so far this right has not been the focus of these promotional initiatives. Therefore, it is important to mainstream the RTD in these initiatives or to adopt a specific resolution on this right.

The African Court on Human Rights, which complements the African Commission, has rendered an important judgement in the Ogiek case. The latter not only confirms the justiciability of the RTD, but also its strong binding value. Through this case, the court was unequivocal in showing that the RTD is indeed an entire part of the human rights discourse. The remedies prescribed went beyond a mere declaration that rights were violated, but to include structural interdict to enable to oversee the implementation of its decision by the government of Kenya. In addition, the Ogiek case displays the complementarity of the African Commission and the African Court on Human Rights and the maturity of the African human rights system.

Recognising that human rights institutions need to be sustained by political will demonstrated through political organs to be effective, Chapter 6 explored the role of the AU political organs in fostering the RTD. It found that the AU governance institutions – specifically the AU Assembly, the Executive Council, the PRC, the PSC, the PAP, the NEPAD and APRM have a massive potential to enhance the realisation of the RTD in Africa. While the AU Assembly as the highest organ of the AU has the crucial power to advance the RTD, it is yet to work toward such an achievement. It needs to be sensitised on the question and should show a strong political will. At the same time, its efficiency and willingness to deal with the RTD depends on the nature of political negotiations conducted at the PRC that will table them to the Executive Council for them to reach the AU Assembly.

The PSC's mandate is fundamentally linked to the achievement of the RTD and it is obliged to work closely with the African Commission in ensuring human rights and the RTD, but so far the PSC is yet to work with the Commission for their mutual success. The PAP is very likely to achieve the RTD, but needs to work in direct collaboration with the African Commission as well as other continental institutions to unleash its potential to realise the RTD.

Finally for NEPAD and the APRM, although criticised for their neoliberal features, their main goals and objectives indicate their orientation and potential towards achieving the RTD. Although unsatisfactory for many, the ultimate goal of these initiatives centred on poverty eradication is vital for the RTD to flourish. To advance the responsiveness of the APRM standards to African problems, it is essential to infuse African values and traditions in the process to reinforce its legitimacy at the grassroots level.

Overall, the RTD is very well binding in the African human rights system. However, numerous measures have to be taken at various levels to ensure its practical attainment.

7.3. Towards an Africa where the right to development is a reality

While at the global level all stakeholders including IFIs, the WTO and TNCs should take their responsibilities in advancing the RTD, African States have a major role to play as the right is binding on them. Therefore, they should remedy the problem at various levels of their human rights architecture.

7.3.1. At the regional level

The regional African human rights system should be commended for a normative protection of the RTD and the establishment of the quasi-judicial body, the African Commission to monitor the implementation of the RTD. Nevertheless, this valuable institution needs to improve on its operations for the RTD to be fulfilled.

On the protective mandate, one should start by recognising 'the development of the [RTD]' by the African Commission with the communication procedure, through which the nature, content and core feature of the RTD including its individual and collective as well as participatory nature were clarified.

Nevertheless, as far as the on-site protective missions are concerned, the African Commission is yet to use their full potential to focus on the RTD. The Commission should make a conscious decision to focus on the RTD for some of these missions and not exclusively on cases of massive violations of human rights.

Furthermore, given that the missions are generally triggered by a Communication, the Commission should harmonise its work and ensure that the mission reports also capture its background including the specific reference to the Communication from which the mission originated.

Still on the field of harmonisation, the Commission must also finalise the terminology related to the type of mission and make specific difference when it deals with a 'fact-finding mission', 'protective mission' or 'investigative mission' and not use these terms interchangeably without any clarification. This will be useful if an investigative mission on the RTD is undertaken as it will be an investigation to better assist in implanting the right.

The African Commission is also bogged down on its on-site protective mission by state sovereignty as these missions cannot take place without the states' consent. It is imperative to find a way to enable the African Commission to exceptionally discharge its protective mandate without the agreement of the State to be visited, especially because in Africa many states are not doing enough to protect the RTD and will be reluctant to welcome a protective mission focusing on this right.

On the promotional mandate, the state reporting procedure is a great platform through which the African Commission addresses the RTD. Nonetheless, the Commission should be consistent in issuing Concluding Observations and Recommendations related to article 22 of the African Charter. It should seize any opportunity to elaborate on the content of the right as to ensure that reporting States have all the necessary details to assist them in policy making. The guidance provided may include the difference between State's obligations and the progress achieved without neglecting the challenges faced by the State and probably how to overcome such challenges.

Furthermore, besides providing mere recommendations, the Commission shall also establish mechanisms to follow up on the implementation of its recommendations on the RTD as well as other human rights provided for in the Charter.

Aside from the state reporting, the African Commission has much more to do in improving the promotional visits. Amongst other things, it is imperative to find a way to avoid the state consent also needed for on-site protective missions discussed earlier. In addition, it is essential to find the financial resources needed to organise promotional visits with specific attention to the RTD, to organise workshops and seminars on this right and ensure the broad dissemination of the outcome.

It should also ensure the participation of the AU political organs at these workshops and other promotional initiatives as to collaborate and keep them posted on development on the right under discussion. In addition, the RTD should be mainstreamed in most of its activities and the Commission should even adopt resolutions on this right which is essential in dealing with the scourge of poverty in Africa.

As far as the African Court on Human Rights is concerned, while it should be commended for its decision in the Ogiek case, it should keep the pressure on Kenya and ensure that its decision is implemented.

7.3.2. At the sub-regional level

The book has acknowledged that at the sub-regional level numerous RECs Protocol aim to improve people's standard of living, and also provide for human rights explicitly. While this is a positive development, it is important to ensure that while pro-poor policies are adopted, they explicitly mention the RTD as to ensure its presence and visibility in the RECs documents.

Furthermore, while sub-regional courts or tribunals are a good illustration of the judiciarisation of human rights at the sub-regional level, they should be capacitated financially. These institutions should be opened to the public and not States only. In addition, judges should be trained on various issues including the RTD. In fact, most regional courts should at least learn from the approach of the ECOWAS Court of Justice which acts as a court of first instance and goes a long way in ensuring that national jurisdictions comply with their commitments under the African Charter.

7.3.3. At the national level

At the national level, the RTD should be explicitly provided for in the bill of rights or the binding part of the Constitution to avoid any controversy on its binding character. In addition, African States should subscribe to and implement constitutionalism with a strong separation of powers. They should ensure respect for the rule of law and human rights and foster good governance. They should ensure the meaningful participation of their citizens in development initiative as well as in policy making.

In addition, it is imperative to establish independent national monitoring institutions such as the ombudsman and national human rights commissions and capacitate them to make sure that they discharge their mandate to foster respect for human rights, good governance and social justice. In the same vein, it is important to provide a conducive environment for NGOs and civil society in general to strive and play their role which is to be the watchdog of the society.

7.3.4. The political organs of the AU

The book recognises the significant role of political organs of the AU in fostering the RTD in Africa. Nevertheless, it is also of the view that these organs are far from having delivered African people from poverty and secured their RTD. To remedy this situation, the AU Assembly needs to be sensitised on the nature of this important right, display a political will that translates into measures to turn the RTD into reality across the continent.

Similarly, the PRC which is the diplomatic body of the AU, should also consider the RTD as essential and take necessary measures to ensure that it is included on the agenda to be discussed at the Executive Council and subsequently be discussed in the AU Assembly. In enhancing this possibility, the African Commission should reach out to these institutions in its promotional mandate through workshops and seminars on the RTD. Such a promotional mission could be planned as site events during the ordinary sessions of the AU as participants and various stakeholders are in town and can spare a few hours to discuss human rights and the RTD in particular.

Furthermore, while the work of the PSC is essential for the realisation of the RTD, it needs to work closely with the PAP which has a broad investigatory power on issues including matters of security and human rights. Furthermore, it needs the collaboration of the African Commission which has expertise on human rights and understands the link between peace and security and the RTD. At the same time, the Commission also needs the PSC's expertise to strengthen its work for the realisation of human rights, hence the need for a close collaboration between these AU institutions if the RTD is to become reality.

As for NEPAD, while the continental plan is now part and parcel of the AU, there is a strong need to ensure its implementation. For this to happen, African countries should raise the much-needed funds to cover the cost of the programme. They should ensure that human rights discourse in general and the RTD in particular are explicitly captured in the NEPAD agenda. This can be done by emphasising that services such as education, health care, infrastructure and agriculture delivered under the NEPAD programme are instrumental for the realisation of related human rights and the RTD.

While the objectives of the APRM address respect for human rights, it is equally important to make the link between these rights and the achievement of the RTD. Furthermore, it is important to increase the legitimacy of the process by tapping into the social construct which will encourage individuals and communities to discharge their duties for the improvement of standard of living for all, which is definitely the core objective the RTD.

7.4. What will it take for these prescriptions to become realities?

As demonstrated throughout this book, normatively the RTD is a reality. Nonetheless, time is now ripe to move from normative to practical reality. For this to happen, necessary actions need to be taken by various actors, namely the intellectuals, African governments and civil society organisations (CSOs).

7.4.1. The role of intellectuals

Intellectuals from various fields and especially proponents of global justice should keep researching on development and human rights and explore how to address poverty from a human rights perspective. In this vein, the role and responsibilities of global institutions such as the WTO, the IFIs and other global role players such as TNCs should be embedded in research which will not only keep the question of the RTD on the table, but would also lead these institutions to embark on an introspection which is likely to create a positive change of approaches to development.

There is a need to theorise the Economic Partnership Agreements between the EU and some African countries and interrogate their appropriateness for the realisation of the RTD in Africa. Similarly, while reflecting on the post 2015 agenda and on the AU agenda 2063 for Africa's development, omitting the RTD would be a huge mistake as this concept captures the essence of this agenda which seeks to eradicate poverty and improve the quality of lives in Africa. Essentially, infusing the RTD in the post 2015 and AU 2063 agenda will enable policy makers to seek context responsive solutions to the achievement of these important agendas.

Furthermore, intellectuals should deconstruct the group of emerging economies known as BRICS (Brazil, Russia, India, China and South Africa) and explore the potential of this group to realise the RTD and how BRICS states can lead this process, especially now that they are the alternative to the unipolar world led by the USA. The work of intellectuals should inform African governments' approach to tap into BRICS to better the lives of their people.

The other element to consider is that experts in African laws and studies should examine African national Constitutions in line with article 22 of the African Charter or to the extent that the Bill of Rights in these Constitutions are informed by the need to realise the RTD. There is a strong need to keep the RTD debate in the African development discourse and knowledge production as to inform African governments on what is missing.

The role of intellectuals cannot be overemphasised as it is likely to take the RTD discourse to continental, sub-regional and global policy makers as it intends to seek solutions for sustainable development across the board. In this respect, intellectual analysis on the RTD would benefit international development agencies and non-governmental organisations as they tackle development issues in their professions. Crafting the African development discourse in the RTD concept will enable policy makers to rely on the much needed multidisciplinary approach in tackling Africa's development questions. Similarly, intellectuals should inspire policy makers to move from pure regional economic integration to integration centred on people with extreme focus on human dignity at the centre of the RTD. Put differently, regional integration should be given a human face.

7.4.2. The role of African governments

Given that some hindrances to the realisation of the RTD can be found in 'the game of power' which informs international relations, African governments should partner with each other, strengthen South-South partnerships and more importantly tap into the BRICS nations to challenges the hegemony of the global North sustained by the Bretton Woods institutions. In this perspective, countries from the global South should build coalition with the G77 countries and China to advance the RTD at the global level. They should tap into the G77 'to transform global relations for a just world'.

Furthermore, given the prominence of China and its important place in the BRICS where Africa is represented by South Africa, African countries should rely on both South Africa and China to advance the RTD in global affairs. The leadership of BRICS in advancing the RTD should be visible especially as this new bloc of states seeks relevance in the developing world in general. China is a key player in this endeavour as besides BRICS, it is a member of the UN Security Council and takes part in all global initiatives where it can infuse the RTD agenda. This is to say that a partnership between African governments and China would enhance the prospect to advance the RTD discourse at the global stage.

7.4.3. The role of civil society

Research conducted by intellectuals should prepare the ground for intensive activism by (CSOs). The latter should frame their fight for social justice around the concept of RTD which encompasses all aspects of equality, human dignity and better life for all. A strong civic activism in Africa would not only keep governments under pressure to comply with their obligations under the African Charter in general, but specifically would give effect to the RTD. To this end CSOs should built a strong community-based network to force governments to enforce constitutionalism and respect for the rule of law which are instrumental for the achievement of the RTD.

Furthermore, CSOs should move from the mere development discourse to the RTD one in dealing with poverty. In this vein, it should advance the entitlement formula which will enable the RTD to be mainstreamed in poverty eradication and cascade from laws and policy to action for its realisation with the judiciary as watchdog

In addition, to make a long lasting impact, African CSOs should build a solid coalition with the global civil society to ensure that during world and regional summits, the debates are not limited to economy and poverty, terrorism or other issues, but encompass the RTD discourse as to ensure its visibility and practicality. Overall, turning the RTD into reality in Africa entails a firm commitment by intellectuals who will guide policy makers that are governments, as well as CSOs who should be the watchdog of the entire process. The activities of these key players will filter down to the African human rights system and strengthen its likelihood to become a machine for the realisation of the RTD in Africa.

Selected bibliography

Books

Aaronson, S. A. and Zimmerman, J. M. *Trade Imbalance. The Struggle to Weigh Human Rights Concerns in Trade Policymaking* (Cambridge University Press 2008).

Agubuzu, L; Onimode, B and Adedeji, A *African Development and Governance Strategies in The 21st Century: Essay in Honour of Adebayo Adedeji At Seventy'* (Zed Books in Association with the African Centre for Development & Strategy Studies 2004).

Aguda, T. A. *Human Rights and the Right to Development in Africa* (Nigerian Institute of International Affairs 1989).

Aguirre, D. *The Human Right to Development in a Globalized World* (Ashgate 2008).

Akokpari, J., Ndingfa-Muvumba, A. and Muruthi, T. (eds.). *The African Union and Its Institutions* (Fanele 2008).

Alford, C. F. *Narrative, Nature, and the Natural Law: From Aquinas to International Human Rights* (Palgrave Macmillan 2010).

Alston, P. *Non State Actors and Human Rights* (Oxford University Press 2005).

Andreassen, B. A. and Marks, S. P. (eds.). *Development as a Human Right: Legal, Political and Economic Dimensions*, Nobel Symposium Book 125 (Harvard School of Public Health, Francois Xavier Bagnoud Center for Health and Human Rights 2006).

Ankuma, A. E. *The African Commission on Human and Peoples' Rights: Practice and Procedures* (Martinus Nijhoff 1996).

Asante, M. K. *As I Run Toward Africa* (Boulder, CO: Paradigm 2011).

Banik, D. (ed.). *Rights and Legal Empowerment in Eradicating Poverty* (Ashgate 2008).

Baxi, U. *Human Rights in Post Human World: Critical Essays* (Oxford University Press 2007).

Bilchitz, D. *Poverty and Fundamental Rights: The Justification and Enforcement of Socio-Economic Rights* (Oxford University Press 2007).

Brendon, P. *Decline and Fall of the British Empire 1781–1997* (Vintage books 2010).

Brownlie, I. *Principles of Public International Law* (Oxford University Press 2003).

Cassese, A. and Jouve, E. (eds.). *Pour Un Droit Des Peoples Essaie sur La Declaration d'Alger* (Berger–Levrauld, 1978).

Cheng, B. *International Law Teaching and Practice* (Stevens and Sons 1982).

Chowdhury, S. R., Denters, E. and Waart, P. (eds.). *The Right to Development in International Law* (Martinus Nijhoff 1992).

Cooper, F. *Decolonization and African Society: The Labor Question in French and British Africa* (Cambridge University Press 1996).

Crawford, J. *The Rights of Peoples* (Clarendon Press 1998).

Currie I and de Waal J The Bill of Rights Handbook (JUTA, 2005)

Curtin, P. D. *The Atlantic Slave Trade* (University of Wisconsin Press 1969).

Dupuy, P. M. *Droit International Public* (Dalloz 2008).

Dworkin, R. *Taking Rights Seriously* (Duckworth 1978).

Ebobrah, S. and Tanoh, A. (eds.). *Compendium of African Sub-Regional Human Rights Documents* (PULP 2010).

Falola, T. *The African Diaspora: Slavery, Modernity, and Globalization* (University Rochester Press 2013).

Falola, T. *Colonialism and Violence* (Indiana University Press 2009).

Gumedze, S. *The Peace and Security Council of the African Union- Its relationship With the United Nations, the African Union and Sub-Regional Mechanisms* (Abo Akademi University Press 2011).

Hayden, P. *Cosmopolitan Global Politics* (Ashgate 2005).

Herbert, R. and Gruzd, S. *Le Mecanisme Africain D'evaluation Par Les Pairs: Leçons Des Pionniers* (SAIIA 2008).

Heyns, C. and Viljoen, F. *The Impact of the United Nations Human Rights Treaties in the Domestic Level* (Kluwer Law International 2002).

International Federation for Human Rights. *A Human Rights Approach to the New Partnership for Africa's Development (NEPAD) and The African Peer Review Mechanism (APRM)* (FIDH 2004).

Jones, C. *Global Justice: Defending Cosmopolitanism* (Oxford University Press 1999).

Lovejoy, P. E. and Hogendorn, J. S. *Slow Death for Slavery: The Course of Abolition in Northern Nigeria* (Cambridge University Press 1993).

Marks, S. (eds.). *Implementing the Right to Development: The Role of International Law* (Friedricht Ebert Stiftung 2008).

Mbembe, A. *On the Postcolony* (Wits University Press 2001).

Miers S. and Roberts, R. (eds.). *The End of Slavery in Africa* (University of Wisconsin Press 1988).

Mubangizi, J. C. *The Protection of Human Rights in South Africa: A Legal and Practical Guide* (Juta 2004).

Mudimbe, V. Y. *The Invention of Africa: Gnosis, Philosophy and the Order of Knowledge* (Indiana University Press 1988).

Murray, R. *Human Rights in Africa: From the OAU to the African Union* (Cambridge University Press 2004).

Ngũgĩ wa Thiong'o. *Something Torn and New: An African Renaissance* (Basic Civitas Books 2009).

Ngwena, C. *What Is Africanness to Me? Contesting Nativism in Sexualities, Race and Culture* (PULP 2017).

Nmehielle, V. O. *The African Human Rights System: Its Laws, Practice, and Institution* (Martinus Nijhoff 2001).

Nye, S. *Pan-Africanism and East African Integration* (Harvard University Press 1966).

Nyerere, J. K. *Freedom and unity/ uhuru na umoja* (A Selection from Writings and Speeches 1952–65) (Oxford University Press 1966).

Olowu, D. *An Integrative Rights-Based Approach to Human Development in Africa* (PULP 2009).

Ouguergouz, F. *African Charter on Human and Peoples' Rights – A Comprehensive Agenda for Human Dignity and Sustainable Democracy in Africa* (Kluwer Law International 2003).

Ougergouz, F. *La Charte Africaine des Droits de l'Homme et des Peuples: Historique, Portee Juridique et Contribution a la Protection International des Droits de L'Homme en Afrique* (PUF 1993).

Pogge, T. (eds.). *Freedom From Poverty as a Human Right – Who Owes What to the Poor?* (Oxford University Press 2007).

Pogge, T. *World Poverty and Human Rights: Cosmopolitan Responsibilities and Reforms* (Polity Press 2008).

Rodney, W. *How Europe Underdeveloped Africa* (London and Tanzanian Publishing House 1973). www.Blackherbals.Com/Walter_Rodney.Pdf (Accessed 20 May 2017).

Rukato, H. *Future of Africa – Prospects for Democracy and Development Under NEPAD* (Africa World Press 2010).

Salomon, M. E. *Global Responsibility for Human Rights* (Oxford University Press 2007).

Sen, A. *Development as Freedom* (Knopf 1999).

Sengupta, A., Negi, A. and Basu, M. (eds.). *Reflections on the Right to Development* (Sage 2005).

Shue, H. *Basic Rights* (Princeton University Press 1980).

Skogly, S. I. *The Human Rights Obligations of the World Bank and the International Monetary Fund* (Cavendish 2001).

Snyder, F. and Slinn, P. (eds.). *International Law of Development: Comparatives Perspectives* (Professional Books 1987).

Tan, K-C. *Justice Without Borders: Cosmopolitanism, Nationalism and Patriotism* (Cambridge University Press 2004).

Terreblanche, S. *History of Inequality in South Africa 1652–2002* (University of Natal Press 2002).

The World Bank. *Development and Human Rights: The Role of the World Bank* (The World Bank 1998).

UNDP. *Regional Integration and Human Development: A Pathway for Africa* (UNDP 2011).

Viljoen, F. *International Human Rights Law in Africa* (Oxford University Press /2012).

White, A. R. *Rights* (Oxford University Press 1984).

Williams, C. *The Destruction of Black Civilization: Great Issues of a Race From 4500 B.C. to 2000 A.D* (Third World Press 1974).

Zagorin, P. *Hobbes and the Law of Nature* (Princeton University Press 2009).

Chapters in books

Adésn, J. O., Graham, Y. and Olukoshi, A. *Africa and Development Challenges in the New Millennium-The NEPAD Debate* (Zed Books, 2006).

Akokpari, J. 'Human Rights Actors and Institutions in Africa' In Akokpari, J. and Zimbler, D. S. (eds.) *Africa's Human Rights Architecture* (Jacana 2008).

Alfredsson, G. 'The Right to Development: Perspective From Human Rights Law' In Rehof, L. A. and Gulmann, C. (eds.) *Human Rights in Domestic Law and Development Assistance Policies of the Nordic Countries* (Martinus Nijhoff 1989).

Alston, P. 'Development and the Rule of Law: Prevention Versus Cure as a Human Rights Strategy' In International Commission of Jurists (ed.) *Development, Human Rights and the Rule of Law* (Pergamon Press 1981).

Alston, P. 'The Right to Development at International Level' In F. E. Snyder and S. Sathirathai (ed.) *Third World Attitude towards International Law* (Martinus Nijhoff 1987).

Ama, M. 'Cultural Genocide' In Asante, M. K. and Ama, M. (eds.) *Encyclopedia of Black Studies* (Sage 2005).

Asante, A. K. 'Afrocentric Criticism' In Asante, M. K. and Ama, M. (eds.) *Encyclopedia of Black Studies* (Sage 2005).

Ayittey, G. B. N. 'Can Foreign Aid Reduce Poverty? No' In Haas, P. M. and Hird, J. A. (eds.) *Controversies in Globalisation: Contending Approaches to International Relations* (CQ Press 2009).

Baxi, U. 'From Human Rights to the Right to be Human: Some Heresies' In Kothari, S. and Sethi, H. (eds.) *Rethinking Human Rights* (Tripathy 1989).

Beckman, K. 'Imperialism' In Asante, M. K. and Ama, M. (eds.) *Encyclopedia of Black Studies* (Sage 2005).

Bello, E. 'Article 22 of the African Charter on Human and Peoples' Rights' In Bello, E. and Adjibola, B. (eds.) *Essay in Honour of Judge Taslim Olawale Elias* (Dordrecht: Martinus Nijhoff 1992).

Bourenane, N. 'Theoretical and Strategic Approaches' In Lavergne, R. (ed.) *Regional Integration and Cooperation in West Africa: A Multidimensional Perspective* (Africa World Press 1997).

Brett, R. 'Non-Governmental Actors in the Field of Human Rights' In Hanski, R. and Suksi, M. (eds.) *An Introduction to the International Protection of Human Rights* (Turko/Abo: Institute For Human Rights 2000).

Brietzke, P. H. 'Development as a Human Rite' In *The International Third World Legal Studies Association* (International Center or Law and Development 1984)..

Buhmann, K. 'Navigating From "Train Wreck" to Being "Welcomed": Negotiation Strategies and Argumentative Patterns in the Development of the UN Framework' In Deva, S. and Bilchitz, D. (eds.) *Human Rights Obligations of Business- Beyond the Corporate Responsibility to Respect* (Cambridge University Press 2013).

Bilchitz, D. and Deva, S. 'The Human Rights Obligations of Business: A Critical Framework for the Future' In *Human Rights Obligations of Business- Beyond the Corporate Responsibility to Respect* (Cambridge University Press 2013).

Cohen, J. 'Philosophy, Social Science, Global Poverty' In Jaggar, A. M. (ed.) *Thomas Pogge and His Critics* (Polity Press 2010).

Donnelly, J. 'The Right to Development: How Not to Link Human Rights and Development' In Welch, C. (ed.) *Human Rights and Development in Africa* (State University of New York Press 1984).

Eide, A. and Rosas, A. 'Economic, Social and Cultural Rights: A Universal Challenge' In Eide, A., Krause, C. and Rosas, A. (eds.) *Economic, Social and Cultural Rights* (Dordrecht: Martinus Nijhoff 2001).

Foncesca, R. S. 'The World Trade Organisation: Africa's Dilemma' In Stephan, H. and Power, M. (eds.) *The Scramble for Africa in the 21st Century – From the Old World to the New* (Renaissance Press 2012).

Gawanas, B. 'The African Union: Concepts and Implementation Mechanisms Relating to Human Rights' In Bosl, A. and Diesco, J. (eds.) *Human Rights in Africa – Legal Perspectives on Their Protection and Promotion* (Konrad-Adenauer-Stiftung 2009).

George, R. P. (ed.) *Natural Law Theory: Contemporary Essays* (Clarendon Press 1992).

Jordaan, B., Kalula, E. and Strydom, E. (eds.). *Understanding Social Security Law* (Juta 2009).

Kamga, S. D. 'The Right to Development and the Post-2015 Agenda' In Zondi, S. and Mthembu, P. (eds.) *From MDGs to Sustainable Development Goals* (Institute for Global Dialogue 2017).

Kamga, S. D. *The World Trade Organisation: For Which World? Whose Trade? And Whose Organisation?* (AISA 2014).

Kebonang, Z. and Fombad, C. M. 'The African Peer Review Mechanism: Challenges and Prospects' In Melber, H. (ed.) Current African Issues No 32 *AU, NEPAD and the APRM: Democratisation Efforts Explored* (Upsala: The Nordic Africa Institute 2006).

Kiernan, B. 'From Irish Famine to Congo Reform: Nineteenth-Century Roots of International Human Rights Law' In Provost, R. and Akhavan, P. (eds.) *Confronting Genocide* (Springer 2011).

Kunig, P. 'The Role of "Peoples" Rights in the African Charter of Human and Peoples' Rights' In Ginther, K. and Benedek, W. (eds.) *New Perspectives and Conceptions of International Law an Afro-European Dialogue* (Springer1983).

Lloyd, A. 'The African Regional System for the Protection of Children's Rights' In Sloth-Nielsen (ed.) *Children's Rights in Africa: A Legal Perspective* (Ashgate 2008).

Maas, W. W. 'Trade, Regional Integration, and Free Movement of People' In Roy, J. (ed.) *A New Atlantic Community: The European Union, the US and Latin America* (Miami: European Union Center of Excellence/Jean Monnet Chair, University of Miami 2015).

M'baye, K. 'Introduction' (Part Four) 'Human Rights and the Rights of Peoples' In Bedjaoui, M. (ed.) *International Law: Achievements and Prospects* (The Hague: Martinus Nijhoff 1999).

Miers, S. and Roberts, R. (eds.) *The End of Slavery in Africa* (Madison: University of Wisconsin Press 1988).

Mynnti, K. 'The Right of Indigenous Peoples to Participate in Development Projects' In Scheinen, M. and Suksi, M. (eds.) *Human Rights in Development Yearbook 2002 Empowerment, Participation, Accountability and Non-Discrimination: Operationalising a Human Rights Based Approach to Development* (Martinus Nijhoff 2005).

Okafor, O. C. 'A Regional Perspective: Article 22 of the African Charter on Human and Peoples' Rights' In UN, Human Rights Office of the High Commissioner (ed.) *Realizing the Right to Development – Essays in Commemoration of 25 Years of the United Nations Declaration on the Right to Development* (UN 2013).

Okafor, O. C. '"Righting" The Right to Development: A Socio-Legal Analysis of Article 22 of the African Charter of Human and Peoples' Rights' In Marks, S. (ed.) *Implementing the Right to Development: The Role of International Law* (Friedricht Ebert Stiftung 2008).

Olukoshi, A. 'Governing the African Political Space for Sustainable Development: A Reflection on NEPAD' In Nyong'o, P. A., Ghirmazion, A. and Lamba, D. (eds) *New Partnership for Africa's Development: A New Path*? (Heinrich Boll Foundation 2002).

Pogge, T. 'Assisting the Global Poor' In Chatterje, D. K. (ed.) *The Ethics of Assistance: Morality and the Distant Needy* (Cambridge University Press 2004).

Rosas, A. 'The Right to Development' In Eide, A., Krause, C. and Rosas, A. (eds.) *Economic, Social and Cultural Rights* (Martinus Nijhoff 2001).

Thirlway, H. 'The Sources of International Law' In Evans, M. (eds.) *International Law* (Oxford University Press 2006).

Viljoen, F. 'The African Regional Human Rights System' In Krause, C. and Scheinin, M. (eds.) *International Protection of Human Rights: A Text Book* (2nd ed.) (Abo Akademi, University Institute for Human Rights 2012).

Viljoen, F. 'Introduction to the African Commission and the Regional Human Rights System' In Heyns, C. (ed.) *Human Rights Law in Africa* (Martinus Nijhoff 2004).

Journal articles

Alliot, A. 'Towards the Unification of Laws in Africa' (1965) 14 *International and Comparative Law Quarterly* 366.

Anghie, A. 'Whose Utopia? Human Rights, Development and the Third World' (2013) 22: 1 *Qui Parle: Critical Humanities and Social Sciences* 66.

Baimu, E. 'Human Rights in NEPAD and Its Implementation for the African Human Rights System' (2002) 2 *African Human Rights Law Journal* 301.

Baxi, U. 'The New International Economic Order, Basic Needs and Rights: Note Towards Development of the Right to Development' (1983) 23 *India Law Journal* 235.

Banks, N., Hulme, D. and Edwards, M. 'NGOs, States, and Donors Revisited: Still Too Close for Comfort?' (2015) 66 *World Development* 707.

Bond, P. 'Removing Neocolonialism's APRM Mask: A Critique of the African Peer Review Mechanism' (2009) *Review of African Political Economy* 596.

Brownlie, I. 'The Right of People in Modern International Law' (1995) 9 *Bulletin of Association of Legal Philosophy* 108.

Danilenko, G. M. 'International Jus Cogens: Issues of Law-Making' (1991) 2 *European Journal of International Law* 42.

Donnelly, J. 'In Search of the Unicorn: The Jurisprudence and Politics of the Right to Development' (1985) 15 *California Western International Law Journal* 473.

Doyle, C. and Gilbert, J. 'Indigenous Peoples and Globalization: From "Development Aggression" to "Self-Determined Development"' (2008/9) 7 *European Yearbook of Minority Issues* 219.

Dupuy, P. M. 'Soft Law and the International Law of Environment' (1991) 12 *Michigan Journal of International Law* 420.

Gilbert, J. 'Nomadic Territories: A Human Rights Approach to Nomadic Peoples' Land Rights' (2007) 7: 4 *Human Rights Law Review* 681.

Gordon, L. R. 'African Philosophy's Search for Identity: Existential Considerations of a Recent Effort' (1997) *CLR James Journal* 98.

Harrington, J. 'Special Rapporteurs of the African Commission on Human and Peoples' Rights' (2001) 2 *African Human Rights Law Journal* 248.

Herbert, R. and Gruzd, S. 'Taking Stock of the African Peer Review Mechanism' (2007) 14 *South African Journal of International Affairs* 5.

Heyns, C. 'The African Regional Human Rights System: The African Charter (2004) 108 *Pennsylvania State Law* 691.

Hollie Nyseth Brehm, H. N., Uggen, C. and Gasanabo, J-D. 'Genocide, Justice, and Rwanda's Gacaca Courts' (2014) 30: 3 *Journal of Contemporary Criminal Justice* 333.

Kamchedzera, G. and Banda, C. U. 'Dignified Rural Living, The Right to Development, Multiparty Politics and Legislation in Malawi' (2009) 25 *South African Journal on Human Rights* 73.

Kamga, S. D. 'The Right to Development in the African Human Rights System: The *Endorois* Case' (2011) *De Jure* 381.

Kamga, S. D. and Fombad, C. M. 'A Critical Review of the Jurisprudence of the African Commission on the Right to Development' (2013) 57 *Journal of African Law* 196.

Kinley, D. and Tadaki, J. 'From Talk to Walk: The Emergence of Human Rights Responsibilities for Corporations at International Law' (2003–2004) 44: 4 *Virginia Journal of International Law* 949.

Kiwanuka, R. 'The Meaning of "People" in The African Charter on Human and Peoples' Rights' (1988) 82 *American Journal of International Law* 82.

Manby, B. 'The African Union, NEPAD and Human Rights: The Missing Agenda' (2004) 26 *Human Rights Quarterly* 983.

Mangu Mbata, A. 'Assessing the Effectiveness of the African Peer Review Mechanism and Its Impact on the Promotion of Democracy and Political Good Gouvernance' (2007) 7 *African Human Rights Law Journal* 354.

Mangu Mbata, A. 'The Changing Human Rights Landscape in Africa: Organisation of African Unity, African Union, New Partnership of Africa's Development and The African Court' (2005) 23 *Netherlands Quarterly of Human Rights* 379.

M'baye, K. 'Le Droit Au Development Comme Un Droit De L'homme' (1972) 5 *Revue Des Droits L'homme* 505.

Mbazira, C. 'A Path to Realising Economic, Social and Cultural Right in Africa? A Critique of the New Partnership for Africa Development' (2004) 4 *African Human Rights Law Journal* 40.

Meillan, L. 'Le Droit au Développement et les Nations Unies: Quelques Réflexions' (2003) *Droit en Quart Monde* 14.

Mutua M 'The African Human Rights Court: A two-legged stool?' (1999) 21 *Human Rights Quaterly* 343

Ngang, C. 'Indigenous Peoples' Right to Sustainable Development and the Green Economy Agenda' (2015) 44: 4*Africa Insight* 21.

Ngang, C. 'Towards a Right-to-Development Governance in Africa' (2017) *Journal on Human Rights* 1. (available at http://www.tandfonline.com/doi/pdf/10.1080/14754835.2016.1274645?needAccess=true (access 25 November 2017)

Nkrumah, K. *Africa Must Unite* (Fredericka Praeger Publisher1963).

Nunn, N. 'The Long-Term Effects of Africa's Slave Trades' (2008) 123: 1 *Quarterly Journal of Economics* 139.

Nwauche, E. S. and Nwobike, J. C. 'Implementing the Right to Development' (2005) 2 *Sur International Journal of Human Rights* 93.

Obi, C. I. 'Reconstructing Africa's Development in the New Millennium through NEPAD: Can African Leaders Deliver the Goods?' (2001) 4 *African Journal of International Affairs* 147.

Oduwole, O. 'International Law and the Right to Development: A Pragmatic Approach for Africa' (2014) *International Institute of Social Studies* 1.

Pogge, T. 'World Poverty and Human Rights' (2005) 19 *Ethics and International Affairs* 4.

Senghor, L. 'Address to the Legal Meeting Convened to Draft the African Charter on Human People's Rights, in 1979 in Heyns, C. and Stefisyun, K. (eds) *Human Rights Peace and Justice in Africa: A Reader* (PULP 2006).

Shepherd, G. W. 'The African Right to Development: World Policy and the Debt Crisis' (1990) 37: 4 *Africa Today* 5.

Sohn, L. B. 'The New International Law: Protection of the Rights of Individuals Rather Than States' (1982) 32 *American University Law Review* 50.

Tadeg, M. A. 'Reflections on the Right to Development: Challenges and Prospects' (2010) 10 *African Human Rights Law Journal* 325.

Vandenbogaerde, A. 'The Right to Development in International Human Rights Law: A Call for its Dissolution' (2013) 31: 1 *Netherlands Quarterly of Human Rights* 187–209.

Woods, J. M. 'Justiciable Social Rights as a Critique of the Liberal Paradigm' (2003) 38 *Texas International Law Journal* 763.

Whyte, J. 'Book Review: Development as a Human Right edited by Bard A. Andreasen and Stephen P. Marks, Harvard University Press, London England, 2006' (2007) 1: 1 *The Electronic Journal of Sustainable Development* 1.

Ziya, O. 'The Logic of the Developmental State' (1991) *Comparative Polotics*, October.

Table of cases

Case law – national

South Africa

Basic Education for All and Others v Minister of Basic Education and Others (23949/14) (2014) ZAGPPHC 251; (2014) 4 SA 274 (GP).

Economic Freedom Fighters v Speaker of the National Assembly Others: Democratic Alliance v Speaker of the National Assembly and others (2016) ZACC 11.

Fuel Retailers Association of South Africa V Director-General Environmental Management, Department of Agriculture, Conservation and Environment, Mpumalanga Province and Others (2007) 2 SA 163 (SCA).

Governing Body of the Juma Musjid Primary School and Another v Essay NO and Others (2011) 7 BCLR 651 (CC).

Government of Republic Of South Africa and Others V Grootboom and Others (2000) 11 BCLR 1169 (CC).

The Minister of Basic Education v Basic Education for All (20793/2014) (2015) ZASCA 198 (2 December 2015).

Minister of Health and Others V Treatment Action Campaign and Others (No 2) (2002) 5 SA 721 (CC).

Section27 v Minister of Education (2013) 3 SA 40 (GNP).

India

Bandhua Mukti v Union of India (1984) 3 SCC 161.

Francis Coralie Mullin v The Administrator, Union Territory of Delhi (1981) 2 SCR 516.

Keshavananda Bharati V State of Kerala (1973) 4 SCC 225.

Maneka Gandhi V Union of India (1978) 1 SCC 248.

M.C. Mehta H. Patel V Union of India and Others (1996) SC 2231.

Olga Tellis V Bombay Municipal Corporation (1985) 3 SCC 545.

Shanti Star Builders V Narayan K. Totame (1990) 1 SCC 520.

Supreme Court Legal Aid Committee Representing Under Trials V Union of India (1994) 6 SCC 731, *Citizens of Democracy V State of Assam* (1995) 3 SCC.

Union Territory of Delhi (1981) 2 SCR 516.

Case law – international

Anglo-Iranian Oil Co, Preliminary Objections, United Kingdom V Iran, Judgment (22 July1952) ICJ Reports 93.

France v Turkey PCIJ (7 September 1927), Series A, No. 10.

I.C.J. Advisory Opinion of December 20, 1980, Interpretation of the Agreement of 25 March 1951 between the W.H.O and Egypt, No 10, Rep, 16.

Jurisdiction of the Court of Dantzig, Consultative Opinion 1928, PCIJ. Ser B, No 1.

'Maritime Delimitations and Territorial Questions between Qatar V Bahrain, Jurisdiction and Admissibility'. Judgment, (1994) 1 July. www.Icj-Ij.Org/Docket/Index.Php?Sum=441&Code=Qb&P1=3&P2=3&Case=87&K=61&P3=5 (Accessed 23 May 2017).

Nicaragua v USA) (27 June 1986) (1986) ICJ Reports (1986).

Texaco Overseas Petroleum Company and California Asiatic Oil Company V Libya, 17 International Legal Materials (1978) 1.

Case law – regional

African system (communications)

Burkina Faso v Republic Mali, ICJ (22 December1986) ICJ Reports 554, 566–567.
Communication 136/94 *William A. Courson V Zimbabwe*.
Communication 155/96 *SERAC & another V Nigeria*, ACHPR (2001).
Communication 227/99, *Democratic Republic of the Congo V Burundi, Rwanda, and Uganda* Annex IV, 20th Annual Activity Report of the African Commission.
Communication No 260/2002, AHRLR (2004) *Bakweri Land Claims Committee V Cameroon*.
Communication 276/2003: Centre for Minority Rights Development (Kenya) and Minority.
Communication 266/2003: *Kevin Mgwanga Gumne et al v Cameroon*.
Communications, 25/89, 47/90,100/93; *Free Legal Assistance v Zaire* (2000) AHRLR 74.
Jawara v The Gambia (2000) AHRLR 107, ACHPR (2000).
Katangese Peoples' Congress v Zaire (2000) AHRLR 72, ACHPR (1995).
Rights Group (on behalf of *Endorois* Welfare Council)/Kenya.

Africa-sub-regional

SADC

Campbell and 78 others v Zimbabwe (Campbell case) SADC (T) Case No.2/2007.

ECOWAS

ECCJ decisions *Essien v The Gambia*, Unreported Suit No ECW/CCJ/APP/05/05.
Koraou v Niger, Unreported Suit No: ECW/CCJ/APP/08/08 (27 October 2008).
Manneh v the Gambia, Judgement ECW/CCJ/JJD/03/08, ECOWAS court of justice.
Registered Trustees of SERAP v Nigeria, Judgement ECW/CCJ/APP/08/08 (27 October 2009).

EAC

Anyang' Nyongo and others v Attorney General of Kenya and Others, Reference No 1 of 2006, (27 November 2006).
Katabazi and others v Secretary General of the EAC and another (Reference 1 of 2007, EAC Court (1November 2007) (2007) AHLR 119.

Inter-American system

Inter-American Commission on Human Rights, Report N° 75/02, Case 11.140 *Mary and Carrie Dann Vs United States*.
Inter-American Court of Human Rights *Indigenous Community Yakye Axa V Paraguay* (17 June 2005).

Index

For Product Safety Concerns and Information please contact our EU representative GPSR@taylorandfrancis.com
Taylor & Francis Verlag GmbH, Kaufingerstraße 24, 80331 München, Germany

www.ingramcontent.com/pod-product-compliance
Ingram Content Group UK Ltd.
Pitfield, Milton Keynes, MK11 3LW, UK
UKHW011014180926
475701UK00004B/743

* 9 7 8 0 3 6 7 5 9 3 1 9 3 *